Reverence for Life

THE ALBERT SCHWEITZER LIBRARY

Photograph by Erica Anderson, courtesy of The Albert Schweitzer Fellowship.

REVERENCE FOR LIFE

THE ETHICS OF ALBERT SCHWEITZER

FOR THE TWENTY-FIRST CENTURY

Edited by Marvin Meyer & Kurt Bergel

SYRACUSE UNIVERSITY PRESS

First Edition 2002
        04   05   06   07   6   5   4   3   2

The paper used in this publication meets the minimum requirements of
American National Standard for Information Sciences—Permanence of
Paper for Printed Library Materials, ANSI Z39.48–1984.∞™

Library of Congress Cataloging-in-Publication Data
Reverence for life : the ethics of Albert Schweitzer for the
twenty-first century / edited by Marvin Meyer and Kurt Bergel.—1st ed.
    p. cm.—(The Albert Schweitzer library)
Includes bibliographical references and index.
  ISBN 0–8156–2952–4 (alk. paper)—ISBN 0–8156–2977-X (pbk. : alk.
paper)
1. Schweitzer, Albert, 1875–1965—Ethics. I. Meyer, Marvin W. II.
Bergel, Kurt. III. Albert Schweitzer library (Syracuse, N.Y.)
  B2430.S374 R48 2002
  170'.92—dc21   2002006445

Manufactured in the United States of America

◆　　◆　　◆

Slowly we crept upstream, laboriously navigating—it was the dry season—between the sandbanks. Lost in thought I sat on the deck of the barge, struggling to find the elementary and universal concept of the ethical that I had not discovered in any philosophy. I covered sheet after sheet with disconnected sentences merely to concentrate on the problem. Two days passed. Late on the third day, at the very moment when, at sunset, we were making our way through a herd of hippopotamuses, there flashed upon my mind, unforeseen and unsought, the phrase "reverence for life." The iron door had yielded. The path in the thicket had become visible. Now I had found my way to the principle in which affirmation of the world and ethics are joined together!

I was at the root of the problem. I knew that the ethical acceptance of the world and of life, together with the ideals of civilization contained in this concept, has its foundation in thought.

—Albert Schweitzer, *Out of My Life and Thought,*
reflecting upon a trip on the Ogowe River
in September 1915

One day I asked my father, "You have done so much for Africa. Has it given you anything in return?"

He said, "Yes, nowhere else could I have found the idea of reverence for life than here."

—Rhena Schweitzer Miller, reflecting upon
a conversation with her father in Africa

Marvin Meyer is Griset Professor of Bible and Christian Studies and director of the Albert Schweitzer Institute at Chapman University, Orange, California. He is the author of a number of books, including *Jesus Then and Now: Images of Jesus in History and Christology* and *The Ancient Mysteries: A Sourcebook of Sacred Texts*.

Kurt Bergel was professor emeritus at Chapman University and founder and codirector of the Albert Schweitzer Institute. He published articles and books on Albert Schweitzer and European literary figures, including a translation, with Alice Bergel, of Schweitzer's *Memoirs of Childhood and Youth*.

Contents

Preface

Marvin Meyer

Two recent sets of events give a particular poignancy to this book. In the spring of 2001, my longtime friend and the coeditor of this book, Kurt Bergel, passed away after a brief illness. Kurt spent his life devoted to living according to the ethics of reverence for life, and he died a person of conviction, compassion, and love. In the autumn of 2001, the World Trade Center and the Pentagon were attacked, and many died. Since then, many more have died in Afghanistan, Palestine, Israel, and elsewhere in the world, and the pain and death continue.

If ever there was a time for reflection upon Albert Schweitzer and reverence for life, it is now.

We search to find meaning at such times of pain and death. In the light of recent events, I thought of what Schweitzer wrote more than once about what he called the fellowship of those who bear the mark of pain. In *Out of My Life and Thought* Schweitzer observed, "Those among us who have learned through personal experience what pain and anxiety really are must help to ensure that those out there who are in physical need obtain the same help that once came to us. We no longer belong to ourselves alone; we have become the brothers and sisters of all who suffer." According to Schweitzer, such people constitute the fellowship of those who bear the mark of pain.

We know who these people are. They are the friends and relatives of those who suffer, of those who pass away and leave the rest of us behind. They are the people of New York and Washington, D.C. who carry on through it all. They are the people of the United States who wipe away tears and dig through rubble. They are the Palestinians and the Israelis who see their loved ones die in the streets. They are the people of Afghanistan who have suffered so much for over two decades. They are the many other people throughout the world who have gone through pain, grief, and injustice and have found a way to continue on in their lives. All of us who feel the pain and experience some healing are members of this fellowship. All of us are the brothers and sisters of the suffering; we all belong to each other.

The question and challenge Schweitzer raises, then, is: what shall we do about it? How do we work to alleviate the suffering of our brothers and sisters—whoever and wherever they are in the world? In the present climate that includes the rhetoric of hate and the promise of vengeance, how can we become instruments, not of violence, but rather of justice and healing and peace?

These are some of the questions that this book seeks to address.

Marvin Meyer
Director, Albert Schweitzer Institute
Chapman University
March 2002

Introduction

Marvin Meyer

Whatever Albert Schweitzer, the acclaimed philosopher, theologian, musician, and medical doctor in Lambaréné, Gabon, did, he did with gusto.

As philosopher, Schweitzer earned a doctorate in philosophy, wrote a scholarly work on Immanuel Kant, and developed a philosophy of ethics in *The Philosophy of Civilization*. As theologian, Schweitzer composed revolutionary books on Jesus and Paul, including *The Quest of the Historical Jesus,* which has remained one of the most influential works on Jesus of the twentieth century. Many would consider it the single most important book on Jesus of the modern era. In addition, the theologian Dr. Schweitzer was also the Lutheran minister Rev. Schweitzer, who preached sermons and functioned effectively as pastor and as head of a theological seminary for a number of years.

As musician, Schweitzer was one of the leading organists of his day, and his book on Johann Sebastian Bach and his edition of Bach's chorale preludes established him as a great interpreter of Bach. He used measured tempos when he played Bach—he may be thought to be plodding by contemporary standards—and he said that the organist "who plays too fast will go to hell." He was an advocate of traditional organs and organ building, so that it was said of him, somewhat unkindly and with no particular cultural sensitivity, that at Lambaréné he saved old Africans and in Europe he saved old organs.

As medical doctor, Schweitzer traveled to equatorial Africa to build a hospital and practice medicine. There, at Lambaréné, in the Republic of

Gabon, he was the hospital's architect, builder, director, and chief medical doctor. And when, later in his life, he might have chosen the quiet life of retirement, he learned about the grim realities of nuclear physics and became an outspoken opponent of nuclear testing and an advocate of peace in the world. For the humanitarian and devoted life he lived he was awarded the Nobel Peace Prize in 1953, and in a manner typical of him, he then used the cash award from the prize to build a leper village at Lambaréné.

Of all his accomplishments in his life and thought, his greatest achievements may be found in what he said and did in the name of the ethic termed reverence for life. In his autobiography *Out of My Life and Thought* he says that the phrase "reverence for life" came to him in a flash of insight as he passed, on a boat, by islands and hippopotamuses on the Ogowe River. Later he would say this ethic is actually the same as Jesus' ethic, "the ethic of love widened into universality." He also realized his ethic has much in common with aspects of Chinese and Indian thought—especially the Jain commitment to *ahimsa,* radical nonviolence or noninjury—and he would admit he came up with the concept of reverence for life when he was thinking of the Buddha.

"Basically I am a philosopher," Schweitzer wrote in a letter to Hélène Bresslau, and his philosophical exposition of reverence for life in *The Philosophy of Civilization* and elsewhere may be his clearest presentation. Looking for an appropriate place to begin thinking, Schweitzer rejected Descartes's *cogito ergo sum,* and he told Norman Cousins that he was not impressed with the dictum: "One might as well say, 'I have a toothache, therefore I exist' " (Norman Cousins, *Albert Schweitzer's Mission,* 74). Instead, Schweitzer proposed to locate the beginning point for thinking about ethics in the awareness of our will-to-live in the midst of other wills-to-live. We recognize our own urge to become, to realize our life fully, and we cherish and revere that life. Ethics, then, entails reciprocity: Revere the life of the other, Schweitzer says, as you revere your own life; maintain and encourage the life of the others as you maintain and encourage your own life. If this ethic of reciprocity sounds like Jesus' love command and the Golden Rule in the Sermon on the Mount, Schweitzer confesses that he himself is a philosopher caught by Jesus, "the most divine of all philosophers." We might add that Schweitzer may also be caught by a host of other thinkers and religious figures from a wide variety of traditions who similarly advocated one form or another of the love command or the Golden Rule: Love your neighbor as yourself, and do to others as you want them to do to you.

Schweitzer had high hopes for his ethic of reverence for life. He proposed it as an ethic that applies to all life, human, animal, and plant (and to crystals, he added with Schopenhauer). "Life as such is sacred," he states in *The Philosophy of Civilization,* and all of life is equally sacred. No life is second or third class—all life is equally valuable. Schweitzer's ethic is an ethic of thinking clearly and reasonably, and of making hard decisions based on necessity. The ethic of reverence for life is absolute and limitless; it is "responsibility without limit towards all that lives." Yet the taking of life cannot be avoided in our eating, our drinking, our maintenance of health, our everyday lives. Schweitzer himself acknowledges that as a medical doctor he is a mass-murderer of bacteria. So, he says, face ethical conflicts squarely and honestly, make ethical decisions thoughtfully, and violate the absolute voice of the ethical only if you must. Schweitzer encouraged the maintenance of a guilty conscience, but his preoccupation with guilt may seem overly Lutheran. We may prefer to think, with Mike W. Martin, of regret, responsibility, and healthy realism, rather than guilt, as the appropriate response to the hard ethical decisions in our own lives.

Schweitzer's ethic is an ethic that is practical. It can be lived and is meant to be lived. Schweitzer's ethic has been dubbed a philosophy with calluses on its hands, for it is an ethic that works. Schweitzer lived reverence for life at Lambaréné, and he encouraged others to find their own Lambaréné. And throughout the world, in differing ways, people have.

Schweitzer recommended reverence for life and lived it, but he was no saint. His daughter Rhena Schweitzer Miller recalls his authoritarian traits, and Schweitzer himself describes and deplores his temper. Today we feel properly uncomfortable with his colonial attitudes, his statements about "primitive people" in, for instance, the article from *Christendom* presented in this volume. That he reflected the colonialist and paternalistic attitudes of his generation is no surprise, but that he was able to transcend, to an extent, some such attitudes is encouraging. Sylvère Mbondobari's essay below is very helpful in addressing this matter forthrightly.

Schweitzer was no saint, but rather he was just a sinner, just an ordinary person like the rest of us. But that fact might make his call to reverence for life more powerful, more human. It is not a call from one who is ethically superior to us but from one who is ethically similar to us. It is a call from one of us to the rest of us, and to himself, to consider our lives and the lives of our brothers and sisters among human beings, animals, and plants. Saints may be extolled and put on a shelf, and their words may be admired from a distance and ignored. The words of sinners, of thoughtful but ordinary folks, are more difficult to ignore. We may need to listen and respond.

◆　　◆　　◆

This book is intended to provide an appreciative and critical assessment of the ethic of reverence for life. The contributions bring together three related sets of materials. First, there are several contributions by Albert Schweitzer (and Hélène Bresslau) on reverence for life, from early letters between Albert and Hélène to later, more mature reflections on ethical concerns. Second, many of the contributions in this volume derive from an international conference titled "Albert Schweitzer at the Turn of the Millennium." These contributions include essays by James Brabazon, Marvin Meyer, Sylvère Mbondobari, Erich Gräßer, Mike W. Martin, Ara Paul Barsam, James M. Robinson, and Nikki Lindberg. (The essay by Mike W. Martin is actually not the same as the paper he delivered at the conference. This essay has been incorporated here because of its central significance as a philosophical critique of reverence for life.) Third, the remaining contributions reflect the ongoing interests and commitments of the Chapman University Albert Schweitzer Institute. There is an essay by Kurt Bergel, founder and codirector of the Albert Schweitzer Institute, which he composed shortly after World War II; an introduction to Jainism and *ahimsa* by the late Ronald Huntington, former codirector of the Albert Schweitzer Institute; my translation of the Sermon on the Mount; and several essays by undergraduate students enrolled in the Chapman University course "Albert Schweitzer: His Life and Thought."

The conference "Albert Schweitzer at the Turn of the Millennium" was presented on February 19–21, 1999, on the campus of Chapman University, Orange, California. Held in celebration of the eightieth birthday of Rhena

Schweitzer Miller and the life of Alice Bergel, the conference was convened by Kurt Bergel and Marvin Meyer of the Albert Schweitzer Institute, with the support of the Chapman University Department of Religious Studies, the Griset and Huntington Lectureship endowments, and the Wang-Fradkin Professorship. In addition to the academic papers presented by the Schweitzer scholars mentioned above, the conference featured dramatic, liturgical, and musical presentations. Edith M. Schwartz directed "Albert Schweitzer and Hélène Bresslau: Letters of Devotion," a dramatic reading from the correspondence between Albert and his future wife (see the letters below). Ronald Farmer officiated at an interfaith workshop service, and the Dembrebrah West African Drum and Dance Company played West African music on traditional instruments and performed dances from that region of Africa. Christiane Schweitzer Engel played a Mozart piano concerto, Chapman music faculty member Margaret Dehning sang "A Requiem for Schweitzer," and Chapman students performed as instrumentalists and singers. Antje Bultmann Lemke conducted an interview with Rhena Schweitzer Miller.

The chapters of this book are divided into four parts. In part one, "The Vision of Reverence for Life," Brabazon and I present a twofold introduction to the contemporary discussion of reverence for life. Brabazon's essay is an invitation to consider, with Schweitzer, life and reverence for life as the most fundamental of the values in our lives. In part two, "Albert Schweitzer on Reverence for Life," six contributions by Albert Schweitzer (and Hélène Bresslau) provide reflections on his ethic from different periods in his life. These six contributions are arguably the most significant contributions he made to the discussion of reverence for life. In part three, "Assessing Reverence for Life," several essays explore and critically assess aspects of Schweitzer's ethic. Three opening essays, by an American (born in Germany), an African, and a European (Bergel, Mbondobari, and Gräßer), discuss reverence for life generally, in the context of the Second World War, German and Gabonese literature, and contemporary ethical challenges. The following essay, by Martin, offers a careful philosophical evaluation of the ethic of reverence for life and reveals its complexity. Martin identifies what he judges to be unpalatable features of the ethic but suggests that they can be jettisoned without causing irreparable damage to the ethic itself. The next four essays examine aspects of Jain thought (in Huntington and Barsam) and the life and thought of Jesus (in Robinson and the Sermon on the Mount) in order to shed light on religious dimensions of the ethic of reverence for life. In part four, "Reverence for Life and Education," Lindberg outlines strategies for teaching Schweitzer's thought in elementary, middle, and high school, and university students explore aspects of reverence for life in research papers on the meaning of life and twelve-step programs, ordinary decision making, eating habits, the abortion issue, animal rights, and everyday activism.

◆   ◆   ◆

Albert Schweitzer proposed an ethic that was meant to be global in its outreach. Rooted in a variety of philosophical and religious traditions and reflective of a variety of ethical statements from around the world, the ethic of reverence for life deserves to be evaluated and debated in the current discussion of ethics and religions in a global context. Schweitzer proposed a universal ethic, applicable to all living things. He also proposed reverence for life as "a logical consequence of thought," attainable by all people, regardless of individual differences and beliefs, as long as they think clearly, sincerely, and well. Today, at the beginning of the twenty-first century, we may appreciate Schweitzer's vision anew, for we recognize that we need to discuss creative ways in which life may be revered and maintained throughout the world. In various ways we need to explore, evaluate, and live an ethic like reverence for life. It is our hope that the present book may contribute to such an ethical discussion and such an ethical life.

◆   ◆   ◆

In *Memoirs of Childhood and Youth,* Albert Schweitzer advises us to "allow our inner thankfulness to find expression." He adds, "Then there will be in the world more sunshine and more strength to do good." Here we follow Schweitzer's advice. We acknowledge with gratitude the generous support of the Chapman University Department of Religious Studies, the Griset and Huntington Lectureship endowments, and the Wang-Fradkin Professorship for both the Schweitzer conference and this book. The cooperation of Chapman University faculty, staff, and students helped make the confer-ence a truly memorable event for all the participants. Linden Youngquist has provided excellent assistance in the electronic preparation of the manuscript of this book, and Jonathan Meyer has helped with proofreading. The edito-rial staff of Syracuse University Press has worked with us to produce a vol-ume that we hope will be intellectually and aesthetically pleasing. To these friends and colleagues, and others unnamed, we express our thanks.

PART ONE

The Vision of Reverence for Life

Albert Schweitzer at the Beginning of the Millennium

James Brabazon

British writer James Brabazon, whose classic biography of Albert Schweitzer is now available in a new edition from Syracuse University Press, delivered this presentation as the keynote address at the conference "Albert Schweitzer at the Turn of the Millennium." In this presentation Brabazon assesses the overall significance of Schweitzer and his ethic of reverence for life as we face a new era, and he concludes that reverence for life is the real bottom line as we contemplate the living of our lives together. The presentation is reproduced here as originally delivered at the conference.

If Albert Schweitzer had been alive at the turn of the millennium, he would not have been too excited about the date. Nobody knew more about the historical Jesus Christ, his hero, than he did. And one thing he knew was that Jesus was not born on December 25th in the year dot. (Incidentally, if the calendar is supposed to start with the birth of Jesus, how come his birthday was not January 1st? How can he have been born near the *end* of his own first year?)

Of course Jesus was not born then, and there are many complicated and irrelevant historical reasons why we celebrated the turn of the millennium on what was palpably the wrong day of the wrong year; and this is only one of many reasons why Schweitzer would not have been sitting on top of a mountain at the end of 1999, waiting for the world to end.

All the same, the *perception* of the end of a millennium, or indeed of a

3

century, does have an effect on humanity. And a hundred years ago, Albert Schweitzer, age twenty-five, was a worried young man as he looked ahead at the twentieth century. So how worried would he be facing this new century and a new millennium? What would be his fears and his hopes?

A hundred years ago, of course, few people shared his apprehensions. What a century it was going to be! Strasbourg University, where Schweitzer worked and studied, was close to the heart of intellectual Europe, and intellectual Europe was buzzing! Rip-roaring new ideas were overturning the perceptions of pretty much the entire human race as far back as the eye could see. During the previous century the industrial revolution and the standardization of parts had turned the physical world upside down, and now they were starting on the way the world was perceived. Marx was looking at the problem of society in history, Freud and others were peering into the hidden mysteries of the mind, and Nietzsche was wondering whether there was any special reason why he should be restricted by the conventions of the boring neighbors—why not become a superman?

At the same time, industrialization was making it possible for nations to think in much larger units, units linked by motorized vehicles on tarmac roads, and by signals carried for great distances on long pieces of wire. Nations were changing shape. Germany was only just becoming united, Italy had recently done so, and Turkey was thinking about it. New nationalisms were being born, with new, bold ambitions.

And somewhere behind all this was Charles Darwin and the shattering new theory of the origin of species, the terrifying yet seemingly incontrovertible proposition that human beings did not start with a cozy couple in the Garden of Eden, but had evolved from the primeval slime into their present magnificent status as the lords of the universe—with the implication that they were going to go on evolving, so long as they proved themselves the fittest. Abruptly or gradually, this notion had taken hold of human minds and left them open to all sorts of new theories—especially theories about power. If God did not start it all off, if there was no supreme power, power must somehow be found in humans.

Marx looked for it in the proletariat, Freud looked for it in the subconscious, and Nietzsche looked for it in the ability of human beings to rise above the conventions that had restricted them through the centuries. Before long, Hitler was to find it in the concept of the superrace.

These theories all had this in common: they undermined conventional religion and a traditional God, and each of them carried enough conviction to attract hosts of adherents more fanatical than their founders—such is the attraction of any idea that claims to solve the riddle of living. We desperately need something solid to cling to, and if we cannot find anything solid, we pretend that what we are clinging to is more solid than it really is.

All these theories failed, though it took many years, millions of deaths, and the distortion of millions of minds before it became clear that none of these was in itself the way forward, and that some of them were very bad ideas indeed. Looking back now, this can be seen as the century of the massive mistakes, of grandiose theories that went "pop."

It is not surprising that most people did not foresee the implications of these theories. G. K. Chesterton once remarked that one of the favorite tricks of the human race was to listen very carefully to what the experts said was going to happen, and then go off and do something completely different.

But if Albert Schweitzer were here with us, looking back at two world wars, the Holocaust, nuclear bombs, and the shattering of our confidence of our place in the universe, he would have every right to say, "Very sorry, but I told you so."

What Schweitzer foresaw was the threat to human values that was posed not only by the new theories, but by all the massive movements that were gathering force a hundred years ago: the pressure of nationalism, dividing nation from nation; the pressure of enormous industrial organizations, requiring slavish loyalty; and the pressure with which the adherents of the new ideas demanded total commitment, in the belief that their own particular panacea really was the be-all and end-all, and any challenge to it was not just a matter for discussion but punishable treachery, so that not only the world of politics but also the worlds of industry and psychology were divided into hostile camps, no compromise allowed. Were you a Jungian or a Freudian, a Marxist or a Communist, a capitalist or a socialist? The pressures to declare for one or the other of these juggernauts were very hard to resist. "Come along, now, don't dither, have you no convictions?" Among the intellectuals there was a kind of commitment to commitment. And this meant giving up their individuality. In extreme instances, in the fascist states, it was made explicit. To be an individual was a crime. The obligation was to hand over one's entire being to the service of the party or the state. But in many other areas of life you were also required to relinquish your brains in return for a party ticket.

Well, we learned the hard way. We have seen great dogmas die; we are skeptical where our predecessors were gullible. But though we may feel wiser now, do we not envy the confidence and enthusiasm of those who a century ago set forth so eagerly on one yellow brick road or another, each leading to one wonderful wizard or another who turned out to be no more than an inadequate human being? Are we happier, and are we any nearer to wisdom? The Western world is littered with people who still cannot quite work out what went wrong with the noble principle, "From each according to his ability, to each according to his need." A great emptiness remained after the illusions were blown away.

Some people in this situation have gone back to fundamentalist versions of the religions that were swept aside by the new ideas. Fundamentalist Christianity, Islam, and Judaism have exercised a powerful grip on starving souls. They offer the certainties that elsewhere have disappeared. But in turn they too exert a terrible demand on human beings to leave their individuality, even their humanity, behind.

We would not need Schweitzer to warn of the ease with which fundamentalism becomes fanaticism and fanaticism becomes terrorism. We can all see that happening in several directions today. But I suggest that if he were here today and looking back, while feeling relieved that some of the storms that he saw building up have blown out, some of the lunacies have run their course, and some of the nightmares have faded away, he would be all too aware of the devastating litter that they have left behind, the emptiness of purpose in great areas of the world where seven devils have entered in where one has been driven out, and the urgency of the need to do something about these before they become as destructive as the storms themselves.

And he might be looking with some alarm at another doctrine, more basic than the fascisms, that has a hold on a wide segment of humanity, a bad idea that still thrives. This is what I call the doctrine of the bottom line, the religion of selfishness and greed, the justification of which, like that of the superman and the superrace, is the law of the survival of the fittest.

The bottom line is one of those irritating clichés, such as "at the end of the day" or "when all's said and done," which are designed to suggest that here we have a final conclusion and no further argument is possible. And I do want to take the argument further. It is also, of course, a financial image. I did think of calling my presentation "How to Make Bankers Human," but I abandoned that because that proposition seemed altogether too implausible.

Poor Darwin, of course, was not to blame. He only said that those species survived that best adapted to their environment. He never claimed that those with the biggest muscles, the biggest breasts, and the loudest mouths should inherit the earth. An excellent survivor is lichen, which keeps a very low profile. But this did not and still does not bother those who use the doctrine to justify their own self-aggrandizement. They do not read Darwin. They have a rough idea of what Darwin said and it suits them fine. If you are big, tough, and brutal, nature is on your side. There is nothing like giving intellectual respectability to your selfishness.

Not everybody, fortunately, subscribes to this notion. People like you and me, whose muscles, breasts, and mouths are pretty average, and who do not have an overpowering urge to trample other people on the way to the top, have a bit of difficulty with it. Unfortunately, it is the people who do like trampling on others who tend to subscribe to it, and because of their trampling inclinations and abilities they tend to be at the top. So powerful people believe in power—more and more of it; rich people believe in money—more and more of it; selfish people believe in selfishness; greedy people believe in greed. So it is that the most powerful people in the world, the financiers, arms dealers, and drug dealers (legitimate and otherwise), believe in themselves and in their divine right to unassailable power.

And unassailable they are. No politician would dare to tangle with the major banks, the major arms manufacturers, or the major drug companies. These people make their own laws, and their law is the law of the bottom line, fiercer and more ruthless than the law of the jungle, the law against which there is no appeal.

These thoughts were reinforced by the recent collapse of the Far Eastern economies and the threatened global meltdown, which had resulted largely from a lot of people—bankers and such folk with a lot of money to invest—investing where they should not. And when I say investing, I mean speculating. And when I say speculating, I mean gambling. And when I say money, I mean other people's money—yours and mine. And that is what they were doing, gambling with your money and mine, without consulting us and without considering the long-term consequences of their greed.

I once met a very pretty lady, with rings on her fingers and bells on her toes, who said that she was looking for someone to lend money to. When I made the obvious, banal joke that she need look no further, she smiled pityingly and explained that the money she was talking about was oil money in billions, and what she really had in mind was a South American country that wanted to build a railway—something like that. I never saw her again, but I expect she found her South American country. I expect they built their railway—or part of it. I expect they found they could not keep up the interest payments, that the bank had to write off a huge bad debt and consequently charge me more for my overdraft, and the South American country and its inhabitants were poorer than before. Huge, unnecessary aggravation all around.

The money people justify all this through their belief in a wonderful, self-adjusting mechanism called the market. They subscribe to clichés such as "The market rules okay, you can't buck it," "This thing is bigger than all of us, a law of nature, part of the survival of the fittest," and "At the end of the day, when all is said and done, in the last resort, the bottom line is the economy."

And it is not only bankers who think this way. Most of us have also swallowed the same notion. The whole business world is the slave of that particular bottom line. As a headline in my paper put it, "The Meek May Inherit the World in the Long Run, but Try Telling That to the Boss." Money is reality.

It is true of course that in one simple sense you cannot buck the market. It really does not work to pay people to make things that nobody wants to buy. One of the more amiable imbecilities of our century, called socialism, believed in doing this. In so far as the socialists fought for social justice they were needed and they were right. But they became stuck with this picture of downtrodden workers (defined generally as people who get paid to get their hands dirty) being owed a living by a thing called the government, which was a source of endless funds. It was forgivable, being a reaction to the brutality of the bosses of the industrial revolution, but it was never going to work, either in the large scale of the Soviet Union or the smaller scale of Western industry, though it took a long time for it to sink in that if people stopped buying the coal and steel and things that the workers were producing, the government did not have any money to pay the workers with except what they took from the tax-payers, and the tax-payers were just us, including the workers.

All this was obvious, naturally, to a grocer's daughter named Margaret Thatcher, and she pretty much put an end to socialism in my country, though the facts of life were already doing a reasonably good job of making the situation clear.

But the power of the market at that level was one thing. The theory, unfortunately, was stretched to cover the market in money itself, and in the guesses and gambles of the bankers and the traders.

It is true that while I was thinking about these things, even the bankers noticed that things had gotten a little out of control. Books and articles began to appear about the crisis of global capitalism. The moneymen had managed to frighten even themselves by their shortsightedness. A few questions began to be asked about the possibility of control. It was encouraging to think that I was in the company of people who actually lived in that world—it suggested I might be on the right lines. But the questions were really only to do with adjustment. Nobody still questioned whether the bottom line really was the bottom line.

Of course, money is essential. I have nothing whatever against it. In fact, I really like it. But its importance lies not in itself but in what one does with it. The economy is *not* the bottom line. It just is not. It is some distance from the bottom line. The economy is actually only the housekeeping—the house itself has to be at least one line closer to the bottom. And in this case the house is the world we live in. So maybe it is the ecology. And at least one line lower still are the creatures who live in the house—ourselves and our fellow living beings.

Nor am I arguing against any investment, however large, in the productive economy—provided it is productive of something needed by the community—us. This too can cause great problems and great hardship, but provided it is genuinely needed, properly researched, and properly accounted for, it is vital. But it has been estimated that for every dollar circulating in the productive economy, twenty to fifty are circulating in the world of what they call "pure" finance—that is to say, in speculation, in billion dollar gambling. And the odd thing is that the bigger the gamble, the less efficient seems to be the research and the accounting. When bad debts get big enough, there is nothing one can do except write them off. The people who collude in these investments—that is, the people who desperately want to find somewhere to invest all those billions, and the people who want to get their hands on all those billions—they know that. They fudge up budgets and bottom lines as if there was no tomorrow, in ways that, believe me, would have them sacked in a week if they were working on a movie or a TV show on which I was producer. Or indeed if they were working on any normal business project.

These people live in an unreal world. This is not a place where money is traded for things and things for money. It is a place where money is traded for money; real things do not enter into it. And as a consequence of this they are also out of touch with normal ethics. Where most of us will have some sense of shame if we do something to hurt other people, or even to break the law, for a 100 percent financier one thing only will produce in him a feeling of shame—if he has failed to swindle someone in a deal. I know a man who I swear can never sleep properly if he feels that the deals he did that day were honest—the kind of man who thinks it is a really good idea to set up a bogus charity and pocket the proceeds himself. The word lucrative covers all sins; words such as sincere and compassionate and humane are simply tools for easing money out of suckers.

And this world, like the world of Hollywood, is beset by swarms of hangers-on, desperate for a sniff of a piece of the action and ruthless in their attempts to get there. The few who do have the power have also the assurance that they are untouchable, because if they do breach promises or even legal contracts, they have the money and influence to win any case brought against them.

I need not go on. We all know about this. And we shrug, because that is the way things are, despite the fact that everybody in the world suffers. Nobody is safe from the law of the bottom line, otherwise known as the law of market forces. The bank manager who today cancels your overdraft because the market has decided that your house is worth less than it was last April may well shortly find himself out on the street because his bank has made a billion-dollar investment in a power station on an ill-surveyed site that turns out to be a swamp, and they only find out when it starts to sink. We are all familiar with these funny stories. But they are not very funny. The individual in these situations—that individual with whom Schweitzer was concerned, you and I and the bank manager—we are all expendable. As expendable as the Jews were to Hitler, or the generals, the doctors, and the intellectuals were to Stalin. The bottom line does not actually kill them; it just lets them starve. People starved all over the world because of misleading hopes before the Wall Street crash and are starving today in Russia because of a battle of bottom lines between the superpowers in the seventies and eighties—a battle that appeared to be between ideologies but which turned out to be between economies.

So here's the point. We live in an age when the dictatorship of the faceless banker is as dangerous as the dictatorship of the power-mad fanatic, except that where Hitler and Stalin merely *desired* to dominate the world, the banker actually does it. Thanks to the speed of communications and the ability of speculative bankers to invest anywhere in the world, bad decisions in Japanese banks, or in American banks that invest in Japan, or in British banks that invest in Malaysia, or in German banks that invest in Russia, affect every man, woman, and child everywhere. We are all adrift on a sea of fantasy and guesswork, with the result that nobody knows from day to day how much their house is worth, how much their factory is worth, or their farm, or their farm produce, or their labor.

Thus the real world is at the mercy of the fantasy world. And whereas Hitler and Stalin at least looked after their own people, the speculator does not give a damn for anyone. Hitler and Stalin could die. The law of the bottom line rolls on regardless. And if it destroys economies—that is, reduces millions of people to starvation—well, that is the way it is, like drought or any other natural disaster.

Looking at the problem, it seems at first sight insoluble. There are ways in which a nation can keep some sort of control over transactions within its borders, but when investment of gigantic sums can be made electronically across the globe, the only constraints come from the prudence and foresight of the bankers and speculators who participate. And they do not have prudence and foresight. They rely on this supposedly self-adjusting thing, "the market," before which we all bow down.

But the market consists, like everything else, of people, and people get things wrong. People can be stupid and venal, and when large sums of money are involved it appears to make them more stupid and venal than ever. Even bankers, setting off for a motorboat trip around the bay, will know better than to pile forty passengers onto a boat designed for ten. But when it comes to money, and they see what seems a suitable vessel, they will happily overload it to absurd levels, thus guaranteeing that it will sink with all hands on board. Greed is a really lousy guide. Instead of suggesting that a vessel that already has all one's rivals onboard may not be the best one to clamber onto by hook or by crook, greed will say, "Me too, me too!" and everyone will be hanging onto the sides and spilling over the top like rush-hour commuters on Bombay buses. When it transpires that the pilot has never heard of safety regulations and does not give a damn for any of his passengers except his immediate family, the passengers look at one another and say, "Somebody should do something about this." But there is nobody to do it, because there is no regulation except the market.

The market, of course, will in the end work its self-adjusting magic by ensuring that a lot of foolish rich people are now not nearly so rich and maybe a bit less foolish. But there are always plenty more greedy folk lining up for the next trip. And in the meantime forests have fallen, rivers have been poisoned, fertile country has been concreted over and then abandoned, and the ordinary people who entrusted their savings to the bankers, in the fond belief that the bankers lived in the real world and would take good care of them, these are now evicted from their homes, lose their families, commit suicide, and in some cases starve to death. Never mind. That is just the way it is.

How can this be? All that money, looking for somewhere to go. All that need, unmet. Ridiculous! Obscene! This cannot be the way things are! This is not like a natural disaster! *We* do it! We, the global community, we are responsible. Life is at issue.

How can it be changed? I do not know. I only know that it can be changed if and when we all stop believing that money makes its own laws and remember that, as Jesus said of the Sabbath, money is made for mankind, and not mankind for it.

Perhaps the first thing is to recognize that there actually is no law of nature that decrees that bankers and the system called "the market" are immutable and invincible. The theorists who believed that the survival of the fittest meant that it was a good thing to trample on other people got in a bit of muddle, and still do, between the law of the jungle and the law of the market. They use the law of the jungle to demonstrate that the law of the market is "natural." This theory is so deeply embedded in the commercial awareness of our civilization that it takes quite a wrench to observe that it is rubbish—there is actually a difference between human beings and lions and tigers. One would think it was fairly obvious to anyone who walked around with his eyes open, but it all goes to show that one consequence of keeping one's eyes fixed on stock market computer screens is that it is easy to bump into things like simple facts. As that great naturalist and comedian Billy Connolly has observed, a wildebeest can be forgiven for not knowing that it is a wildebeest, because there are no mirrors on the Serengeti plains. But a banker has a mirror and he has TV. He can see very well that he is not a wildebeest, nor yet a lion nor a tiger nor a chameleon. He is not a swift, savage creature with rippling muscles and a magnificent disregard for the suffering of its prey and the messy entrails that it leaves lying on the plain. He is simply a paunchy, balding banker. Yet he is prepared to behave as though he was governed by the same imperatives as the animal predators. Poor sap! Hundreds of thousands of years of evolution have passed him by, years that have created vast differences in the impulses that govern us.

But what we believe about the world, how we see ourselves, is very important. As we see ourselves, as we see life, so we behave. If we believe that something gives us leave to behave badly, a great many of us will do just that. How we love our excuses, our justifications! Do not blame me, blame head office. Do not blame me, blame company policy. Blame Communist Party policy. Blame history. Blame the Führer. How easily many of us can become animals if some higher power gives us leave! It was the *ideas* of the master race, of the Communist Party that was all-knowing and all-wise, that gave people distorted ideas about themselves and allowed millions of men and women who might have lived civilized lives to become monsters. We tend to concentrate on the evil of those regimes, forgetting the sheer philosophical *wrongness* that gave that evil its justification.

Among potent but I think misleading ideas, there is this notion that it must be good to be "natural." The principal aim of human beings, after all, has been to escape as far as possible from nature, or at least to control it—to get out of the wet, to cook food before we eat it, to sleep somewhere more comfortable than the lumpy ground, to breed varieties of grass that we can grind and mill and turn into bread and pasta, and to turn our grunts into speech and our speech into literature. And the entire process of civilization has been to moderate the more basic natural impulses so that our communities can live in increasingly complex relationships and achieve increasingly complicated objectives.

Yet recently "natural" has become an "in" word. We are told on the one hand that aggressive behavior in business is natural, because animals eat one another, and on the other hand that other animals never kill except for food, so we should do the same. Both are rubbish. Pretty little foxes love to get in a henhouse and kill as many hens as they can just for fun. Adorable otters will kill fish just for fun. Cute little mink will kill anything that comes their way.

I suggest to you that this whole identification of ourselves with animals is a highly misleading sentimentality—and I say it in full awareness of Schweitzer's solidarity with the animal world, because that is a different thing. Britain's best-loved and most-respected naturalist and presenter of wildlife TV programs, David Attenborough, was called by an interviewer an animal lover. "Don't be ridiculous," said Attenborough. "I've been sat on and shat on by too many of them. I'm fascinated by them and I respect their right to their proper place on the planet. But I certainly don't feel obliged to love them." And this is important, this realism, this refusal of sentimentality. There are animals that have the most revolting eating and breeding habits, which, if we were to copy them in Orange County or in the city of London, would raise the most liberal eyebrows—apart from being exceedingly difficult to perform.

Schweitzer was never sentimental. What he felt, and spoke about, was a unity and a responsibility far deeper than that. And he certainly never suggested that we humans should learn aggression and hostility from the animals.

We have to do better than the animals, not copy them! And I suggest that the law of the market and its justification by the law of the jungle is just another of the great twentieth-century follies, like communism and fascism, and like them it may well be due for the chop. Communism and fascism, once seemingly all-powerful, faded away not only through the efforts of their enemies but through their own internal tensions, pressures, and defiance of the basic laws of common humanity, which will finally break through any oppression as grass will finally break through concrete.

And if I am right, that is what will happen here too. But it took a lot of effort to get rid of those other lunacies, and I am suggesting we should perhaps engage in a campaign against this particular lunacy, against the dominance of the irresponsible financier, just as Schweitzer campaigned against the hydrogen bomb tests, which at that time also threatened whole societies with destruction.

What Schweitzer was saying, with his reverence for life, was that grass is the bottom line. Life is the bottom line, not profit, not success, not conquest. And if we think he is right, let us say so, loud and clear, as a philosophy, as a way of thinking, as a bottom line, as a way of looking at the world that has close and permanent connections with a way of living.

We do need something solid to cling to. And I suggest to you that there is nothing so solid as reverence for life! That is the bottom line, and that is what we must try to make people realize. Money has its place. Religions have their place. Nations have their place. None of them is the bottom line. If we treat them as such, we are assuredly at risk of intolerance and indifference toward those who do not share our race or our religion or our color. *Life* is what links us. The recognition of this is what it means to be human. We are not lions and tigers. We share life with the animals and indeed with the plants, but we alone are aware of it. That gives us responsibility—the responsibility of being human.

Let us note here how dangerous the idea of reverence for life is. It takes away our excuses. It says that *nothing*—no faith, no political or theological or economic theory, no sense of revenge for historical wrongs—can justify cruelty and inhumanity. On the other hand, it gives us leave to do something that a great many of those trapped in slave states secretly longed to do—to be human. We are very lucky, you and I. We live in a time and a place that give us leave to be human and make it easy to do so—if we wish. In a world where we all need some solid base to build on, some polestar to guide us, let us be thankful that we have a chance to go for a base that is unshakable, life itself, nothing less profound.

Now, there is something else that has happened to us in the twentieth century. Along with the crazy theories and the violent nationalisms, there has been an outburst of what one can only call by the question-begging name "humanity." Professor Dawkins, in his theory of the selfish gene, claims that we are all impelled toward activities that preserve and propagate our genetic survival. He could be right. One never knows with scientists, they sometimes are. But if it is so, we have to stretch the meaning of selfishness pretty far if it is to include the activities of people impelled to work in dangerous and horribly uncomfortable conditions in order to help and to heal less-fortunate fellow humans who have no possible chance of repaying their benefactors.

Schweitzer claimed that living for others is the greatest happiness. An enjoyable way of passing the time is to discuss with friends the limits of enlightened self-interest, the extent to which putting oneself through hardship can be regarded as fun, and whether people who devote themselves to other people are just masochists (as if that description solved the problem). Indeed, Schweitzer claimed that it would have been a hardship for him *not* to have done what he did for the people of Gabon. But what is evident is that any of these ways of finding satisfaction has evolved a very long way from the simple adaptation to one's environment that was the thesis of Charles Darwin. The proposition that almost all of us would rather survive than perish, and would rather be happy than miserable, is hardly worth putting on paper. The interesting thing is that altruism, empathy, and concern for others, and not just other humans but other species and forms of life, have found such a ringing response, especially in the last century and in the latter half of it, and with the young—especially, one could say, post-Schweitzer.

A while ago I had occasion to read the book I wrote about Schweitzer in the 1970s. I wanted to find out how much of it was now out-of-date. A depressing discovery was how much I once knew and had now forgotten. More cheerful, however, was to find that I am now far less pessimistic about human beings than I was then. Humanity has developed a more tender skin in recent years—sometimes to the point of folly, as happened recently in England when ardent lovers of wildlife released hundreds of ferocious mink from captivity, which gave the little darlings a chance to gorge on chickens, cats, dogs, and babies. But every movement has its fanatics, and they do not invalidate the main point. One thing Schweitzer never did was lose his grip on common sense.

It may be somewhat hopeful to expect drunken Serbian youths with Kalashnikovs slung over their shoulders to listen to sermons on compassion from self-righteous politicians, but little by little new areas of the world are being affected by this novel notion that we really are members one of another, that the selfish gene, if it exists at all, is smart enough to know that its true self-interest is in peace, not conflict, in cooperation, not confrontation.

When the United States first dropped atom bombs on Hiroshima and Nagasaki, there was of course a profound shock throughout the world that such power now existed, that human beings now possessed the ability to destroy their planet. This was the apocalypse, no less. I saw something rather different, and I wrote a little piece for our parish magazine called "The Hope of the Atom Bomb." What it said was that hitherto the human race had always had Daddy God to rely on to look after things. But now he had given us the key of the door and had said, in effect, "Right, now you're big girls and boys, and now if you throw tantrums and fling the furniture around, you clear up your own messes, and you pay for the damage. And if you're really stupid enough to burn the house down, that's your problem. Don't come whining to me."

I seem to remember saying in the article that it might take fifty years for the idea to sink in, for the world to sober up from its present inebriated condition (this, remember, was just at the end of World War II) and settle down to being grown-up.

Well, I may be going soft in my old age, but it seems that in many continents a generation is growing up to whom it is simply obvious that we *are* responsible for ourselves, that our environment is all-important, that the bottom line is not the economy, it is the ecology, it is life.

Since the latter half of the last century this generation's awareness of the environment has started to stretch across the world, helped by the technologies of travel and of communication. These too have made an astonishing

difference to our world since Schweitzer was staring at the coming twentieth century. Electricity, then the internal combustion engine—the very
thing that made wars so much more devastating—have totally changed our
perspective on the world. Yes, we boast about the new discoveries and new
developments, but do we remember how recently the vast majority of
mankind was still limited to horse-drawn transport, to information that was
mostly gossip and hearsay, to cities that were lit at best by gas? Do we realize
the effects of the new discoveries on the ability of the peoples of the world
to learn about one another, thanks to the way in which journalists can pen-
etrate to far and fearsome places and transmit their information instanta-
neously to anyone with a radio or TV set? How extraordinary that
laser-guided missiles can target with considerable accuracy the most vulnerable places of an enemy country, and our own journalists can send us pictures of it as it happens. It is not just the technology that would have been
inconceivable a hundred years ago, but it is the awareness that it gives to the
world as a world that shows us unmistakably what human beings are doing
to one another.

What is happening, at an ever-increasing rate, is a fantastic increase in
knowledge—knowledge of two kinds. First, knowledge of the extraordinary things we can now do; then, knowledge of what has gone wrong, what
unforeseen consequences are devastating the planet as a result of the first
knowledge. The technology that enabled us to make bigger and better cars,
planes, tanks, and bombs has been followed by the technology that enables
us to see the damage the earlier technology was unwittingly doing. A hundred years ago, factories flung filth into the air and the water with never a
thought of the poisoning of the plants and the birds and the insects and the
fish. Now, we have people who analyze the effects of this on wildlife in the
farthest corners of the globe and bring back close-ups to our living rooms.

The damage comes first, and the awareness follows. On the whole I feel
that humanity *is* learning from its information, *is* catching up with technology. There are places where bitter, inhuman conflict still rages, but these are
in general the places where access to world awareness is still at a low level.
There are places where pollution is still appalling, but these are in general
places where poverty, rather than lack of knowledge, is the reason it persists.
It is a race between the damage done and the ability to overcome it. But

overall, the understanding of the situation and the will to deal with it have grown and grown. Even in politics there seems to me to have been a sea change. The famous "third way" of my prime minister, which seems to have powerful similarities with the policies of your president, seems to me to be a switch from concentrating on defeating opponents to concentrating on defeating problems. And because our understanding of the situations facing humanity is increasing, it is harder than it was before for different parties to take up different stances. So, to the bewilderment of political analysts who have been trained to spot policy differences and exciting confrontations, both sides grow closer and closer together. Trade union officials appear on TV explaining the economic problems of the management and what they are prepared to do to help. The diehards are outraged. What is the world coming to? Coming to its senses, maybe. Humanity has become increasingly human and increasingly able to express its humanity. The selfish gene has begun to recognize that its survival depends on the survival not of one side or the other, but of the whole lot of us.

Another scientist, Rupert Sheldrake, a highly qualified biologist who also knows his quantum physics, has suggested that there might be a series of force fields, as yet as undetected as electricity was a couple of hundred years ago, that binds together every kind of unit in the universe, from the smallest particle to the universe itself—and not only objects, not only individual creatures, but communities—each field nested in the next largest, like Chinese boxes. It is an unproven theory, but it would explain a huge number of puzzles about ourselves and our world that are normally dismissed as not just insoluble but as too weird to worry about. It would also give a scientific basis to our sense of oneness, first with our family, then with our football team, then with our nation, then with the planet earth, and finally perhaps with the universe itself.

For Sheldrake also suggests, as others have suggested, that the universe itself is evolving, learning as it goes along. And we are learning with it. And if, as now seems clear, matter and mind are made of the same stuff, then the mystics and the scientists are both working toward the same common goal. The main reason I would like to live to be two hundred or more years old is that I want to be there when the scientists and the theologians meet, like people who have started from different sides of the earth meeting at the

North Pole, and each group says to the other, "What on earth are *you* doing here? And how on earth did you get here?"

It is bound to happen, because the truth is the truth, and there can only be one truth. And the way to the truth is, as Schweitzer showed, not by piling argument on argument, but by stripping away falsehood and going to the bottom of things, to the place where he found reverence for life. The place that is peace and joy, the Paradiso, the white light that is made from all the colors, the final bottom line, the still center—maybe the quantum soup.

The stillness of that center is not the stillness of a top lying on its side; it is the stillness of a top spinning perfectly—absolutely stable, motion and energy perfectly balanced, maybe singing a quiet song.

"God" is a word that Schweitzer avoided, because it means so many different things to different people. But whatever else it means, it must mean the bottom line. It must mean the enhancement of life. When it is used, as it so often is, to justify or excuse conflict, it is surely the wrong bottom line. It leads to reduced life. When it is used, as it can be by priests and preachers, to gain power over others or to raise large sums of cash for the aggrandizement of the preacher, it is the wrong bottom line. It leads to reduced life—even for the preacher.

Let me offer three phrases: "to reverence life," "to be in harmony with the ultimate energy of the universe," and "to love God." They all mean the same thing.

When Schweitzer found reverence for life, he had been covering sheet after sheet of paper with scribbled thoughts as he searched for the base he believed must exist, where ethics and reality met. The phrase finally came to him from nowhere—or maybe from everywhere. And I like to think that at that moment all the pieces of paper blew away in a gust of wind and settled for a moment on the surface of the Ogowe River before sinking forever out of sight. And I hope they were biodegradable.

The right bottom line leads to enhanced life. And this is what I hope for the world, and individually for all of us: that we can gain the insight to ditch all the crummy and inadequate bottom lines that we are surrounded with—financial, religious, political, and interpersonal—and settle for nothing less than that ultimate place where Schweitzer found reverence for life, where he said we cannot help finding reverence for life, because that is what is there.

Once we have found it, we will be in a position to assess all the other bottom lines.

And there is no time to be lost. We live with the aftermath of the great mistakes. The wounds that the twentieth century has inflicted on our planet are deep and terrible, sometimes seeming beyond hope of curing. And they are not only physical; they are mental as well. Russia has its economic breakdown and its despair. The former beautiful Yugoslavia continues to tear itself to pieces, creating ever-new hatreds. African tribalism and the consequences of white misrule erupt in horrendous slaughter and bitterness. The inner cities of Europe and America have become deserts where young lives are wasted in hopelessness and frustration, and their vital energies are poured into destructive, drug-ridden craziness. The whole world has its pollution.

With all these danger points, and with the ability of an increasing number of nations to wield weapons of mass destruction, the new millennium offers a frightening number of powder kegs ready to blow. The coming century is going to be a race between the destroyers of the environment and the preservers, with the preservers having a lot of catching up to do. That is why we need the right bottom line *now*. That is why reverence for life is just as important now as when Schweitzer first spoke of it—and always will be. The difference is that now the soil is far more fertile. The members of the new generation are not stupid. They have seen what a shambles the old systems made, and most of them have seen too that opting out is not an option, that the "me" generation got them nowhere. They have the information about what is wrong, they have the technology to put much of it right, and they have their hearts and minds in the right place. But they need all the help we can give them.

Schweitzer did not believe in great movements—he believed in individuals and their individual hearts and minds. He believed in happiness and health. He believed that when individuals are free, in happiness and health, to be fully themselves, their compasses would inevitably swing to the magnetic north of reverence for life. I think that is what he would wish for the new millennium—that enough of us, as individuals, would find that magnetic north, and in whatever sphere we found ourselves, add our small but absolutely essential contribution to the direction of our world.

CHAPTER 2

Affirming Reverence for Life

Marvin Meyer

Marvin Meyer, director of the Chapman University Albert Schweitzer Institute, pre-sented this essay at the conference "Albert Schweitzer at the Turn of the Millennium" as a scholarly meditation in the context of an all-faiths service, which also included an ecumenical liturgy, a recording of organ music of Bach played by Schweitzer, and African music and dance. In this essay Meyer surveys the various ways in which Schweitzer—and we—can articulate and affirm an understanding of reverence for life.

One of the vivid images, among others, that comes to mind when I think of Albert Schweitzer affirming reverence for life is the image of Schweitzer with his ants. This image has been made memorable by the dentist, artist, and author Frederick Franck, who lived and worked with Schweitzer for a time in the late 1950s and described his experiences in his book *Days with Albert Schweitzer: A Lambaréné Landscape.*[1] Among the charm-ing drawings in the book is one with the caption "Dr. Schweitzer entertains his ants." Frederick was kind enough to present me with an artist's proof of the drawing, and I have mounted it appropriately in my study among other drawings and prints. The drawing shows Schweitzer at eighty-six, bushy of hair, mustache, and eyebrows, hunched over his writing table, with pages of a manuscript tacked to a wall, sheets of paper on the table, and ants crawling over the sheets. Frederick describes Schweitzer encountering his ants: "For some years he has been watching this particular family of ants, a few hundred or a few thousand quite benign and harmless ones, which live in a nest

22

somewhere under the floor boards of his room. After every meal he puts a little piece of fish under the kerosene lamp on his table; immediately the ants crawl up the table leg, walk in a neat line across the top piled with papers, and start to tackle the fish offering from all sides. It requires five or six of the tiny insects to transport a huge fragment of two cubic millimeters of fish across the table, down the leg to their residence. Dr. Schweitzer and I watched with delight how first the softer pieces of fish were chosen in preference to older, harder ones." [2]

Schweitzer affirming reverence for life: certainly reverence for life is expressed in Schweitzer's treatment of his ants, as well as his mosquitoes, his chickens, and his pelican, Parsifal, but it should not be trivialized as being reducible to only that. Schweitzer considered reverence for life to be the elemental and universal ethical concept, the foundation for all sound moral thought and action, the necessary conclusion of clear thinking and reflection. When Schweitzer affirmed reverence for life, he affirmed the solidarity of all living things and the moral obligation of people who live in the midst of living things.

Schweitzer affirming reverence for life: certainly Schweitzer was neither the only person nor the first person to advocate love and solidarity among humans and all living things. But when he affirmed reverence for life, he did so in his own inimitable way, with the variety of formulations and affirmations typical of the man who did so many different things so well.

It is my intention in this meditation to examine four ways in which Albert Schweitzer articulated his understanding of reverence for life.

◆　　◆　　◆

First, Schweitzer affirmed reverence for life autobiographically. In his *Memoirs of Childhood and Youth* Schweitzer traced his sensitivity to the pain and suffering in the world back to his childhood, and he recounted stories, now familiar to many of us, of his concern for living things from the days of his early childhood.[3] I quote from the recent translation by Kurt and Alice Bergel: "Already before I started school it seemed quite incomprehensible to me that my evening prayers were supposed to be limited to human beings. Therefore, when my mother had prayed with me and kissed me goodnight, I secretly added another prayer which I had made up myself for all living beings. It went like this: 'Dear God, protect and bless all beings that breathe, keep all evil from them, and let them sleep in peace.' "[4] Again: "I had an experience during my seventh or eighth year which made a deep impression on me. Heinrich Bräsch and I had made ourselves rubber band slingshots with which we could shoot small pebbles. One spring Sunday during Lent he said to me, 'Come on, let's go to the Rebberg and shoot birds.' I hated this idea, but I did not contradict him for fear he might laugh at me. We approached a leafless tree in which birds, apparently unafraid of us, were singing sweetly in the morning air. Crouching like an Indian hunter, my friend put a pebble in his slingshot and took aim. Obeying his look of command, I did the same with terrible pangs of conscience and vowing to myself to miss. At that very moment the church bells began to ring out into the sunshine, mingling their chimes with the song of the birds. It was the warning bell, half an hour before the main bell ringing. For me, it was a voice from heaven. I put the slingshot aside, shooed the birds away so that they were safe from my friend, and ran home. Ever since then, when the bells of Passiontide ring out into the sunshine and the naked trees, I remember, deeply moved and grateful, how that day they rang into my heart the commandment 'Thou shalt not kill.' "[5] Schweitzer told other stories about an old horse being dragged to the slaughterhouse in Colmar, about his own dog, Phylax, and his neighbor's dog, Löscher, about the revolting experience of impaling worms and hooking fish, and about the treatment extended to Mausche the Jewish dealer when he passed through Günsbach.

When reflecting on his childhood, Schweitzer observed that the commandment not to kill and torture impacted him in a powerful way in his childhood and youth, and such may well be the case. It may well be that Schweitzer was predisposed from childhood and influenced by childhood experiences to feel a kinship with other living beings, a feeling that may anticipate his later affirmations of reverence for life. Yet Schweitzer's reflections, published in his *Memoirs of Childhood and Youth,* are based upon his sessions in 1923 with the psychologist and pastor Oscar Pfister in Zurich, when Schweitzer was depressed and in need of counsel. His reflections in his *Memoirs* allowed him the subsequent opportunity to present his own interpretation of the experiences of his childhood and youth, and while James Bentley's charges of "emotional duplicity" seem to me to put the matter too strongly,[6] I suggest that Schweitzer may in fact have projected his values as an ethical thinker in his mid-forties back upon the experiences of his childhood. In his *Memoirs* we may learn as much about the values of the adult Schweitzer as we do about young Albert in and around Günsbach.[7]

◆　◆　◆

Second, Schweitzer affirmed reverence for life exegetically. Albert Schweitzer grew up as a preacher's child, and from an early age he was exposed to the interpretation of the Bible in an open, liberal, Lutheran context. He was given a copy of the New Testament, he says, at age eight, and he apparently entered the world of critical biblical scholarship already in his youth. If wise men from the East visited baby Jesus and offered him valuable gifts, young Albert asked, why was the holy family so poor? If shepherds saw the holy child in the manger, he wondered, why did none of them become followers of Jesus? And, not to leave out critical questions pertaining to the Hebrew Scriptures, how could a rainstorm lasting forty days and forty nights produce a cataclysmic flood according to Genesis, he questioned, when a similarly heavy rain in Günsbach produced nothing of the kind? (His father's answer: in the old days it came down in bucketfuls, not in drops as it does today.)

Later, as a young man involved in military service for Germany, Schweitzer spent some of his leisure time opening his Greek New Testament and reading a text that was to play a powerful role in his exegesis of the Bible and in his interpretation of the person of Jesus: Matthew 10. (Today I might prefer to refer to this as the Matthean version and revision of the mission speech in the synoptic sayings source Q.[8]) In Matthew 10, Jesus sends out the twelve followers to announce that heaven's kingdom is near, and he reassures them that, although they will be opposed, they will not finish going through the towns of Israel before the child of humankind—conventionally called the Son of Man—comes. The child of humankind who is coming, Schweitzer recognized, is the apocalyptic figure, announced in the book of Daniel and elsewhere, who will return to usher in God's kingdom at the end of time.

Schweitzer's radical proposal, following Johannes Weiss, was eventually published in *The Mystery of the Kingdom of God* and *The Quest of the Historical*

Jesus.[9] The latter work in particular was a masterful piece; James M. Robinson observes that the reader must be "amazed at the undistracted persistence with which Schweitzer worked out a brilliant thesis as he worked his way through enormous masses of literature."[10] Schweitzer proposed that Jesus was convinced—mistakenly, tragically—that the end was at hand, and that he was to be the instrument by whom the final kingdom would be brought in. Through Jesus' efforts, and through his death, God's kingdom would come. Of this Jesus was convinced, but he was wrong, heroically wrong, dead wrong. Schweitzer depicted Jesus' grand and misguided efforts in this manner: "There is silence all around. The Baptist appears, and cries, 'Repent, for the kingdom of heaven is at hand.' Soon after that comes Jesus, and in the knowledge that he is the coming Son of Man lays hold of the wheel of the world to set it moving on that last revolution which is to bring all ordinary history to a close. It refuses to turn, and he throws himself upon it. Then it does turn, and crushes him. Instead of bringing in the eschatological conditions, he has destroyed them. The wheel rolls onward, and the mangled body of the one immeasurably great man, who was strong enough to think of himself as the spiritual ruler of humankind and to bend history to his purpose, is hanging upon it still. That is his victory and his reign."[11]

Jesus, according to Schweitzer, is a stranger to our modern world. "He comes to us," Schweitzer writes in his memorable conclusion to his *Quest,* "as one unknown, without a name."[12] Schweitzer scoffed at the many scholars who engaged in a quest for the historical Jesus and ended up creating a modern Jesus in their own image, after their own likeness, reflecting their own values of their own world. Thus with regard to Ernest Renan's *Life of Jesus,* Schweitzer charges, "It is Christian art in the worst sense of the term— the art of the wax image. The gentle Jesus, the beautiful Mary, the fair Galileans who formed the retinue of the 'amiable carpenter,' might have been taken over in a body from the shop-window of an ecclesiastical art emporium in the Place St. Sulpice."[13]

Schweitzer's reconstruction of the life and death of Jesus is not above reproach, however. In the face of a great deal of the scholarship of his day, and scholarship to the present day, Schweitzer stressed the primary place and importance of the Gospel of Matthew (along with the Gospel of Mark). He chose his own scholarly path, passing by his brilliant teacher Heinrich

Holtzmann, who championed the hypothesis of the primacy of Mark among the synoptic Gospels. I believe in this respect Holtzmann was probably right and Schweitzer was probably wrong. Yet Schweitzer also needed Matthew: he needed Matthew 10 and the apocalyptic historical Jesus of Matthew 10 in order for his strange, foreign Jesus to emerge as the eschatological child of humankind. Though scholars in his day and ours have seen Matthew 10 as the creation of the later Christian church imposing its apocalyptic vision upon its portrait of Jesus, Schweitzer disagreed. He thought the apocalyptic Jesus to be the historical Jesus. Schweitzer's apocalyptic Jesus has remained one of the truly compelling images of Jesus throughout the twentieth century, but it is no wonder that many of us now gravitate to a different paradigm of Jesus, a nonapocalyptic paradigm of Jesus as a teacher of wisdom.[14]

It was not that Schweitzer was willing to bypass the wisdom of Jesus. Schweitzer was touched by Jesus' ethic of love, and he was moved by the Sermon on the Mount as much as Tolstoy, Bonhoeffer, Gandhi, and others were.[15] For Schweitzer, the sayings of Jesus communicated the message of love that was to remind him, increasingly, of reverence for life. Already in 1905, in a sermon he preached at St. Nicolai's Church on Sunday, November 19, he exclaimed, "What kind of a living person is Jesus? Don't search for formulas to describe him, even if they be hallowed by centuries. I almost got angry the other day when a religious person said to me that only someone who believes in the resurrection of the body and in the glorified body of the risen Christ can believe in the living Jesus. . . . Let me explain it in my way. The glorified body of Jesus is to be found in his sayings."[16] If for Schweitzer those sayings are the sayings of an apocalyptic preacher announcing the end of the world, they remain the purer and stronger because of that. They are the charged, ethical sayings about the life of love in the interim, in the brief time before the end. They are the sayings about how to love when everything is at stake, when there is no room for weakness and vacillation. In his *Quest* Schweitzer also describes our encounter with Jesus and his sayings as an encounter with "Jesus as spiritually risen within people," and Schweitzer himself becomes a proponent of "Jesus mysticism." And as Schweitzer puts it, from the early days of his career, this sort of ethical life, this strong commitment to love in the face of God's kingdom, may be called "practical eschatology," and Schweitzer refers to his Lambaréné hospital as an "outpost of the kingdom of God."[17]

Later Schweitzer emphasized the sayings of Jesus even more emphatically, when he suggested that Jesus actually used only the language of apocalyptic to communicate his primary message, his ethical message of love. In his 1950 preface to *The Quest of the Historical Jesus* he wrote, "It was Jesus who began to spiritualize the ideas of the kingdom of God and the Messiah. He introduced into the late-Jewish conception of the kingdom his strong ethical emphasis on love, making this, and the consistent practice of it, the indispensable condition of entrance. By so doing he charged the late-Jewish idea of the kingdom of God with ethical forces, which transformed it into the spiritual and ethical reality with which we are familiar. Since the faith clung firmly to the ethical note, so dominant in the teaching of Jesus, it was able to reconcile and identify the two, neglecting those utterances in which Jesus voices the older eschatology."[18]

For Schweitzer, then, Jesus becomes preeminently the proclaimer of love, and for Schweitzer Jesus becomes—like Schweitzer himself—the proclaimer of reverence for life. In the epilogue to *Out of My Life and Thought* Schweitzer puts it quite succinctly: reverence for life is the ethic of Jesus, "the ethic of love widened into universality."[19] (On the universality of reverence for life, we may think with Schweitzer of God as infinite life, or of the Jain ethical principle of *ahimsa,* nonviolence toward all life. More on both of these matters below.) Suddenly Jesus, who was said to come to us as one unknown, does not seem so much a stranger to our times after all. He seems to be, as Henry Clark put it, the first liberal Christian, who under the guise of old-world apocalyptic preached a modern, humanitarian message of love and compassion.[20] It is somewhat ironic but perhaps also indicative of Schweitzer's own humanity that the person who called scholars to a self-critical stance in the face of their modernizing portraits of Jesus concluded that he and Jesus articulated the same basic ethical message for today.

◆　　◆　　◆

Third, Schweitzer affirmed reverence for life religiously through his study of world religions. Schweitzer was a student of world religions, but he was no disinterested student. Rather, he betrayed the nearly desperate spirit of a scholar who—one of my colleagues noted—was writing his books on world religions "as a drowning man looking for something—anything—to grab onto." [21] He frantically searched—that same colleague said he ransacked— the religions of the world to find an appropriate ethic that would allow for an active affirmation of life. The result of his academic and personal search was *Christianity and the Religions of the World, Indian Thought and Its Development,* and the still unpublished *Chinese Thought and Its Development.* [22] Schweitzer examined and evaluated, in addition to Christianity, ancient Mediterranean religions and Asian religions. I find it unfortunate that he did not pay any particular attention to the African religions around him, just as he did not learn an African language or study African music. Among the world religions that he did study, he appreciated features of many of them, particularly ancient Stoicism, Chinese religions, and aspects of Indian religions.

Schweitzer was especially fascinated with the ethical piety of Lao-tse and Meng-tse, among others, from China. In *Indian Thought and Its Development* Schweitzer cites several Chinese maxims and stories that are indicative of the ethical stance of active compassion that he found so attractive in Chinese sources, such as "Have a pitiful heart for all creatures"; "One must bring no sorrow even upon worms and plants and trees"; "One does evil who shoots birds, hunts animals, digs up the larvae of insects, frightens nesting birds"; and "Do not allow your children to amuse themselves by playing with flies or butterflies or little birds. It is not merely that such proceedings may result in damage to living creatures: They awaken in young hearts the inclination to cruelty and murder." Such statements of ethical wisdom are reminiscent of Schweitzer's own statements, stories, and actions having to do with birds, worms, and insects—recall Schweitzer's ants. (Could Schweitzer have carried these Chinese maxims into his own writing and his own life?) Compare also the following story about the wife of a Chinese soldier. She was, it is said, ill and near death: "As a remedy she was ordered to eat the brains of a hundred sparrows. When she saw the birds in a cage, she sighed and said, 'Shall it come to pass that to cure me a hundred living creatures shall be slain? I will rather die than allow that suffering shall come to them.' She opened the cage and let them fly. Shortly after, she recovered from her illness." [23]

Schweitzer at times returned to a conviction that Christianity, and particularly the gospel of Jesus, may represent the best articulation of a living spirituality and of reverence for life. He once wrote, "Christianity alone is ethical mysticism,"[24] whereas the union with the divine found in Eastern religions represents a less active form of personal spirituality. Schweitzer was not appreciative of the renunciation of the world, of life, and of action that he considered (rather unfairly) characteristic of Indian religions. Nonetheless, I am convinced, with Ara Paul Barsam, that Schweitzer was deeply influenced by religious expressions from China and India.[25] An Indian ethical principle that seems to have made a significant impression upon Schweitzer was that of *ahimsa,* nonviolence or noninjury, as preached and practiced among Jains and others. Jainism was established in the sixth century B.C.E. by Mahavira, a reformer of Hinduism. The Jains believe that the universe is alive with suffering souls and agonizing lives: a person is hurt, an insect is crushed, a tree is cut, a stone is kicked—in our infinite cycle of births and deaths and rebirths, *samsara,* our souls have known indescribable pains. Since our human lives are bound together with the existence of all other beings in the world, Mahavira affirmed, "One who neglects or disregards the existence of earth, air, fire, water, and vegetation disregards his own existence which is entwined with them."[26] To live rightly and well in this sort of world requires that we repudiate all the violence and the killing that can increase the stain of *karma* (the causality that shapes our destiny and determines the character of birth and rebirth). Thus, the Jain Sutras proclaim, "All things breathing, all things existing, all things living, all beings whatever, should not be slain or treated with violence, or insulted, or tortured, or driven away."[27] A deep commitment to a life of *ahimsa* may be seen in the everyday practices of observant Jains. Jains ordinarily observe a strict vegetarian diet, and even the vegetables—that are, after all, living things to be killed or eaten—are evaluated for their karmic weight. Jains advocate that kindness and consideration be shown to animals, and they support programs for the prevention of cruelty to animals. Some Jains even wear masks to prevent the inadvertent slaughter of tiny insects that otherwise might be killed as people breathe in and out; some sweep the surface of the ground ahead of them lest they trample living things. Such radically nonviolent practices, extreme as they sometimes are, illustrate a lifestyle that is mindful of the precariousness of life all around and the need to exercise care and gentleness in the presence of other living things. Jains compare this restrained and gentle life to that of "the bee [that] sucks honey in the blossoms of a tree without hurting the blossom and strengthens itself." [28]

In his evaluation of *ahimsa,* Schweitzer admitted that the proclamation of *ahimsa* is of great importance in the development of ethical thought. "The laying down of the commandment not to kill and not to damage is one of the greatest events in the spiritual history of humankind," Schweitzer announced in *Indian Thought.* "Starting from its principle, founded on world and life denial, of abstention from action, ancient Indian thought—and this in a period when in other respects ethics has not progressed very far—reaches the tremendous discovery that ethics knows no bounds! So far as we know, this is for the first time clearly expressed by Jainism." [29] Schweitzer goes on to praise Buddha (with qualifications) for making this ethic of nonviolence an ethic of compassion, and he lauds Gandhi for transforming *ahimsa* into a principle of active compassion and affirmation of life—an ethic comparable, as Gandhi also recognized, to the ethic of Jesus as enunciated in the Sermon on the Mount.

Schweitzer's affirmation of reverence for life compares well, in several respects, with the ethic of *ahimsa* of Jains and others. If *ahimsa* is an all-encompassing ethical principle that fundamentally shapes the nonviolent lives and commitments of Jains and others, so does reverence for life for Schweitzer. If *ahimsa* embraces the value of all life—humans, animals, and plants—and proclaims solidarity among humans and all living things, so does reverence for life for Schweitzer. Schweitzer goes so far, in his *Philosophy of Civilization,* as to see, with Schopenhauer, a will to live not only in humans, animals, and plants, but even in crystals. [30] (In his first sermon on reverence for life, in 1919, Schweitzer also notes how the snowflake, with its delicate and intricate pattern, melts and dies in one's hand: "The flake, which fell upon your hand from infinite space, which glistened there, quivered, and died—that is you. Wherever you see life—that is you!" [31]) And if *ahimsa* implies something of a gloomy, pessimistic assessment of life in the world—we cannot, finally, avoid the taking of life—so does reverence for life for Schweitzer. Mike W. Martin notes the guilt-mongering of Schweitzer and prefers to employ the concept of responsibility—a concept that Schweitzer also embraces. [32] James Brabazon reminds us that we might equally well speak of debt rather than guilt.[33] Schweitzer says that since we cannot avoid destroying and injuring life, we necessarily incur guilt or indebtedness. He writes, "Ethics is responsibility without limit towards all that lives"—and then a few pages later he adds, "The good conscience is an invention of the devil."[34]

It is not entirely surprising, after all, to remember what Schweitzer told Charles Joy about the origin of the idea of reverence for life: "The idea of reverence for life came to me as an unexpected discovery, like an illumination coming upon me in the midst of intense thought while I was completely conscious. And when the idea and the words had come to me, it was of Buddha I thought."[35]

◆　　◆　　◆

Fourth, Schweitzer affirmed reverence for life philosophically. In his correspondence with his soon-to-be wife, Hélène, Schweitzer acknowledged that he was essentially a philosopher, though a philosopher who was caught by Jesus. ("Basically I am philosopher—but I let myself be caught by him, the greatest, the most divine of all philosophers, in whom the most sublime thought leads back to the most simple. Because of this obedience he will forgive my heresies."[36]) In his correspondence with Oskar Kraus, Schweitzer explained that in his philosophical writings he employed exclusively the language of philosophy and logical thinking, and thus referred to "the universal will-to-live" rather than "God."[37] Schweitzer's most complete and arguably most compelling discussion of reverence for life is given in his philosophical writings, specifically in *The Philosophy of Civilization*.[38] There he considers Descartes's starting point for philosophical discourse, the dictum *cogito ergo sum,* and pronounces it paltry and arbitrary. Instead, Schweitzer suggests that true philosophy begins with another sort of immediate awareness, in which each of us lives and moves, he claims, day by day. Like Arthur Schopenhauer, as well as Friedrich Nietzsche, Schweitzer proposes the primacy of the will, but he puts a very different spin on the place of the will. He writes that true philosophy or true ethics begins with an awareness and affirmation of the will to live: "I am life which wills to live, in the midst of life which wills to live." From this awareness Schweitzer derives disarmingly simple and straightforward definitions of ethics, of moral goodness, and of evil: "Ethics consists, therefore, in my experiencing the compulsion to show to all will-to-live the same reverence as I do to my own." And, as for good and evil: "It is good to maintain and to encourage life; it is bad to destroy life or to obstruct it."[39] Schweitzer never allows these descriptions of good and evil to degenerate into either relativism or legalism. Reverence for life remains absolute, to be sure, and all of life is sacred to the truly ethical person. But the application of reverence for life in concrete situations, in which we inevitably must make hard decisions that will sometimes—but only when necessary—destroy and obstruct life, requires the application of thoughtful reflection and ethical responsibility. Hence, as we have seen, Schweitzer's assertions about the need for clear thinking and a sensitive conscience.

Schweitzer's belief that all of life is sacred is a belief rooted in his metaphysics, Mike Martin suggests, and this belief leads Schweitzer to the formal conviction that killing any life form is reprehensible. While this conviction is a refreshing departure from self-serving attempts to minimize the value of so-called "lower" life forms, his reluctance to rank the relative value of different forms of life may present us with an ethical challenge. Killing life forms may be reprehensible, but is the killing of all life forms equally reprehensible? Are all life forms of equal value? Martin objects to Schweitzer's reluctance to rank life forms, and he considers Schweitzer's ethic to be arbitrary in this regard.[40]

Of course, Schweitzer himself made practical decisions, as a medical doctor and ethical person, that may imply an informal ranking of values. He acknowledges that he is a mass-murderer of bacteria, so that he and his patients may live. He kills fish, so that young or wounded birds may be fed—compare *The Story of My Pelican*.[41] The crucial matter, Schweitzer claims, is that there be clear thinking and ethical reflection, in individual cases.

In a letter from Africa, Schweitzer reflects upon this important ethical issue: "I have just killed a mosquito that was buzzing around me in the lamplight. In Europe, I wouldn't kill it even if it were bothering me, but here, where mosquitoes spread the most dangerous form of malaria, I take the liberty of killing them, although I don't like doing it. The important thing is for all of us properly to mull over the question of when damaging and killing are permissible. . . . Much will be achieved once people become reflective and wisely realize that they should damage and kill only when necessary.

That is the essence." In this letter, Schweitzer gives another example of such decision-making—four injured pelicans who need to be fed fish in order to live—and he writes, "I always pity the poor fish to the depths of my soul, but I have to choose between killing the fish or the four pelicans who would surely starve to death." The difficulty of this choice leads Schweitzer to conclude, "I do not know whether I am doing the right thing in deciding one way instead of the other." Killing, after all, is always regrettable. [42]

Schweitzer maintained that this exposition of reverence for life discloses that reverence for life is a logical consequence or necessity of thought. James Brabazon is helpful in his discussion of what Schweitzer meant by "thought," *denken*. When Schweitzer asserts that reverence for life is a necessity of thought, Brabazon explains, he is not referring only to intellectual argumentation and logical proof but also to other sorts of reflection: meditation, intuition, and mystical reflection. Brabazon quotes Schweitzer approvingly in this regard: "If rational thought thinks itself out to a conclusion, it arrives at something non-rational which, nevertheless, is a necessity of thought." [43] In spite of the best efforts of Schweitzer and Brabazon, I still do not think a strong case is made for reverence for life as a necessity of thought. Schweitzer himself admits that "the world is a ghastly drama of will-to-live divided against itself," that the world is, as we also recognize to our grief, a dog-eat-dog world or, for Schweitzer, a hippo-eat-hippo world. [44] For this question, this issue, Schweitzer has no answer, and he calls the contrast between creative will and destructive will an enigma. Further, even if necessity of thought is not judged to be logical necessity, few thinkers other than committed Schweitzerians buy into the necessary relationship Schweitzer poses between rational and nonrational thought, nor do ethicists feel compelled to draw the same conclusion as Schweitzer. Reverence for life remains a powerful, appealing ethical option, but it does not appear to be a necessity of thought.

Nevertheless, it may be possible, in another way, to demonstrate a universalizing tendency in the principle of reverence for life. Foundational to reverence for life, I would propose, is reciprocity, the recognition that it is right and proper to balance my expectations and actions for myself with my expectations and actions for others. Thus Jesus, speaking out of his Jewish tradition, advises, "So in everything, act toward others the way you want others to act toward you" (the Golden Rule, which sometimes is articulated in the negative as the so-called Silver Rule),[45] and he commands, "Love your neighbor as yourself" (love that includes love for enemy, as Jesus states in the Sermon on the Mount).[46] On February 16, 1919, Schweitzer preached his first sermon on reverence for life, and it was a sermon on love for neighbor and for God. God, Schweitzer proclaimed in that sermon, is infinite life, and hence love for God is love for all life. "Reverence before the infinity of life," Schweitzer said, "means the removal of the strangeness, the restoration of shared experiences and of compassion and sympathy. . . . And reason discovers the connecting link between love for God and love for humankind: love for all creatures, reverence for all beings, a compassionate sharing of experiences with all of life, no matter how externally dissimilar to our own."[47] Such ethical rules of reciprocity are to be found all around the world among devotees of the religions of the world. Hinduism praises one who looks on neighbor as self. Buddhism announces a universal love for all beings, a love that overcomes the hatred of others. Confucianism proclaims, "Do not do to others what you would not want them to do to you." The *Tao Te Ching* observes, "One who loves the world as one's own body can be entrusted with the world." With these affirmations we are close indeed to Schweitzer's affirmation of reverence for life.[48]

◆   ◆   ◆

In September 1915, Schweitzer says, he came up with the phrase "reverence for life" while passing through a herd of hippopotamuses on the Ogowe River, and thereafter he found a variety of ways to affirm reverence for life—autobiographically, exegetically, religiously, and philosophically. But there is an additional way, perhaps the most important way, in which Schweitzer affirmed reverence for life. He did so daily, actively, in his life. He lived reverence for life. As a medical doctor for Africans and Europeans who were in need of medical attention and as the head of a village hospital that welcomed and nurtured people and animals, Schweitzer practiced reverence for life for half a century at Lambaréné and in the equatorial jungle around. For Schweitzer, reverence for life was a practical philosophy with "calluses on its hands."[49] Like Goethe in *Wilhelm Meister,* Schweitzer chose reverence as the category to explain life in the world, and like Goethe in *Faust,* Schweitzer considered the opening of the Gospel of John, "In the beginning was the word [Greek, *logos*]," and understood it as "In the beginning was action."[50] Before going to Africa, Schweitzer promised to be quiet as a fish, and he maintained that his life was his argument. Schweitzer found reverence for life when he found Lambaréné and lived in Lambaréné.

It remains for us, then, to evaluate for ourselves these affirmations of reverence for life. I do not anticipate that many of us will emulate Schweitzer by encountering and entertaining our own family of ants, but what shall we do? How shall we understand the challenges of moral goodness, evil, and ethics in the world? How shall we see ourselves in the context of other living beings in the world? How shall we assume our responsibilities and act upon them in a world of painful and perplexing ambiguities? Finally, our consideration of Schweitzer's understanding of reverence for life may become a call to us, not unlike the call that Schweitzer describes at the end of *The Quest of the Historical Jesus,* the call to which he responded by going to live and work in Africa. This call has been issued, in different places and at different times, by Buddha, Mahavira, Jesus, and others, and in Schweitzer this call is a call to ethical action. How do we understand reverence for life? How shall we affirm life and reverence for life? How shall we find our own Lambaréné?

PART TWO

Albert Schweitzer on Reverence for Life

CHAPTER 3

Letters, 1902–1905

Albert Schweitzer and Hélène Bresslau

Albert Schweitzer and Hélène Bresslau carried on an active correspondence with each other prior to their marriage and departure for Lambaréné. The letters included here, from 1902 to 1905, discuss friendship, love, and commitment, and portions of the letters anticipate later, more developed reflections on reverence for life. Particularly interesting in the letters is the contribution of Hélène, since her voice is heard less often than Albert's in discussions of these issues. These letters, translated by Antje Bultmann Lemke, are part of a larger collection being published by Syracuse University Press. Explanatory comments in brackets have been added by Kurt Bergel. Kurt and Kitty Bergel have also made minor changes in the translation.

From Hélène Bresslau

[Strasbourg] May 5–6, 1902

My friend,

You made me feel good, but you have also hurt me; therefore, I would like to continue our discussion. Actually, I would like to thank you because I have advanced through our exchange quite a bit.

You are probably correct in your views about development, as far as we think of it as a slow, gradual becoming. I believe that everything that lies in us is dark, and we are not conscious of it until a word or an event coming from the outside suddenly brings it to our consciousness or puts it into a new

39

light. In this way, rather by spurts, we advance a step and recognize it only afterward. This is what happened to me.

I often asked myself in the past: Are all these thousands of girls who are destined to be happy so much better than I am?—and while I am aware of my faults, I think that I am not really a bad person. And further: Why does God put this boundless desire for happiness into our hearts if he denies us fulfillment? One is inclined to feel only then that much, perhaps the best, can come to fruition—and one wants to rebel against being excluded from this fulfillment! That was my struggle and the end of my philosophy: If we can only attain fulfillment through harmonious unfolding of our powers— and must not this be our goal?—how else could we accomplish what we are meant to accomplish?—what happens if it is denied us?

You too must know the struggle of that part in us that is so filled with longing. How else could you have understood the silent cry of the cherry trees in Günsbach? Or did you always know that your path to life would pass by the closed gate of happiness? You see, my friend, this is the very new insight that you gave me yesterday: here is not the end; here the road only divides, and your path leads ahead; it goes further, wherever it may lead; what matters is the "moving ahead," the way beyond that I was not able to find. And now this seems so simple and clear to me, so reassuring. And yet, I never would have found this on my own; I wanted to convert you to my theory, which seemed so much kinder and brighter, yet it only led me to despair. You must not believe that what I told you yesterday made me helpless; that is overcome and buried—if it were not so, I could not have told you. It was only the indirect cause; it left me so little resistance that any agitation caused me physical pain, and every thought of my rudderless drifting upset me.

To be sure, I do not yet know my way—it is so much easier for a man whose profession gives him direction—will you help me to find mine? "Why would we need friends if we did not need them?" I always despised that phrase, but there is some truth in it. A young woman is dependent upon her talents, and if she does not have any special ones, she is in a predicament. Perhaps in this case, too, I might receive sudden help, as happened yesterday.

My friend, don't be angry with me that I tell you all of this. I feel as if these renunciations contain a hidden trait of sympathy between us. Make this a part of our discussions that is of no concern to any third person. If you want to tell me anything before we meet again, just write—if you send it with the morning mail it will reach me directly—my parents know about our friendship. They know as much as they have to so they don't draw the wrong conclusions. This is not a breach of trust; what our friendship is and what it means to us is between us alone. A young woman has to account for her ways differently than a man who is independent. You will understand, my friend, won't you: in addition to this, our friendship will remain a well-kept secret with my parents.

So again: I thank you!

Always in good friendship.
Hélène Bresslau

From Albert Schweitzer

Saturday, July 19, 1902
9:00 in the evening

Now I have done my duty for tomorrow and can come to you to thank you for your words which I read on my way to the university and which moved me so deeply. I had no way of knowing that yesterday, when I came home, sat in my armchair, and closed my eyes with a single thought not to think about anything, that just at that time you thought of me, that you wrote to me to bring me joy today; so I was egotistical, not you.

I should not have shown you that I was so sad, but I could not help it. I lacked the energy to make the effort to hide my feelings. I was so downcast and the future seemed so utterly hopeless. And now you came this morning and you lifted this hopelessness from me, so the blue sky was smiling for me, too. How can I thank you? I don't want you to reproach yourself—no. You are not the cause of my restlessness; neither am I; it is the movement of the needle of the compass until it finds the pole. We will find it. I ask too much of you, yet in spite of my anxieties, what you give makes me happy. Your lines reveal the noble soul of a woman and a willingness for self-sacrifice that is given only to women. That is a precious gift for him receiving it, more precious than anything in this world because it is uplifting: it ennobles. Is it not the greatest, deepest truth in the encounter of two human beings that they ennoble each other? I do not want you to look up to me, because all I have has been given to me by women, and especially by the one to whom I was closest [his Aunt Mathilde Schweitzer, who had died in Paris on February 2, 1902]—and what I missed in this loneliness, I felt for the first time today again: the fresh breath, a woman who—perhaps with pain and sacrifice—wants to be there for me. For this I thank you. I know that we will find the right path.

In deep gratitude I hold your hand.

Your friend, A. S.

From Albert Schweitzer

[Günsbach] Monday morning

July 8–9, 1902

I am sitting on my rock and am reading Schleiermacher's beautiful lectures on religion. My rock lies above the valley—a small wilderness surrounded by vines: honeysuckle and blackberries fight for first place; blue sloes and red rosehips tell about the beauty of last spring. Now the modest fall flowers are still in bloom, and dry grass blades shiver in the east wind. Everything is enveloped in a blue, gossamer veil out of which the distant mountain chain shows like a silhouette. In the meadows they are mowing, and the fragrance of the hay invigorates the air up here. Late butterflies look for fluttering companions; trees appear in harsh outlines on the bare fields, as if they painted the skeletons of bodies that are still filled with lush vitality. But I see everything in its splendor.

Now, however, I have to turn to my work, although I would love to dream in this vigorously breathing autumnal atmosphere.

Now the blanket has to be folded and I am going home.

From Albert Schweitzer

Again in Günsbach

October 9, 1902, on the rock

What a parting!—The cows graze in the dark green fields. A blue mist hovers above. Everything looks subdued; the mountains are shrouded, out of this blue translucent sea you can hear the sounds of the cowbells, from far and near, unreal in rhythm and harmony—I feel like reading in a story-book—a red ladybug runs over my paper—the brown blades of grass and last little flowers shiver in the wind—could I only capture this last hour of peaceful autumn—yet early tomorrow morning I have to leave for Paris—Much is difficult and some things are more so than I imagined—

This last quiet hour of parting—a fear I cannot suppress. The path of duty as a higher destiny of our existence is hard. One has to fight and struggle for the hours of pure happiness, of rising above this world—but they are so beautiful—I have read aloud the Apology of Socrates at Saar-Union [a town in which members of his faculty lived]. We were all moved—and I felt that I understand this human being, understand him totally—

Now I am picking the last flowers beside this rock for the grave at Père Lachaise [the cemetery in Paris where his Aunt Mathilde was buried]—a small bouquet, unpretentious among the luxuriant flower arrangements by which her grave will be adorned—but it carries a peace and the melancholy of autumn, the rays of the setting sun and wondrous memory. At night fragrant dreams of past happiness and abiding love rise from the fading blossoms. Goodbye fields, goodbye woods, goodbye mountains. I thank you.

From Albert Schweitzer

October 11, 1902

Between Troyes and Paris in the express train, 4:30 p.m.

One can vaguely feel Paris in the distance. The sun is setting on the horizon and the trees with their golden leaves cast long shadows. I have read the letters of St. Ignatius in Greek, but the saint would not be pleased with me if he knew how much nature distracted me. Is it strength or weakness to live in such a mystical union with nature, to feel the effects of its smile and its tears deeply in one's soul?—I have seen about a hundred pictures by Millet [a French social realist painter]—it felt as if he and I looked at everything together—

Paris—Paris

From Albert Schweitzer

Strasbourg, Saturday morning, 10:30
July 4, 1903

I have come home from my lecture and will begin to write my little sermon for tomorrow afternoon. But I am not in the mood for it: I am too sad, too indifferent to have higher thoughts. Come, take the armchair, move it toward the table, and we will talk to each other—how good it would be if you could chat with me a little. You don't mind that I am wearing an old jacket? It is a little worn at the sleeves and one button is missing.

All week I had a fever; it was there already on Sunday evening when I visited you; that's why I was so taciturn. I was awfully thirsty. And then I had to take quinine. That makes the head tired. And when I came home yesterday I found a letter telling about a boy from my confirmation class of last year who had to have his leg amputated. He is a nice fellow who liked me very much. Why does all this happen? During his illness I visited him several times and tried to comfort him, but to see him in this desperate condition drives me to despair.

You don't answer me, but you look at me with your kind glance. Is it still true that you are happy when you fall asleep and when you wake up? I have thought about both of us frequently in these days. Always this question: do I not ruin your life? Your path would be straight if I had not met you, or at least if I had acted with my usual indifference. You certainly would have found a home and a family, all that—and now I think that I have led you astray, and everything I accept from you is stolen from your happiness. That discourages me. I see you leaving for Russia; I know the grief this causes your parents—and if I did not exist you would remain here, I know this, because it is not your destiny to roam and struggle in this world, but to be a true woman in the circle of her family. Sometimes I could cry—what is the solution? And then again, I tell myself: Did she not tell you that she is happy, do believe it—and I force myself to believe it, but I ask myself whether this fire may not die down, and then only dim memory will remain in your heart and your life will be cold. If you only knew how much I admire you! I never have been able to tell you. If you only knew how the esteem you show me helps me on my way, how your affection raises me up. It and your deep love are a source of strength. I want my whole life, including my thoughts, to be completely open before you, and I do not want you to experience any disappointment—but you pay for this too dearly. You idealize me, I know this, and that adds to my strength, your affection warms my heart—but you, what do you get out of this? Letters, enjoyable triumphs, moments of deep happiness—and then a great emptiness.

Don't say anything, this is the way it is. We must not talk—

Give me both your hands—we are at the Rhine, I imagine—the smell of the hay—just as at that time when I revealed the secret of my life to you. You were so happy to be the sister of my thought, and I felt miserable because I had opened myself up so completely. But then I did not regret it—now I feel relieved in the knowledge that you, such an honest and noble soul, know my inner thoughts, and to talk about them with somebody gives me happiness. And even when I worry about you—it is not only in sadness.

God bless you. Each of us will go our way and you will find happiness. What kind? That is not the essential point. But tell me often that you are happy—I must hear that—

Noon—for more than one and a half hours I have been talking to you. I feel as if I woke up. But I feel better now.

Thank you. A. S. I will now write my sermon.

P.S. To look for a text, I am opening my New Testament and my eye falls on the second letter of Paul to Timothy, 2:5, "And if a man strives for mastery, he is not crowned, except *he competes according to the rules.*" [Schweitzer's emphasis]

From Albert Schweitzer

Sunday morning
November 1, 1903

I think that I don't have to tell you anything else. Only that I hold you in high esteem and that I admire you very much. I do not have the courage to tell you what you mean in my life, and all that you have become for me; you are my friend if ever a woman was the friend of a man. Why do I tell you this? I am always afraid to tie you too closely to me and to block your road to happiness. But tell me—have you become richer with me, have you become somebody, have you also found happiness? The horizon of your life has changed, it has become brighter—please tell me; I know it, but I want to hear it from you. Is it true that I have given you the true concept of life? Do you feel that I awakened a sound that slumbered in you, but that nobody had been able to bring to life? And is the happiness I brought you something precious to you? Tell me and look deep into my eyes.

You, too, have given me much: you have forced me to open up; you have torn my thoughts out of me, you told me with pride: I have a right to know them—when I was lonely and sad you came to me and you gave me everything a woman can give that is noble and beautiful, not without struggle, but without egoism. You were a woman, we drowned the professor's little daughter in the Rhine [Schweitzer refers to their previous conversation by the Rhine]—You have given me great support: the esteem and the affection of a noble person that watches over you everywhere, to the depth of your thoughts, and that does not permit you to falter because one always thinks: What would she say? Would I still be worthy of speaking to her as I do, of looking into her eyes, of accepting her respect and her friendship?—every noble woman is something of a guardian angel. You came to me when I was alone, when the first guardian angel [Mathilde Schweitzer] had left me. I fought against you; I did not want you to take her place, out of respect for her, and in order not to awaken the jealousy of the dead one because you were a German and only a (marriageable) young girl—you have vanquished and overcome me, and I was forced to make room for you in my thoughts and my life. And only now do I fully recognize the woman in you. Because I know you differently from the others who take you only as a young girl, I cannot treat you in company in a natural manner and wish to keep secret from others that I know you, and fear that they might interfere with our friendship—

I think of you with pride and concern—but I know that whatever happens, will be "good"—

[Hélène Bresslau began her nurse's training at Stettin in 1904.]

From Hélène Bresslau

Stettin, January 13, 1904
City Hospital

My friend,

I had intended to write you a long letter—it is impossible! Thus only these few lines, bringing you all my best wishes for tomorrow [Schweitzer's birthday]. Do you remember how last year another letter and I were the only ones who congratulated you on your birthday? I write in a hurry because I am at the women's surgical floor where I currently work, and I use the two minutes of rest I have in between feeding a patient and our own meal. I intended to take this afternoon off (we always have one free afternoon a week), but there is so much to do that I have to stay. We work from six o'clock in the morning to eight in the evening—one feels pretty tired in the evening. But in spite of it, one loves the work; only once in a while thoughts come to mind that one should probably not pursue. I have a large room with old women—for most of them I wish a peaceful, quick death, and I think that it is almost immoral to keep them alive for a life that brings them only suffering.

I think of you so much; I wonder if you are still alone. Please write me as frequently as possible, would you do that? And send me the *Kirchenbote* [an Alsatian newspaper]—in the isolation of the hospital I hear nothing about what is going on in the world. But I learn much, very much. The other night I intended to write you, but I was too tired, and tonight we have "Pastor's Hour" (!) until 10 o'clock. If you would like to, you could address your letters to "Sister Hélène Bresslau" or to Miss, it does not matter. My name here is Sister Hélène. I'll remain until April 1st.

Somebody is calling me; today we have major operations. I enjoy being in the room where wounds are dressed; it is very interesting. But the other day when I had to be in the operating theater for the first time, I felt very ill.

Goodbye, my friend. Tomorrow I will be with you in my thoughts, and wish that the year that you begin will be a happy and blessed one.

Please answer soon.

God bless you!

From Albert Schweitzer

At the seminary

Tuesday evening, January 19, 1904

Can you imagine that I would miss the opportunity to call you "Sister Hélène"? Oh no. Good evening, Sister Hélène. Take the armchair; wait a moment—I will move it more closely to the table, now sit down, Sister Hélène. Are you comfortable, Sister Hélène? And now I am there for you, let us have a long conversation. Excuse me for one moment, I have to stoke the fire, so we will not get cold. And now give me your good hand, Sister Hélène.

On the 14th I was at Hausbergen; my sister's boy was baptized; the weather was horrible, by the way. When I returned in the evening, I found eight letters. Since I was very tired, I lay down immediately and read the letters, one after another. Guess which one I opened first and read several times before I took up another one! Can you guess? Just admit that you know exactly that it was yours. Then I put my head on the pillow, put both my hands over my eyes (a position I learned from you), and surrendered myself to the feeling of bliss. Yes, it was bliss. Finally again an enlivening touch; I needed it. I took a deep breath. How wonderful it is to have somebody who has the right to wish you a happy birthday and puts so many thoughts into this one wish. I thank you with all my heart—your friendship is at this moment the most precious possession I have in my life. I am forgetting that I want you to detach yourself from me and tell you that I went to sleep, happy as a child. Since that time I have often reread your letter, and I always feel as if everything is now easy when I see you in the distance with your simple and noble thoughts and with your soul that has grown much through much struggle.

Do you know that, until today, I fought a battle with myself? Tomorrow a great celebration will take place in Paris, at the occasion of my uncle's nomination as a member of the Legion of Honor. All our friends and family will be there, and I had planned, with Madame Harth, my aunt's sister, to arrive as a surprise; but today I sent her a telegram to tell her that I cannot come. Now, after the decision has been made, I am not nervous anymore. One must have courage, don't you agree?

I am still by myself. You know that I asked Dr. Schwander to let me know when there are abandoned boys or orphans because I know somebody who would like to raise them. None have been found so far. I also wrote to a minister in a workers' settlement at Mulhouse and made him the same offer; no answer so far. I have also decided to put an advertisement in the newspaper and to let nature take its course. Once in a while, when I think of the difficulties such a project will cause, I tell myself: you can still withdraw, look, it's not necessary; you just pursue a fantasy—but then, immediately, I regain my clear vision and know that this is my calling, that I must follow this path, in spite of everything. And the good spirit returns, and then I feel as if you look at me and speak with me. What good fortune that I spoke with you about everything, and that you now understand me and can make everything easier—Sister Hélène. Oh yes, you are my sister, my good sister, and you share my lofty thoughts. As soon as I am not alone anymore, I will let you know with just a short note. I have to interrupt for a moment—I have to catch my breath, because I have spoken with you without interruption, without knowing where to begin and where to end.

I know that I have forgotten the most important things which I intended to write about. That is the reason I take up the pen again. My last sermons exhausted me—I have, if that is possible, put too much of my heart into them. I am going to send you the recent one from last Sunday and two from last summer. Next time you will get the Advent sermons. Tell me your opinion about the article in the *Kirchenbote,* my dear critic. I am very happy at the seminary. The students show great sympathy toward me and accept my authority without any difficulty. I even was able to take back a student who had been dismissed last year and to keep another one who has also been in trouble. I care for them as a father, try to point them in the right direction by encouraging them to work. One of them just interrupted us. He did not see you—are you invisible to the others? I see you very clearly in the armchair.

I did not write you any letters—I was not able to; I was too tired. But on New Year's Eve I spoke with you. Here is the short page—

I am concluding now, Sister Hélène. Are you happy in your work? Sometimes I imagine that I walk between your patients' beds, and I would like to take a quick glance at your hall. I recently visited your parents and had a good conversation with your mother—

God bless you, Sister Hélène.

Thank you for writing me in French. I know why you did it: to take increasingly the place of the one who died. You write admirably. Would we ever have thought that one day we would exchange our thoughts in French? You remember that I declined when you first offered it?

From Albert Schweitzer

Strasbourg, January 30, 1904

For me pagan thoughts coexist with the Christian and I am not able to separate them. In all of us there is something pagan, something mightily proud and grand that Christ did not know and that does not go well with Christianity and the ideas of Christ. Have you noticed that in his parables he never mentions woods as we know them, as dark, mysterious, impenetrable, as they correspond to the equally dark, equally mysterious, and equally impenetrable character of us, people of the northern countries. Whenever I am in the woods, as soon as I hear their melodies, there awakens something in me that slumbers deep in my heart, something pagan, yet religious, some feeling of pride and energy, of harshness and haughtiness that I cannot define.

What would have become of the Germanic religion without Christianity, if it had developed independently, entirely on the force of its own thought? Would it have been better for us to have this noble religion, rather than this foreign religion of the Great One from Nazareth, which has some touch of decadence, from broken pride of his nation? Yes, everybody loves his neighbor as he loves himself, makes sacrifices for him, yet deep down he despises him and does not want to let him share in his innermost life, so that it may not be desecrated. There are people whom I love only because I have allowed myself to detest them: it took me a long time to realize this, and to recognize that everything else would be a lie and cowardice.

Recently, when I looked through old papers I found a thought jotted down casually: "The great thinkers conquered the world; yes, but how many other thinkers have they killed, who is aware of that?" Thinkers whom we would have needed! The great ones have crushed and destroyed those—and now we have a religion—and mindlessness, and all that is great and true in this world dies—from religion or from nonthinking. Do you comprehend this?

From Hélène Bresslau

Stettin, City Hospital
February 2, 1904
In my room

You are surprised that I answer so late?—but you know how little time I have, and I thought that you would not always expect an answer from me in order to write again, my friend. How much I enjoyed your long letter—that I do not have to tell you. You see, I received thirty letters and cards for my birthday; as answers I send little thank-you cards, that goes quite quickly, and one can produce half a dozen in a few free minutes while on duty—would you like such a card? I only write letters to my parents; in the evening I am too tired.

You ask me of my opinion about the articles in the *Kirchenbote*. But no, I am too dumb right now, I have nothing on my mind but my patients. And I only read what is sent to me, and even that I cannot finish. I did read one of your sermons, "And he preached forcefully," and articles in the *Kirchenbote;* among those "Jesus and the Wise Men" I like best. In it I recognize you, my friend, and you know that I almost think like you. In it you are yourself: arrogant and humble—and slightly paradoxical. Are you annoyed that I tell you that? But you know how I mean it. And sometimes I have the impression that you know exactly if and that you have gone a little too far. And I feel that you are right; only through exaggeration can we shake the spirits, when we force them into contradiction (while I write this word "contradiction" I am not sure whether it exists, I don't have a dictionary—don't laugh at me!). When I write in French, I do so without even thinking about it—it comes naturally, just as it was natural when I spoke French with you, but I realize that I make many mistakes—you must excuse me!

I am very, very happy here and I don't even suffer anymore from the physical exhaustion as I did in the beginning. But I would not like to stay here forever, even if I had the permission of my parents—which I would never receive—And why not? Because I am too egotistical, too much of an individual, and because I do not want to give up my life as an individual and sacrifice it forever. Here our work absorbs us completely—physically and mentally—

I was interrupted and now I have barely a quarter of an hour to conclude this letter. I have been very happy because I have almost always been alone in my room (the sister whom I share it with had night duty), so in the four weeks since I arrived, I have always been alone in the evening and night, and she had used the room during the day. Tomorrow she leaves. Who will be my next roommate? I am afraid because I have always been used to having a room to myself. Here everything changes, and very fast. On my floor I have already changed my hall. In the former I saw three of my patients dying, severe cases, for whose death I had hoped because of their great suffering. Then young people came and the hall lost its character as a museum room—that was quite a change. And now I have two halls with young women; in one: nice, well behaved; in the other: girls from another world, the kind everyone tries to hide from "well brought up" young women. All in all thirty patients (more than one-half of the whole floor); they are, however, not seriously ill, and most of them can get up, and they help willingly, so I have less work, at least less heavy and less unpleasant work than with my twelve old women. I like it there very much. I do a little of what the pastor spoke of the other day (but can you imagine: not because he spoke of it!): physician of the soul, inner mission—and I believe that I don't do it entirely in his way! The "Pastor's Hour"—you are entirely correct in what you think about it. He is an "honorable servant of God," entirely honey and water—but shallow water!—You can imagine that, on those evenings, I would rather go to bed! Since that is impossible, I keep myself busy with a collection of howlers—if you are interested, I will send you some.

We have other classes too—Medical Theory with two of our doctors—they are much more interesting.

My friend, play music, much music, also for me! You don't know how I long for it—it would be another reason why I could not spend the rest of my life in a hospital—for the first time in four months I played a little today—how to find time for such things?

Good night, my friend.

Thank you, special thanks for the short note from New Year's Eve!

From Albert Schweitzer

Atheism—could it not be a religion too? The most beautiful and the most difficult, the religion that will follow the religion of Christ. Did he not say when he faced death, "My God, my God, why have you forsaken me?" So he died as an atheist?

Who has the courage to pursue this thought?

March 15, 1904. Meditation on the train, in the darkness of night.

From Albert Schweitzer

[Strasbourg] Sunday morning
May 1, 1904

The leaves have grown in recent days—soon they will be as large as those that dropped when I wrote the letters for your trip—You know how I urged you at that time to accept the hand of a sympathetic man, if you met one on your way. Have you not met anyone for whom you feel more than indifference? I always thought that you might be engaged when you return, and you know that this would give me genuine pleasure. So, just tell me, you see how indiscreet I am becoming—but between us, can there be any indiscretion? I would like so very much to see you happy—but you will, of course, in happiness preserve your noble spirit.

Everything must be blossoming around my rock, why can't I go there?

Yesterday your father delivered an extraordinary address! It was the most brilliant synthesis between scholarship and the arts that one could imagine. Next winter, at the president's ball you will be the queen. I will look at you bashfully from the distance. According to your letter you lead quite a fashionable life in Hamburg. I beg you, could you once give me a quiet evening with your thoughts? That would make me feel good—very good. If I think how hard it was for me to tell you my plans for the future—the thought that you know everything now gives me courage to hold onto my plan. I have undertaken the following. I would like to have two boys between six and eight who do not have anybody. As a first step I have contacted Dr. Schwander, the director of the welfare programs at Strasbourg. He promised to notify me when he finds somebody. (I have not told him that I am the one who would like to take in the boys.) Next I wrote to Mulhouse. They also made promises, and so did the people in Paris, whom I asked about children from Alsace. I want to realize my plans at last. If you discover anything in Hamburg, please let me know—it would be most wonderful if the solution came from you. This long wait has been painful, but on the other hand it has given me time to think over everything. How often have I told myself: if you want it, you can turn around, you will be happy, just as others are, and you can do much good—but the inner voice told me every time: you see the road you want to follow, do so, only in this way are you true to yourself, honest and strong. There was not the slightest struggle, my feelings were so strong that, if I were to act otherwise, I would be destroyed. I don't fight my destiny; I follow it as quietly and happily as rarely a person has done. This alone is my life. Soon I will be thirty years old—I know very well that every word I say in a sermon would drop to the floor the moment it came out of my mouth, if I did not follow my road. I must continue. It is moving to see your life so absolutely clearly before yourself, and to know that spiritual happiness is enough to fill our lives—and to feel the communion of thought with a few noble souls who have the right to know.

Sometimes it seems to me as if I had arrived beyond the clouds and stars, and could see the world in the most wonderful clarity, and therefore have the right to be a heretic. To know only Jesus of Nazareth; to continue his work as the only religion, not to have to bear anymore what Christianity has absorbed over the years in vulgarity. Not to be afraid of hell, not to strive for the joys of heaven, not to live in false fear, and the false submission that has become an essential part of our religion—and yet to understand the one Great One, and to know that one is his disciple. Last night before I went to sleep, I read the twenty-fifth chapter of the Gospel of St. Matthew because I especially love the verse, "Truly I tell you, just as you did it to one of the least of these who are my brothers, you did it to me." But when it came to the last judgment and the separation of the "sheep from the goats" I smiled: I do not want to belong to the sheep, and in heaven I would certainly meet quite a lot whom I do not like: St. Loyola, St. Jerome, and a few Prussian church leaders—and to act friendly with them, to exchange a brotherly kiss? No, I decline. Rather to hell. There the crowd will be more congenial. With Julian the Apostate, Caesar, Socrates, Plato, and Heraclitus one can have a decent conversation. Yet, I serve him, because of him, only because of him—because he is the only truth, the only happiness.

From Albert Schweitzer

[Strasbourg] Sunday afternoon
May 1, 1904
Coming from the church

I preached to my good women about gratitude—which is not difficult, if one's heart is so filled with gratitude toward "God" as mine is. I often ask myself whether I thank him enough for all the gifts he has given me. Do you know that we performed a St. Matthew's Passion that was considered by the critics totally faithful to the classic tradition? We had rehearsed for it with great enthusiasm. My lectures last semester were most successful; it is truly marvelous to lecture in a full hall and to feel that you are carried by the sympathy of the young people. At the seminary it also went very well last winter: no incidents, either with the students or personnel. The chief cook is a cow, touchy as the devil: I disarm her with even-tempered and special politeness. You would have a good laugh if you could see me in that role. But those are insignificant things: I feel that I have brought to the seminary a certain spirit, that I can convey something that those who have lived with me here will carry with them. I was touched by the expressions of sympathy of several students when they left the seminary. That gives me courage. Yes, I will not have lived in vain. I have a certain vision of immortality: that which is immortal and immaterial in us is our thoughts. We live when our thoughts are reborn in others. This is why Socrates and Christ live. That is living immortality! Why do we need another one?

Since I am somewhat rested, my head is filled with philosophical thoughts. It is painful. Basically I am a philosopher—but I let myself be caught by him, the greatest, the most divine of all philosophers in whom the most sublime thought leads back to the most simple. Because of this obedience he will forgive my heresies: I am like one of those satraps [Roman governors] who were sent to the border of the empire and enjoyed certain freedoms because they defended and protected the country.

From Hélène Bresslau

Hamburg, June 5, 1904
26 Papenhuderstrasse

Just a brief word, you shall have it! I am so happy that the book on Bach is completed—tell me what you are doing now; have you returned to philosophy? Do you realize that you walk like a crab? You go exactly where I came from. Your ideas concerning immortality, these impassioned visions, that our thoughts are reborn in the people who follow us, these I had before I arrived at those which I told you on the road to Günsbach—do you remember?—In this respect, and in all humility I came closer to the great Kant—and this gave me great joy. And now, when I reflect upon this, I find a union of both: when our thoughts live in others—after our own life has come to an end—and when they reappear, perhaps in a purer form, is that not the sign of the highest perfection of which Kant speaks?—Even if he did not think of immortality in human form and on this earth. But has this philosophy not existed for a long time in the concept of transmigration of souls? If this is nonsense, please forgive me, but I have not studied philosophy! If this is what you call atheism, I have been an atheist for many years. I remember a discussion I had with Kuck and Rudolph Spindler on our return trip from Weissenburg to Wingen, and that I told them, "All in all I am a heretic," and they answered, "You must admit that you cannot dissociate yourself from Christ; to be a Christian does not simply imply anything but to love Jesus Christ." How often have I thought of this when I spoke with people who have ideas similar to mine, but they did not dare to call themselves Christians. What else is that but a question of name? A name is a sound and smoke. [Hélène is quoting here from Goethe's *Faust*.] I wish that a minister, instead of calling himself secretly an atheist, would tell those who think independently and who reject the formalities, the trimmings and all that goes with it, those who have lost the courage to call themselves Christians (because unfortunately they came to the conclusion that these formalities were the essence of Christianity), those who are not always strong enough to stand on their own, I wish that this minister would say freely and openly what true Christianity is: to love Jesus Christ and those who do should follow him. He will find out what I frequently observed: that their atheism is nothing that is in conflict with Christianity—and he can tell them much better than I ever could and can—

Yes, people are "fashionable" at Hamburg; but we find life only in this world, and I had to find it. This means that I too was flying high and above the clouds, but a little too high, because I had little understanding and feeling for the value of life—now I have found it again. You would probably be surprised to see me quite often happy and content as a child. The reason for this lies in the fact that we both—as I believe—have found in each other a trustworthy support, and in this way have learned to walk alone, totally alone, not to depend on anybody—inwardly, of course.

I attended here two wonderful performances: *The Three Herons' Feathers* [a play by Hermann Sudermann, 1889] and *Tristan and Isolde,* the latter conducted by Nikisch [1855–1922, famous German conductor].

I read a little (even Ernst Haeckel [1824–1919, zoologist]) and I will recommend some books to you when I return.[. . .] My brief word grew into a long one—but I was really quite proud of you, and hope to be even more so! Therefore, much strength and good work, but not at night, please do remember!—and tell me how you progress! Now I must close, Adieu!

From Albert Schweitzer

1904–5, midnight

The bells ring midnight. I conclude the last year with thoughts of you and begin this year thinking of you. You are the most precious thing I have in this world. There are people who are devoted to me, and to whom I am devoted because they are my relatives, or because I got to know them well and over a long period of time, longer than we have known each other. With these I share some of my daily life, and we exchange some thoughts— but you are the person I "revere" most; you have the greatest power over me. Do you think that that is sentimental? You have something genuine, great, and pure that draws me to you. This is something that surpasses love and is not tied to any emotion. When I am facing struggles and temptations, when I am in danger of losing the foundation that is the basis of my noblest thoughts, you immediately stand before me in my mind, whether they are great or little things. In everything I do wrong, I have the feeling that I betray you, to belie the opinion that you have of me. That helps me to pursue my path.

I thank you in this last and first hour of the year for what you are for me. You are somewhat like a little guardian angel for me here on earth. I cannot say that often, but I have to tell you once, I have to.

I wish you nothing for the coming year, because our wishes are futile, and if I could shape your life through my wishes, I would not know how to do it. Accept things as they come to you. This is my only wish: to be strong, noble and good in everything you encounter, strong and noble, as my aunt used to say. I, for my part, will try to do the same.

We ask too much from life, too much inner happiness, which we hide defiantly, so we have the right to ask fate to fulfill our wishes. The only prayer I directed to God, the great Spirit, at the first ring of the bell after midnight was the plea to keep me pure and of noble spirit for what I must achieve on this earth. Aside from that, whatever has to come may come. I kiss your hand for a long time.

From Albert Schweitzer

Saturday evening, February 26 [25], 1905
(at the seminary)

At last! I long to speak with you. I have to tell you so much, and sad things. If you were with me you would find it difficult to comfort me. Everything is lost! I searched in vain. Either the children I try to find do not exist, or people don't want me to have them and take my plans for fantasies. I had to swallow a lot. Some people, however, are quite touching, for example Pastor Belin from the Neuhof institution. I now have approached Metz. If that should work out, I have to wait for some new chance, while I have lost another illusion. Have I told you that I have changed my plan? I would like to take in young men who leave school, so they may learn something solid, or to see that they can become teachers. You see, I have so much love to give; I will be so happy. When I meet a homeless person—and they come around every day—and when I hear that he grew up as an orphan, I tell myself that he would not be in this condition if I had met him.

I am in the grip of a terrible despondency. But I never tell myself that my ideas are fantasies. I am too logical, too rational to indulge in fantasies. What I want cannot be fantasy. I am too realistic. But I want to free myself from this bourgeois life that would kill everything in me; I want to live; I want to do something as a disciple of Jesus. That is the only thing in which I believe—and in your friendship. Because I believe in it! But people don't allow us to step outside the ordinary, to detach the conventional ties. Yes, I would perish in those. I must free myself.

If you only knew how sad I am. I was sure I would find my way. Now I am at a loss, forced into the useless existence of a "young man" who desires a "good opportunity to marry." This is how people see my situation.

Look, I do good deeds. I gave all my money to the poor. On New Year's I had nothing in my pockets. But what I want to give, my love, my life, my time—that I am not permitted to give. And that is for me a true need, more than my life. See, Lene, I don't deceive myself. This thought not just to contribute through scholarship, but through my life, came to me in an unexpected way. Like a small cloud from the distance, on the horizon—so it seemed to me. While I wrote my book on Kant, I felt the cloud coming closer: its shadow enveloped me. In my Kant I have said more than I realized at the time: I destroyed everything that is essential in religion; I left the categorical imperative as the only reality. And now the cloud has become larger. I see nothing of what I once saw. Scholarship has become pale—I feel only one thing: I must act. Everything else feels like a comedy. I feel like I am playacting; as long as I have not accepted this reality, my whole life is a comedy. Yes, if I could realize my plan, and at the same time educate future ministers at the seminary. I am happy at the seminary because I can do good and Nowack [the director of the seminary] genuinely respects me, but the rest? For the others I am a young man who lives a pleasant life in a very pleasant home and earns three thousand marks, and it is exactly that that makes me so defenseless in their eyes. Always waiting. I have had enough of it. Will I have the energy to write the third part of my book on the Last Supper? I will write it without enthusiasm! But I will write it, because the book will have its value. I already have everything in my head. I will need one year, or at most, a year and a half. I will force myself to write it. You will be satisfied with me. But my heart is not in it, as it was in my sketch of the life of Jesus. I expect something different, something that concerns my own life! I have given up the ambition to become a great scholar; I want to be more—simply a human. That will become the theme of your book *Wir Epigonen*. We are not true humans, but beings who live by a civilization inherited from the past, that keeps us hostage, that confines us. No freedom of movement, nothing. Our humanness, indeed, everything in us, is killed by our calculations for our future, by our social position and rank. You see, I am not happy—yet I am happy. I suffer, but that is part of life. I live, I don't care about my existence, and that is the beginning of wisdom, i.e., to search for a value for this existence which the others don't know at all, and which they don't accept. Not a professorship, a comfortable life—but something different. I have found it; I believe that I possess this value: to serve Jesus. I am less at peace than if my only goal were to attain a professorship and a good wife, but I live. And that gives me the tremendous feeling of happiness, as if one would see a ray of light in a deep pit, as if one would hear music. One feels uprooted, because one asks, what lies ahead, what decisions should I make—but more alive, happier than those who are anchored in life. To drift with released anchor.

I know one thing: if I cannot realize my plan to educate, to take care of young boys, I cannot remain here: I would despair. I would envy all those who serve Jesus, even the lowliest woman at the Salvation Army. I would conclude that I have to search for another kind of realization and would offer my services to the French Mission in the Congo or at the Sambesi River, because people are needed there. If I would listen to myself, I would leave here tomorrow instead of playing this comedy as I waste away. But first I have to write the history of the Last Supper and then, as my last book, our book, your book *Wir Epigonen*. That will take three years, in which I will be tied to the seminary. Three years of waiting, of testing, of maturing. After that nothing can restrain me. All these thoughts had already taken shape and occupied my thinking when we listened to the mission sermon of Gerold [Theodor Gerold, minister at St. Nicolai's Church] together. I try to push them away, yet they always reappear. When I become totally absorbed in my study of the Last Supper, they will be temporarily suppressed. But look, all these thoughts that entered into my life, which from some distance gradually came closer and closer and at last finally conquered me. It is my horrible logic which attracts these thoughts, which delivers me to them, this logic that does not allow me any escape and forces me to search what may fulfill my life!

I am at this point. It is difficult to write you this instead of telling it as "in the beginning," on the bank of the Rhine surrounded by flowers and sun. But look, difficult issues begin with an idyll, then the idyllic parable perishes, and what remains is the burden. This burden, however, unites those who know each other so well. But the idyll was beautiful—wasn't it!—I would never want to lose a second of it. All is well as it comes to us.

I am so happy that you found a great task! [Hélène's nursing program] It is like that: the last will be the first, and the first will be the last. Earlier I was closer to the goal than you, and now you are active, while I am simply a Privatdozent [a title that corresponds to assistant professor]—a human who lectures, who does not act. I am so happy for you; now I don't blame myself anymore for having you uprooted. Now you will find your way. And you will be happy. And if home and family expect you, you will be very happy, and when you have to go your way alone, your life will nevertheless be fulfilled.

Do you remember that I have a promise from you, from the bank of the Rhine: "If you need somebody some day, promise that you will call me." I promised you—and I often think of that. If I ever need you, I will call you, you can be sure. I guard your promise as something precious, like a jewel to pawn.

CHAPTER 4

First Sermon on Reverence for Life

Albert Schweitzer

On February 16, 1919, Albert Schweitzer preached his first sermon on reverence for life during the morning service at St. Nicolai's Church in Strasbourg. Based on the reading in Mark 12:28–34, this sermon links the ethic of reverence for life to the command to love God and neighbor in the teachings of Jesus. Schweitzer appeals to both the heart and reason in support of reverence for life, and love and compassion for all of life. The sermon is reproduced here, with the permission of the publisher, from Albert Schweitzer, A Place for Revelation: Sermons on Reverence for Life, *trans. David Larrimore Holland (London: Collier Macmillan, 1988), 3–12.*

A nd one of the scribes came up and heard them disputing with one another, and seeing that he answered them well, asked him, 'Which commandment is the first of all?' Jesus answered, 'The first is, Hear, O Israel: The Lord our God, the Lord is one; and you shall love the Lord your God with all your heart, and with all your soul, and with all your mind, and with all your strength. The second is this, You shall love your neighbor as yourself. There is no commandment greater than these.' And the scribe said to him, 'You are right, Teacher; you have truly said that he is one, and there is no other but he; and to love him with all the heart, and with all the understanding, and with all the strength, and to love one's neighbor as oneself, is much more than all whole burnt offerings and sacrifices.' And when Jesus saw that he answered wisely, he said to him, 'You are not far from the kingdom of God.' And after that no one dared to ask him any question" (Mark 12:28–34, RSV).

The scribe who poses the question to Jesus about the greatest commandment is eager to learn. He wants information about something that
concerns him and many of his comrades. In the Gospel according to
Matthew, in chapter 22, the scribes pose this question to Jesus in order to
tempt him. But the Evangelist Mark surely has the better memory when he
describes the congenial encounter in which Jesus and the scribes understand
each other for a moment, look into each others' hearts, and then go their
separate ways again.

In those days, thinking Israelites were considering the problem of how
all of the commandments, both great and small, might be traced back to one
basic law. We, too, have a similar need. *What is intrinsic good?* I have read to
you the eternal words of our Lord about forgiveness, mercy, love, and all of
the other characteristics we as his disciples are to prove true in the world. But
we all seem to think of these qualities as only colors refracted from the white
light of some basic ethical attitude, such as he requires from us.

I want to reflect with you now on this question: What is this basic ethical attitude? Later on I shall devote several meditations to the questions of
Christian ethics upon which I have been ruminating in distant lands, in the
isolation of the primeval forest, but always with these services in Saint
Nicolai's in mind and in the confident hope of being able someday to speak
to you about them.

The question of exactly what this basic ethical attitude might be im-
poses itself upon us nowadays. We are forced into a recognition that earlier
generations and, until recently, even we ourselves refused to accept. We cannot escape it, however, if we want to be truthful: *Christian ethics has never become a power in the world.* It has never penetrated very deeply into the human
soul but, rather, has been accepted only superficially, more acknowledged in
words than practiced in deeds. Mankind acts as if the words of Jesus did not
exist for them, as if there were no ethics for them at all.

That is why it is useless simply to rehearse and interpret the ethical
commandments of Jesus again and again, as if that would somehow in the
end produce their general acceptance. That would be like painting with
beautiful colors on a wet wall. We must first of all create a *foundation for understanding* those commandments and guide our world into a frame of mind
in which Jesus' teachings have meaning. And it is by no means easy to inter-

pret the words of Jesus so that they can be used practically in life. For example, let us take the sayings about the greatest of the commandments. What does it mean to love God with all your heart and only to do good out of love for him? Follow up on this idea and a world of considerations opens up before you. When in life have you chosen to do good out of love for God when you otherwise would have chosen to do evil? And take the other commandment: "You should love your neighbor as yourself." Truly, that is wonderful. I could expound it to you in the most charming examples. *But can it be carried through?* Suppose for the moment that, beginning tomorrow, you wanted literally to live according to that commandment. What would the results be in a few days?

That is the greatest riddle in Christian ethical teaching. We cannot simply apply the words of Jesus directly to life, however holy our desire to serve him. And from that comes the great danger that we shall give a respectful reverence to Jesus' words and praise them as "ideal" but in reality leave them unnoticed.

Still another misunderstanding endangers the realization of Christian morality. The attempt easily makes us arrogant. If we forgive our enemies, we think ourselves terribly virtuous. If we assist someone who needs our help, we consider ourselves very noble. For in doing the few things that, in the spirit of Christ, we can do differently from and better than other people, we feel ourselves superior to them. This unethical self-satisfaction seems frequently almost to make us more unethical than those who do not even acknowledge the commandments of Jesus or endeavor to follow them. Precisely because they demand something so extraordinary, it is difficult for us to regard the demands of Jesus as *ordinary.* Yet that is precisely what he asks us to do, to see his demands as ordinary. For he says that, however much we have done, we should still regard ourselves as useless servants.

That is why we must think together concerning the intrinsic good. We want to understand how the highly exalted demands of Jesus are to be fulfilled in daily life, and we want to be able to comprehend them, though highly exalted, as the ordinary duty of mankind.

We want to grasp the fundamental principle of all ethics and to derive from that underlying principle, as from a supreme law, all ethical actions. Yes, but can morality be grasped at all? Is it not a matter of the heart? Does it not depend on love? That has been said to us repeatedly for two thousand years. And what is the result?

Let's observe humanity around us, both collectively and individually. Why are people so often unprincipled? Why are even the most pious among them—and often these in particular!—able to let themselves be carried along by prejudice and nationalist passion into judgments and actions that are no longer ethical at all? Because they lack a morality based on reason and founded logically in reason. Because for them ethics is not something given with reason as a natural endowment.

Reason and the heart must work together if a true morality is to be established. And herein lies the problem for all abstract ethical questions as well as for practical decisions in daily life.

When I say reason, I refer to an understanding that penetrates to the depths of things and that embraces the wholeness of reality, extending even into the realm of the will.

We experience a noteworthy duality when we seek to understand ourselves in light of the ethical will within us. We observe, on the one hand, that the moral will is connected to reason. On the other hand, we are pressed toward decisions that are not rational, in ordinary terms, but correspond, rather, to demands that would ordinarily be regarded as extravagant. In this duality, in this strange tension, lies the essence of ethics. The fear that an ethic based on reason would be something focused too low, would be too detached and heartless, is unfounded. When reason truly plumbs the depths of questions, it ceases to be cool reason and begins willy-nilly to speak with the melodies of the heart. And the heart, when it seeks to fathom itself, discovers that its realm reaches over into that of reason and that it must go through the land of reason in order to get to the further reaches of its own territory. How can that be?

Let's then explore the basic notion of goodness, first from the point of view of the heart and then from that of reason, and see if they converge.

The *heart* says that ethics is based on love. Let's examine that word "love." Love means harmony of being, community of being. Originally it applied to groups of persons who belonged to each other in some fashion so that they stood in some inner, reciprocal connection with each other: children and parents, married couples, and intimate friends. But now ethics requires that even people whom we do not know should not be regarded as strangers. The same applies to those who are worse than strangers to us because we have an aversion to them or because they have shown hostility toward us. We are, however, to treat them as if they were close to us. In the final analysis, then, the commandment of love means this: For you there are no strangers, only people whose well-being must be your concern. We often assume it to be natural to be concerned for those who are close to us and to be indifferent to those who are not. This natural disposition is not, however, permitted by ethical standards. And Jesus eliminated our behaving toward one another as strangers altogether when he said, The other person must mean as much to you as you do to yourself. You must feel what concerns him or her as that which concerns you directly.

The heart should explain the first commandment: "You should love God with all your heart and with all your mind and with all your strength." To love God, that remote, unfathomable being! Here it indeed becomes clear that the word "love," when it is used ethically, is used in a figurative sense. We ought to love God, who needs nothing from us, as if he were a creature we confront in daily life. In a human context, love means sharing experiences, having compassion, and helping each other. Toward God, however, love means something akin to reverential love. God is everlasting life. Thus, the most elementary principle, when grasped by the heart, means that out of reverence for the incomprehensible, infinite, and living One whom we call God, we should never consider ourselves strangers toward any person, rather, we are to coerce ourselves into being helpful to him and to share his experiences.

This, then, is what the heart says when it tries to give the most general meaning to the commandment of love for God and neighbor.

Now let *reason* speak. Let's assume that nothing about ethics has passed down to us and see how far we can get by pondering the forces that influence our actions. Will reason also make us step outside ourselves?

One usually hears it said that the only thing confirmed in reason is egotism. How can I make things good for myself? That is reason's wisdom, nothing more. At best, it can teach us a certain decency and justice, because these more or less belong to the feeling of happiness. Reason is the desire for knowledge and the desire for happiness, and both are mysteriously connected to each other in an inner way.

Desire for knowledge! You may seek to explore everything around you, you may push to the farthest limits of human knowledge, but in the end you will always strike upon something that is unfathomable. It is called life. And this mystery is so inexplicable that it renders the difference between knowledge and ignorance completely relative.

What difference is there between the scholar who observes the smallest and least expected signs of life under a microscope and the old peasant, who can scarcely read and write, when he stands in his garden in the spring and contemplates the blossoms bursting open on the branches of his tree? Both are confronted with the riddle of life! The one can describe it more thoroughly than the other, but for both it is equally inscrutable. All knowledge is finally knowledge of life. All realization is astonishment at this riddle of life—*reverence for life* in its infinite, yet ever new, manifestations. For what does it mean for something to come into being, live, and pass away? How amazing that it renews itself in other existences, passes away again, comes into being once more, and so on and so forth, from infinity to infinity! We can do all things and we can do nothing, for in all our wisdom we are not able to create life. Rather, what we create is dead!

Life means strength, will coming from the abyss and sinking into it again. Life means feeling, sensitivity, and suffering. And if you are absorbed in life, if you see with perceptive eyes into this enormous animated chaos of creation, it suddenly seizes you with vertigo. In everything you recognize yourself again. The beetle that lies dead in your path—it was something that lived, that struggled for its existence like you, that rejoiced in the sun like you, that knew anxiety and pain like you. And now it is nothing more than decomposing material—as you, too, shall be sooner or later.

You walk outside and it is snowing. Carelessly you shake the snow from your sleeves. It attracts your attention: a snowflake glistens on your hand. You cannot help looking at it, whether you wish to or not. It glistens in its wonderful design; then it quivers, and the delicate needles of which it consists contract. It is no more; it has melted, dead in your hand. The flake, which fell upon your hand from infinite space, which glistened there, quivered, and died—that is you. Wherever you see life—that is you!

What is this recognition, this knowledge apprehended by the most learned and the most childlike alike? It is reverence for life, reverence for the impenetrable mystery that meets us in our universe, an existence different from ourselves in external appearance, yet inwardly of the same character with us, terribly similar, awesomely related. *The dissimilarity, the strangeness, between us and other creatures is here removed.*

Reverence before the infinity of life means the removal of the strangeness, the restoration of shared experiences and of compassion and sympathy. And thus the final result of knowledge is the same, in principle, as that which the commandment to love requires of us. Heart and reason agree together when we desire and dare to be people who attempt to fathom the depths of things.

And reason discovers the connecting link between love for God and love for humankind: love for all creatures, reverence for all being, a compassionate sharing of experiences with all of life, no matter how externally dissimilar to our own.

I can do no other than be reverent before everything that is called life. I can do no other than to have compassion for all that is called life. That is the beginning and the foundation of all ethics. Once one has experienced this and continues to experience it—and whoever experiences it once always continues to experience it!—that person is ethical. He bears his morality in him and can never lose it, and it continues to develop in him. Whoever has not experienced it has only a superficially acquired morality. His ethical theories are not grounded in him, do not belong to him, and can drop away. And the terrible thing is that our entire generation possesses only such a superficially acquired ethic. When the time came for our ethic to be tested, it fell away from us. For centuries the human race has been trained with only a superficial ethic. We were brutal, ignorant, and heartless without suspecting it, because we did not yet have an adequate standard of value. We possessed no reverence for life.

You ought to *share life* and *preserve life* —that is the greatest commandment in its most elementary form. Another, and negative, way of expressing it is this: You shall *not kill.* We take this prohibition so lightly, thoughtlessly breaking flowers, thoughtlessly treading on the poor insect, and then—in terrible self-delusion, since everything avenges itself!—we thoughtlessly disregard the suffering and the lives of men and offer them to trivial earthly goals.

Much is said in our time about building a new humanity. How are we to build a new humanity? Only by leading people to a true, proper, inalienable ethic that is capable of development. But it will not succeed unless many individuals transform themselves from blind into seeing people and begin to spell out this great commandment, which says reverence for life. More hangs on this than on the law and the prophets. It is the whole ethic of love in its deepest and in its highest sense. And it is the source of renewal again and again for the individual and for humankind.

CHAPTER 5

The Philosophy of Civilization

Albert Schweitzer

Arguably the best and most compelling presentation of reverence for life from a philo-sophical point of view is to be found in Albert Schweitzer's volume The Philosophy of Civilization *(originally published in 1923) in chapter 26, entitled "The Ethics of Reverence for Life"* (The Philosophy of Civilization, *trans. C. T. Campion [Buf-falo: Prometheus Books, 1987], 307–29). This presentation of reverence for life fol-lows a lengthy and largely critical survey of the unsuccessful attempts of other ethical thinkers to offer a satisfactory system of ethics. Schweitzer himself proposes what he calls "the most universal definition of good and evil": "It is good to maintain and to encourage life; it is bad to destroy life or to obstruct it." The chapter is reproduced here (modified slightly for style) with the permission of Rhena Schweitzer Miller.*

Complicated and laborious are the roads along which ethical thought, which has mistaken its way and taken too high a flight, must be brought back. Its course, however, maps itself out quite simply if, instead of taking apparently convenient short cuts, it keeps to its right direction from the very beginning. For this three things are necessary: it must have nothing to do with an ethical interpretation of the world; it must become cosmic and mystical, that is to say, it must seek to conceive all the self-devotion which rules in ethics as a manifestation of an inward, spiritual relation to the world; it must not lapse into abstract thinking, but must remain elemental, under-standing self-devotion to the world to be self-devotion of human life to every form of living being with which it can come into relation.

The origin of ethics is that I think out the full meaning of the world-affirmation which, together with the life-affirmation in my will-to-live, is given by nature and try to make it a reality.

To become ethical means to begin to think sincerely. Thinking is the argument between willing and knowing which goes on within me. Its course is a naïve one, if the will demands of knowledge to be shown a world which corresponds to the impulses which it carries within itself, and if knowledge attempts to satisfy this requirement. This dialogue, which is doomed to produce no result, must give place to a debate of the right kind, in which the will demands from knowledge only what it really knows.

If knowledge answers solely with what it knows, it is always teaching the will one and the same fact, namely, that in and behind all phenomena there is a will-to-live. Knowledge, though ever becoming deeper and more comprehensive, can do nothing except take us ever deeper and ever further into the mystery that all that is, is will-to-live. Progress in science consists only in increasingly accurate description of the phenomena in which life in its innumerable forms appears and passes, letting us discover life where we did not previously expect it, and putting us in a position to turn to our own use in this or that way what we have learned of the course of the will-to-live in nature. But what life is, no science can tell us.

For our conception of the universe and of life, then, the gain derived from knowledge is only that it makes it harder for us to be thoughtless, because it ever more forcibly compels our attention to the mystery of the will-to-live which we see stirring everywhere. Hence the difference between learned and unlearned is entirely relative. The unlearned person who, at the sight of a tree in flower, is overpowered by the mystery of the will-to-live which is stirring all around knows more than the scientist who studies under the microscope or in physical and chemical activity a thousand forms of the will-to-live but, with all his knowledge of the life course of these manifestations of the will-to-live, is unmoved by the mystery that everything which exists is will-to-live while he is puffed up with vanity at being able to describe exactly a fragment of the course of life.

All true knowledge passes on into experience. The nature of the manifestations I do not know, but I form a conception of it in analogy to the will-to-live which is within myself. Thus my knowledge of the world becomes experience of the world. The knowledge which is becoming experience does not allow me to remain in face of the world someone who merely knows, but forces upon me an inward relation to the world and fills me with reverence for the mysterious will-to-live which is in all things. By making me think and wonder, it leads me ever upward to the heights of reverence for life. There it lets my hand go. It cannot accompany me further. My will-to-live must now find its way about the world by itself.

It is not by informing me what this or that manifestation of life means in the sum total of the world that knowledge brings me into connection with the world. It goes about with me not in outer circles but in the inner ones. From within outward it puts me in relation to the world by making my will-to-live feel everything around it as also will-to-live.

With Descartes, philosophy starts from the dogma "I think, therefore I exist." With this paltry, arbitrarily chosen beginning, it is landed irretrievably on the road to the abstract. It never finds the right approach to ethics and remains entangled in a dead world- and life-view. True philosophy must start from the most immediate and comprehensive fact of consciousness, which says, "I am life which wills to live, in the midst of life which wills to live." This is not an ingenious dogmatic formula. Day by day, hour by hour, I live and move in it. At every moment of reflection it stands fresh before me. There bursts forth from it again and again, as from roots that can never dry up, a living world- and life-view which can deal with all the facts of Being. A mysticism of ethical union with Being grows out of it.

As in my own will-to-live there is a longing for wider life and for the mysterious exaltation of the will-to-live which we call pleasure, with dread of annihilation and of the mysterious depreciation of the will-to-live which we call pain; so is it also in the will-to-live all around me, whether it can express itself before me or remains dumb.

Ethics consists, therefore, in my experiencing the compulsion to show to all will-to-live the same reverence as I do to my own. There we have given us that basic principle of the moral which is a necessity of thought. It is good to maintain and to encourage life; it is bad to destroy life or to obstruct it.

As a matter of fact, everything which in the ordinary ethical valuation of the relations of people to each other ranks as good can be brought under the description of material and spiritual maintenance or promotion of human life, and of effort to bring it to its highest value. Conversely, everything which ranks as bad in human relations is in the last analysis material or spiritual destruction or obstruction of human life, and negligence in the endeavor to bring it to its highest value. Separate individual categories of good and evil which lie far apart and have apparently no connection at all with one another fit together like the pieces of a jigsaw puzzle as soon as they are comprehended and deepened in this, the most universal definition of good and evil.

The basic principle of the moral which is a necessity of thought means, however, not only an ordering and deepening, but also a widening of the current views of good and evil. Someone is truly ethical only when he or she obeys the compulsion to help all life which he is able to assist and shrinks from injuring anything that lives. Such a person does not ask how far this or that life deserves one's sympathy as being valuable, nor, beyond that, whether and to what degree it is capable of feeling. Life as such is sacred to him. Such a person tears no leaf from a tree, plucks no flower, and takes care to crush no insect. If in summer this person is working by lamplight, he prefers to keep his windows shut and breathe a stuffy atmosphere rather than see one insect after another fall with singed wings upon his table.

If this person walks on the road after a shower and sees an earthworm which has strayed on to it, he bethinks himself that it must get dried up in the sun if it does not return soon enough to ground into which it can burrow, so he lifts it from the deadly stone surface and puts it on the grass. If he comes across an insect which has fallen into a puddle, he stops a moment in order to hold out a leaf or a stalk on which it can save itself.

This person is not afraid of being laughed at as sentimental. It is the fate of every truth to be a subject for laughter until it is generally recognized. Once it was considered folly to assume that people of color were really human and ought to be treated as such, but the folly has become an accepted truth. Today it is thought to be going too far to declare that constant regard for everything that lives, down to the lowest manifestations of life, is a demand made by rational ethics. The time is coming, however, when people will be astonished that humankind needed so long a time to learn to regard thoughtless injury to life as incompatible with ethics.

Ethics is responsibility without limit toward all that lives.

As a general proposition the definition of ethics as a relationship within a disposition to reverence for life does not make a very moving impression. But it is the only complete one. Compassion is too narrow to rank as the total essence of the ethical. It denotes, of course, only interest in the suffering will-to-live. But ethics includes also feeling as one's own all the circumstances and all the aspirations of the will-to-live, its pleasure, too, and its longing to live itself out to the full, as well as its urge to self-perfecting.

Love means more, since it includes fellowship in suffering, in joy, and in effort, but it shows the ethical only in a simile, although in a simile that is natural and profound. It makes the solidarity produced by ethics analogous to that which nature calls forth on the physical side, for more or less temporary purposes, between two beings which complete each other sexually, or between them and their offspring.

Thought must strive to bring to expression the nature of the ethical in itself. To effect this it arrives at defining ethics as devotion to life inspired by reverence for life. Even if the phrase reverence for life sounds so general as to seem somewhat lifeless, what is meant by it is nevertheless something which never lets go of the one into whose thought it has made its way. Sympathy, and love, and every kind of valuable enthusiasm are given within it. With restless living force reverence for life works upon the mind into which it has entered and throws it into the unrest of a feeling of responsibility which at no place and at no time ceases to affect it. Just as the screw which churns its way through the water drives the ship along, so does reverence for life drive the person.

Arising, as it does, from an inner compulsion, the ethic of reverence for life is not dependent on the extent to which it can be thought out to a satisfying conception of life. It need give no answer to the question of what significance the ethical person's work for the maintenance, promotion, and enhancement of life can be in the total happenings of the course of nature. It does not let itself be misled by the calculation that the maintaining and completing of life which it practices is hardly worth consideration beside the tremendous, unceasing destruction of life which goes on every moment through natural forces. Having the will to action, it can leave on one side all problems regarding the success of its work. The fact in itself that in the ethically developed person there has made its appearance in the world a will-to-live which is filled with reverence for life and devotion to life is full of importance for the world.

In my will-to-live the universal will-to-live experiences itself otherwise than in its other manifestations. In them it shows itself in a process of individualizing which, so far as I can see from the outside, is bent merely on living itself out to the full, and in no way on union with any other will-to-live. The world is a ghastly drama of will-to-live divided against itself. One existence makes its way at the cost of another; one destroys the other. One will-to-live merely exerts its will against the other and has no knowledge of it. But in me the will-to-live has come to know about other wills-to-live. There is in it a yearning to arrive at unity with itself, to become universal.

Why does the will-to-live experience itself in this way in me alone? Is it because I have acquired the capacity of reflecting on the totality of Being? What is the goal of this evolution which has begun in me?

To these questions there is no answer. It remains a painful enigma for me that I must live with reverence for life in a world which is dominated by creative will which is also destructive will, and destructive will which is also creative.

I can do nothing but hold to the fact that the will-to-live in me manifests itself as will-to-live which desires to become one with other will-to-live. That is for me the light that shines in the darkness. The ignorance in which the world is wrapped has no existence for me; I have been saved from the world. I am thrown, indeed, by reverence for life into an unrest such as the world does not know, but I obtain from it a blessedness which the world cannot give. If in the tenderheartedness produced by being different from the world another person and I help each other in understanding and pardoning, when otherwise will would torment will, the division of the will-to-live is at an end. If I save an insect from a puddle, life has devoted itself to life, and the division of life against itself is ended. Whenever my life devotes itself in any way to life, my finite will-to-live experiences union with the infinite will in which all life is one, and I enjoy a feeling of refreshment which prevents me from pining away in the desert of life.

I therefore recognize it as the destiny of my existence to be obedient to this higher revelation of the will-to-live in me. I choose for my activity the removal of this division of the will-to-live against itself, so far as the influence of my existence can reach. Knowing now the one thing needful, I leave on one side the enigma of the universe and of my existence in it.

The surmisings and the longings of all deep religiousness are contained in the ethics of reverence for life. This religiousness, however, does not build up for itself a complete philosophy, but resigns itself to the necessity of leaving its cathedral unfinished. It finishes the chancel only, but in this chancel piety celebrates a living and never-ceasing divine service.

◆   ◆   ◆

The ethic of reverence for life shows its truth also in that it includes in itself the different elements of ethics in their natural connection. Hitherto no system of ethics has been able to present in its parallelism and interaction the effort after self-perfecting, in which a person acts upon himself without outward deeds, and activist ethics. The ethics of reverence for life can do this, and indeed in such a way that it not only answers academic questions, but also produces a deepening of ethical insight.

Ethics is reverence for the will-to-live within me and without me. From the former comes first the profound life-affirmation of resignation. I apprehend my will-to-live as not only something which can live itself out in happy occurrences, but also something which has experience of itself. If I refuse to let this self-experience disappear in thoughtlessness and persist in feeling it to be valuable, I begin to learn the secret of spiritual self-realization. I win an unsuspected freedom from the various destinies of life. At moments when I had expected to find myself shattered, I find myself exalted in an inexpressible and surprising happiness of freedom from the world, and I experience therein a clarification of my life-view. Resignation is the vestibule through which we enter ethics. Only someone who in deepened devotion to his own will-to-live experiences inward freedom from outward occurrences is capable of devoting himself in profound and steady fashion to the life of others.

Just as in reverence for my own will-to-live I struggle for freedom from the destinies of life, so I struggle too for freedom from myself. Not only in face of what happens to me, but also with regard to the way in which I concern myself with the world, I practice the higher self-maintenance. Out of reverence for my own existence I place myself under the compulsion of veracity toward myself. Everything I might acquire would be purchased too dearly by action in defiance of my convictions. I fear that if I were untrue to myself, I should be wounding my will-to-live with a poisoned spear.

The fact that Kant makes, as he does, sincerity toward oneself the central point of his ethics testifies to the depth of his ethical feeling. But because in his search for the essential nature of the ethical he fails to find his way through to reverence for life, he cannot comprehend the connection between veracity toward oneself and activist ethics.

As a matter of fact, the ethics of sincerity toward oneself passes imperceptibly into that of devotion to others. Such sincerity compels me to actions which manifest themselves as self-devotion in such a way that ordinary ethics derives them from devotion.

Why do I forgive anyone? Ordinary ethics says, because I feel sympathy with him. It allows people, when they pardon others, to seem to themselves wonderfully good, and allows them to practice a style of pardoning which is not free from humiliation of the other. It thus makes forgiveness a sweetened triumph of self-devotion.

The ethics of reverence for life does away with this crude point of view. All acts of forbearance and of pardon are, for this system of ethics, acts forced from one by sincerity toward oneself. I must practice unlimited forgiveness because, if I did not, I should be wanting in sincerity to myself, for it would be acting as if I myself were not guilty in the same way as the other has been guilty toward me. Because my life is so liberally spotted with falsehood, I must forgive falsehood which has been practiced upon me; because I myself have been in so many cases wanting in love, and guilty of hatred, slander, deceit, or arrogance, I must pardon any want of love, and all hatred, slander, deceit, or arrogance which have been directed against myself. I must forgive quietly and unostentatiously; in fact I do not really pardon at all, for I do not let things develop to any such act of judgment. Nor is this any eccentric proceeding; it is only a necessary widening and refining of ordinary ethics.

We have to carry on the struggle against the evil that is in humankind, not by judging others, but by judging ourselves. Struggle with oneself and veracity toward oneself are the means by which we influence others. We quietly draw them into our efforts to attain the deep spiritual self-realization which springs from reverence for one's own life. Power makes no noise. It is there, and works. True ethics begins where the use of languages ceases.

The innermost element then, in activist ethics, even if it appears as self-devotion, comes from the compulsion to sincerity toward oneself and obtains therein its true value. The whole ethics of being other than the world flows pure only when it comes from this source. It is not from kindness to others that I am gentle, peaceable, forbearing, and friendly, but because by such behavior I prove my own profoundest self-realization to be true. Reverence for life which I apply to my own existence, and reverence for life which keeps me in a temper of devotion to other existence than my own, interpenetrate each other.

◆   ◆   ◆

Because ordinary ethics possesses no basic principle of the ethical, it must engage at once in the discussion of conflicting duties. The ethics of reverence for life has no such need for hurry. It takes its own time to think out in all directions its own principle of the moral. Knowing itself to be firmly established, it then settles its position with regard to these conflicts.

It has to try conclusions with three adversaries: thoughtlessness, egoistic self-assertion, and society.

To the first of these it usually pays insufficient attention, because no open conflicts arise between them. This adversary does, nevertheless, obstruct it imperceptibly.

There is, however, a wide field of which our ethics can take possession without any collision with the troops of egoism. A person can accomplish much that is good without having to require of himself any sacrifice. And if there really goes with it a bit of his life, it is so insignificant that he feels it no more than if he were losing a hair or a flake of dead skin.

Over wide stretches of conduct the inward liberation from the world, the being true to oneself, the being different from the world, yes, and even the self-devotion to other life, is only a matter of giving attention to this particular relationship. We fall short so much because we do not keep ourselves up to it. We do not stand sufficiently under the pressure of any inward compulsion to be ethical. At all points the steam hisses out of the boiler that is not tightly closed. In ordinary ethics the resulting losses of energy are as high as they are because such ethics has at its disposal no single basic principle of the moral which acts upon thought. It cannot tighten the lid of the boiler; indeed, it does not ever even examine it. But reverence for life, being something which is ever present to thought, penetrates unceasingly and in all directions a person's observation, reflection, and resolution. A person can keep himself clear of it as little as the water can prevent itself from being colored by the dyestuff which is dropped into it. The struggle with thoughtlessness is started and is always going on.

But what is the position of the ethics of reverence for life in the conflicts which arise between inward compulsion to self-sacrifice and the necessary upholding of the ego?

I too am subject to division of my will-to-live against itself. In a thousand ways my existence stands in conflict with that of others. The necessity to destroy and to injure life is imposed upon me. If I walk along an unfrequented path, my foot brings destruction and pain upon the tiny creatures which populate it. In order to preserve my own existence, I must defend myself against the existence which injures it. I become a persecutor of the little mouse which inhabits my house, a murderer of the insect which wants to have its nest there, a mass-murderer of the bacteria which may endanger my life. I get my food by destroying plants and animals. My happiness is built upon injury done to my fellow human beings.

How can ethics be maintained in face of the horrible necessity to which I am subjected through the division of my will-to-live against itself?

Ordinary ethics seeks compromises. It tries to dictate how much of my existence and of my happiness I must sacrifice, and how much I may preserve at the cost of the existence and happiness of other lives. With these decisions it produces experimental, relative ethics. It offers as ethical what is in reality not ethical but a mixture of nonethical necessity and ethics. It thereby brings about a huge confusion and allows the starting of an ever-increasing obscuration of the conception of the ethical.

The ethics of reverence for life knows nothing of a relative ethic. It makes only the maintenance and promotion of life rank as good. All destruction of and injury to life, under whatever circumstances they take place, it condemns as evil. It does not keep in-store adjustments between ethics and necessity all ready for use. Again and again and in ways that are always original it is trying to come to terms in a person with reality. It does not abolish for him all ethical conflicts, but compels him to decide for himself in each case how far he can remain ethical and how far he must submit himself to the necessity for destruction of and injury to life, and therewith incur guilt. It is not by receiving instruction about agreement between ethical and necessary that someone makes progress in ethics, but only by coming to hear more and more plainly the voice of the ethical, by becoming ruled more and more by the longing to preserve and promote life, and by becoming more and more obstinate in resistance to the necessity for destroying or injuring life.

In ethical conflicts a person can arrive only at subjective decisions. No one can decide for him at what point, on each occasion, lies the extreme limit of possibility for his persistence in the preservation and furtherance of life. A person alone has to judge this issue, by letting himself be guided by a feeling of the highest possible responsibility toward other life.

We must never let ourselves become blunted. We are living in truth when we experience these conflicts more profoundly. The good conscience is an invention of the devil.

◆　　◆　　◆

What does reverence for life say about the relations between humankind and the animal world?

Whenever I injure life of any sort, I must be quite clear whether it is necessary. Beyond the unavoidable, I must never go, not even with what seems insignificant. The farmer who has mown down a thousand flowers in his meadow as fodder for his cows must be careful on his way home not to strike off in wanton pastime the head of a single flower by the roadside, for he thereby commits a wrong against life without being under the pressure of necessity.

Those who experiment with operations or the use of drugs upon animals, or inoculate them with diseases, so as to be able to bring help to people with the results gained, must never quiet any misgivings they feel with the general reflection that their cruel proceedings aim at a valuable result. They must first have considered in each individual case whether there is a real necessity to force upon any animal this sacrifice for the sake of people. And they must take the most anxious care to mitigate as much as possible the pain inflicted. How much wrong is committed in scientific institutions through neglect of anesthetics, which to save time or trouble are not administered! How much, too, through animals being subjected to torture merely to demonstrate to students generally known phenomena! By the very fact that animals have been subjected to experiments, and have by their pain won such valuable results for suffering humanity, a new and special relation of solidarity has been established between them and us. From that springs for each one of us a compulsion to do to every animal all the good we possibly can. By helping an insect when it is in difficulties, I am only attempting to cancel part of humanity's ever new debt to the animal world. Whenever an animal is in any way forced into the service of humanity, every one of us must be concerned with the sufferings which for that reason it has to undergo. None of us must allow to take place any suffering for which he himself is not responsible, if he can hinder it in any way. He must not soothe his conscience with the reflection that he would be mixing himself up in something which does not concern him. No one must shut his eyes and regard as nonexistent the sufferings of which he spares himself the sight. Let no one regard as light the burden of his responsibility. While so much ill-treatment of animals goes on, while the moans of thirsty animals in railway trucks sound unheard, while so much brutality prevails in our slaughterhouses, while animals have to suffer in our kitchens painful death from unskilled hands, while animals have to endure intolerable treatment from heartless people, or are left to the cruel play of children, we all share the guilt.

We are afraid of making ourselves conspicuous if we let it be noticed how we feel for the sufferings which people bring upon the animals. At the same time we think that others have become more "rational" than we are, and regard what we are excited about as usual and a matter of course. Yet suddenly they will let slip a word which shows us that they too have not yet learned to acquiesce. And now, though they were strangers, they are quite near us. The mask in which we deceived each other falls off. We know now, from one another, that we feel alike about being unable to escape from the gruesome proceedings that are taking place unceasingly around us. What a making of a new acquaintance!

The ethics of reverence for life guards us from letting each other believe through our silence that we no longer experience what, as thinking people, we must experience. It prompts us to keep each other sensitive to what distresses us, and to talk and act together, just as the responsibility we feel moves us, and without any feeling of shyness. It makes us join in keeping on the lookout for opportunities of bringing some sort of help to animals, to make up for the great misery which people inflict on them, and thus to step for a moment out of the incomprehensible horror of existence.

In the matter also of our relation to other people, the ethics of reverence for life throws upon us a responsibility so unlimited as to be terrifying.

Here again it offers us no rules about the extent of the self-maintenance which is allowable; again, it bids us in each case to thrash the question out with the absolute ethics of self-devotion. I have to decide, in accordance with the responsibility of which I am conscious, how much of my life, my possessions, my rights, my happiness, my time, and my rest I must devote to others, and how much I may keep for myself.

In the question of possessions, the ethics of reverence for life is outspokenly individualist in the sense that wealth acquired or inherited should be placed at the service of the community, not through any measures taken by society, but through the absolutely free decision of the individual. It expects everything from a general increase in the feeling of responsibility. Wealth it regards as the property of society left in the sovereign control of the individual. One person serves society by carrying on a business in which a number of employees earn their livings, another by giving away his wealth in order to help his fellows. Between these two extreme kinds of service, let each decide according to the responsibility which he finds determined for him by the circumstances of his life. Let no one judge his neighbor. The one thing that matters is that each shall value what he possesses as means to action. Whether this is accomplished by his keeping and increasing his wealth, or by surrender of it, matters little. Wealth must reach the community in the most varied ways, if it is to be of the greatest benefit to all.

Those who possess little to call their own are most in danger of holding what they have in a purely selfish spirit. There is profound truth in the parable of Jesus which makes the servant who had received least the least loyal to his duty.

My rights too the ethics of reverence for life does not allow to belong to me. It forbids me to still my conscience with the reflection that, as the more efficient person, by quite legitimate means I am advancing myself at the cost of someone who is less efficient than I. In what the law and public opinion allow me, it sets a problem before me. It bids me think of others and makes me ponder whether I can allow myself the inward right to pluck all the fruit that my hand can reach. Thus it may happen that, in obedience to consideration for the existence of others, I do what seems to ordinary opinion to be folly. Yes, it may even show itself to be folly by the fact that my renunciation has not been any use to the one for whom it was made. And yet I was right. Reverence for life is the highest court of appeal. What it commands has its own significance, even if it seems foolish or useless. We all look, of course, in one another, for the folly which indicates that we have higher responsibilities making themselves felt in our hearts. Yet it is only in proportion as we all become less rational, in the meaning given it by ordinary calculation, that the ethical disposition develops in us and allows problems to become soluble which have hitherto been insoluble.

Nor will reverence for life grant me my happiness as my own. At the moments when I should like to enjoy myself without restraint, it wakes in me reflection about misery that I see or suspect, and it does not allow me to drive away the uneasiness I feel. Just as the wave cannot exist for itself, but is ever a part of the heaving surface of the ocean, so must I never live my life for itself, but always in the experience which is going on around me. It is an uncomfortable doctrine which the true ethics whispers into my ear. You are happy, it says; therefore you are called upon to give much. Whatever more than others you have received in health, natural gifts, working capacity, success, a beautiful childhood, harmonious family circumstances, you must not accept as being a matter of course. You must pay a price for them. You must show more than average devotion of life to life.

To the happy the voice of the true ethics is dangerous, if they venture to listen to it. When it calls to them, it never damps down the irrational which glows within it. It assails them to see whether it can get them off their smooth track and turn them into adventurers of self-devotion, people of whom the world has too few. . . .

Reverence for life is an inexorable creditor! If it finds anyone with nothing to pledge but a little time and a little leisure, it lays an attachment on these. But its hard-heartedness is good and sees clearly. The many modern people who as industrial machines are engaged in callings in which they can in no way be active as people among people are exposed to the danger of merely vegetating in an egoistic life. Many of them feel this danger and suffer under the fact that their daily work has so little to do with spiritual and ideal aims and does not allow them to put into it anything of their human nature. Others acquiesce; the thought of having no duties outside their daily work suits them very well.

But that people should be so condemned or so favored as to be released from responsibility for self-devotion as people to people, the ethics of reverence for life will not allow to be legitimate. It demands that every one of us in some way and with some object shall be a human being for human beings. To those who have no opportunity in their daily work of giving themselves in this way, and have nothing else that they can give, it suggests their sacrificing something of their time and leisure, even if of these they have but a scant allowance. It says to them, find for yourselves some secondary activity, inconspicuous, perhaps secret. Open your eyes and look for a human being, or some work devoted to human welfare, which needs from someone a little time or friendliness, a little sympathy, or sociability, or labor. There may be a solitary or an embittered fellow human being, an invalid, or an inefficient person to whom you can be something. Perhaps it is an old person or a child. Or some good work needs volunteers who can offer a free evening or run errands. Who can enumerate the many ways in which that costly piece of working capital, a human being, can be employed? More of him is wanted everywhere! Search, then, for some investment for your humanity, and do not be frightened away if you have to wait or to be taken on trial. And be prepared for some disappointments. But in any case, do not be without some secondary work in which you give yourself as a person to people. It is marked out for you, if you only truly will to have it. . . .

Thus does the true ethics speak to those who have only a little time and a little human nature to give. Well will it be with them if they listen and are preserved from becoming stunted natures because they have neglected this devotion of self to others.

But to everyone, in whatever state of life someone finds himself, the ethics of reverence for life does this: it forces him without cessation to be concerned at heart with all the human destinies and all the other life destinies which are going through their life course around him, and to give himself, as a person, to the human who needs a fellow human being. It will not allow the scholar to live only for his learning, even if his learning makes him very useful, nor the artist to live only for his art, even if by means of it he gives something to many. It does not allow the very busy person to think that with his professional activities he has fulfilled every demand upon him. It demands from all that they devote a portion of their life to their fellows. In what way and to what extent this is prescribed, the individual must gather from the thoughts which arise in him, and from the destinies among which his life moves. One person's sacrifice is outwardly insignificant. One can accomplish it while continuing to live a normal life. Another is called to some conspicuous act of self-sacrifice and must therefore put aside regard for his own progress. But let neither judge the other. The destinies of people have to be decided in a thousand ways in order that the good may become actual. What a person has to bring as an offering is the secret of each individual. But one with another we have all to recognize that our existence reaches its true value only when we experience in ourselves something of the truth of the saying "Whoever loses his life shall find it."

◆　　◆　　◆

The ethical conflicts between society and the individual arise out of the fact that the latter has to bear not only a personal but also a suprapersonal responsibility. When my own person only is concerned, I can always be patient, always forgive, always exercise forbearance, always be merciful. But each of us comes into a situation where we are responsible not for ourselves only, but also for a cause, and then we are forced into decisions which conflict with personal morality.

The craftsman who manages a business, however small, and the musician who conducts public performances cannot be human beings in the way they would like to be. The one has to dismiss a worker who is incapable or given to drink, in spite of any sympathy he has for him and his family; the other cannot let a singer whose voice is the worse for wear appear any longer, although he knows what distress he thus causes.

The more extensive a person's activities, the oftener he finds himself in the position of having to sacrifice something of his humanity to his suprapersonal responsibility. From this conflict customary consideration leads to the decision that the general responsibility does, as a matter of principle, annul the personal. It is in this sense that society addresses the individual. For the soothing of consciences for which this decision is too categorical, it perhaps lays down a few principles which undertake to determine, in a way that is valid for everybody, how far in any case personal morality can have a say in the matter.

No course remains open to current ethics but to sign this capitulation. Current ethics has no means of defending the fortress of personal morality because it has not at its disposal any absolute notions of good and evil. Not so the ethics of reverence for life. It possesses, as we can see, what the other lacks. It therefore never surrenders the fortress, even if it is permanently invested. It feels itself in a position to persevere in holding it, and by continual sorties to keep the besiegers on the *qui vive*.

Only the most universal and absolute purposiveness in the maintenance and furtherance of life, which is the objective aimed at by reverence for life, is ethical. All other necessity or expediency is not ethical, but only a more or less necessary necessity, or a more or less expedient expediency. In the conflict between the maintenance of my own existence and the destruction of, or injury to, that of another, I can never unite the ethical and the necessary to form a relative ethical; I must choose between ethical and necessary and, if I choose the latter, must take it upon myself to incur guilt by an act of injury to life. Similarly I am not at liberty to think that in the conflict between personal and suprapersonal responsibility I can balance the ethical and the expedient to make a relative ethical, or even annul the ethical with the purposive; I must choose between the two. If, under the pressure of the suprapersonal responsibility, I yield to the expedient, I become guilty in some way or other through failure in reverence for life.

The temptation to combine with the ethical into a relative ethical the expedient which is commanded me by the suprapersonal responsibility is especially strong, because it can be shown, in defense of it, that someone who complies with the demand of this suprapersonal responsibility acts unegoistically. It is not to his individual existence or his individual welfare that someone sacrifices another existence or welfare, but he sacrifices an individual existence and welfare to what forces itself upon him as expedient in view of the existence or the welfare of a majority. But ethical is more than unego-istic. Only the reverence felt by my will-to-live for every other will-to-live is ethical. Whenever I in any way sacrifice or injure life, I am not within the sphere of the ethical, but I become guilty, whether it be egoistically guilty for the sake of maintaining my own existence or welfare or unegoistically guilty for the sake of maintaining a greater number of other existences or their welfare.

This so easily made mistake of accepting as ethical a violation of rever-ence for life, if it is based upon unegoistic considerations, is the bridge by crossing which ethics enters unawares the territory of the nonethical. The bridge must be broken down.

Ethics goes only so far as does humanity, humanity meaning considera-tion for the existence and the happiness of individual human beings. Where humanity ends, pseudoethics begin. The day on which this boundary is once for all universally recognized, and marked out so as to be visible to everyone, will be one of the most important in the history of humankind. Thenceforward it can no longer happen that ethics which is not ethics at all is accepted as real ethics, and deceives and ruins individuals and peoples.

The system of ethics hitherto current has hindered us from becoming as earnest as we ought to be by the fact that it has utterly deceived us as to the many ways in which each one of us, whether through self-assertion or by ac-tions justified by suprapersonal responsibility, becomes guilty again and again. True knowledge consists in being gripped by the secret that every-thing around us is will-to-live and in seeing clearly how again and again we incur guilt against life.

Fooled by pseudoethics, a person stumbles about in his guilt like a drunkard. If he gains knowledge and becomes serious, he seeks the road which least leads him into guilt.

We are all exposed to the temptation of lessening the guilt of inhuman-ity, which comes from our working under suprapersonal responsibility, by withdrawing as far as possible into ourselves. But such freedom from guilt is not honestly obtained. Because ethics starts with world- and life-affirmation, it does not allow us this flight into negation. It forbids us to be like the housewife who leaves the killing of the eel to her cook, and compels us to undertake all duties involving suprapersonal responsibility which fall to us, even if we should be in a position to decline them for reasons more or less satisfactory.

Each one of us, then, has to engage, insofar as we are brought to it by the circumstances of our life, in work which involves suprapersonal responsibility. But we must do this not in the spirit of the collective body, but in that of the person who wishes to be ethical. In every individual case, therefore, we struggle to preserve as much humanity as is possible, and in doubtful cases we venture to make a mistake on the side of humanity rather than on that of the object in view. When we have become aware and earnest, we think of what is usually forgotten: that all public activity has to do not only with the facts which are to be made actual in the interest of the collective body, but also with the creation of the state of mind which promotes the welfare of that body. The creation of such a spirit and temper is more important than anything directly attained in the facts. Public activity in which the utmost possible effort is not made to preserve humanity ruins the character. Someone who under the influence of suprapersonal responsibility simply sacrifices human beings and human happiness when it seems right accomplishes something. But he has not reached the highest level. He has only outward, not spiritual influence. We have spiritual influence only when others notice that we do not decide coldly in accordance with principles laid down once and for all, but in each individual case fight for our sense of humanity. There is too little among us of this kind of struggle. From the most insignificant person who is engaged in the smallest business, right up to the political ruler who holds in his hands the decision for peace or war, we act too much as people who in any given case can prepare without effort to be no longer human beings, but merely the executive of general interests. Hence there is no longer among us any trust in a righteousness lighted up with human feeling. Nor have we any longer any real respect for one another. We all feel ourselves in the power of a mentality of cold, impersonal, and usually unintelligent opportunism, which stiffens itself with appeals to principle, and in order to realize the smallest interests is capable of the greatest inhumanity and the greatest folly. We therefore see among us one temper of impersonal opportunism confronting another, and all problems are resolved in a purposeless conflict of force against force because there is nowhere at hand such a spirit as will make them soluble.

It is only through our struggles for humanity that forces which work in the direction of the truly rational and expedient can become powerful while the present way of thinking prevails. Hence the person who works with suprapersonal responsibilities has to feel himself answerable not only for the successful result which is to be realized through him, but for the general disposition which has to be created.

Thus we serve society without abandoning ourselves to it. We do not allow it to be our guardian in the matter of ethics. That would be as if the solo violinist allowed his bowing to be regulated by that of the double bass player. Never for a moment do we lay aside our mistrust of the ideals established by society, and of the convictions which are kept by it in circulation. We always know that society is full of folly and will deceive us in the matter of humanity. It is an unreliable horse, and blind into the bargain. Woe to the driver who falls asleep!

All this sounds too hard. Society serves ethics by giving legal sanction to its most elementary principles and handing on the ethical principles of one generation to the next. That is much, and it claims our gratitude. But society is also something which checks the progress of ethics again and again by arrogating to itself the dignity of an ethical teacher. To this, however, it has no right. The only ethical teacher is the one who thinks ethically and struggles for ethics. The conceptions of good and evil which are put in circulation by society are paper money, the value of which is to be calculated not by the figures printed upon it, but by its relation to its exchange value in the gold of the ethics of reverence for life. But so measured, the rate of exchange is revealed as that of the paper money of a half-bankrupt state.

The collapse of civilization has come about through ethics being left to society. A renewal of it is possible only if ethics becomes once more the concern of thinking human beings, and if individuals seek to assert themselves in society as ethical personalities. In proportion as we secure this, society will become an ethical, instead of the purely natural, entity, which it is by origin. Previous generations have made the terrible mistake of idealizing society as ethical. We do our duty to it by judging it critically and trying to make it, so far as possible, more ethical. Being in possession of an absolute standard of the ethical, we no longer allow ourselves to make acceptable as ethics principles of expediency or of the vulgarest opportunism. Nor do we remain any longer at the low level of allowing to be current, as in any way ethical, meaningless ideals of power, of passion, or of nationalism, which are set up by miserable politicians and maintained in some degree of respect by bewildering propaganda. All the principles, dispositions, and ideals which make their appearance among us we measure, in their showy pedantry, with a rule on which the measures are given by the absolute ethics of reverence for life. We allow currency only to what is consistent with the claims of humanity. We bring into honor again regard for life and for the happiness of the individual. Sacred human rights we again hold high, not those which political rulers exalt at banquets and tread underfoot in their actions, but the true rights. We call once more for justice, not that which imbecile authorities have elaborated in a legal scholasticism, nor that about which demagogues of all shades of color shout themselves hoarse, but that which is filled to the full with the value of each single human existence. The foundation of law and right is humanity.

Thus we confront the principles, dispositions, and ideals of the collective body with humanity. At the same time we shape them in accordance with reason, for only what is ethical is truly rational. Only so far as the current disposition of people is animated by ethical convictions and ideals is it capable of truly purposive activity.

The ethics of reverence for life puts in our hands weapons for fighting false ethics and false ideals, but we have strength to use them only so far as we—each one in his or her own life—preserve our humanity. Only when those people are numerous who in thought and in action bring humanity to terms with reality will humanity cease to be current as a mere sentimental idea and become what it ought to be, a leaven in the minds of individuals and in the spirit of society.

CHAPTER 6

Memoirs of Childhood and Youth

Albert Schweitzer

In 1924 Albert Schweitzer published Memoirs of Childhood and Youth, *from which this selection is taken* (Memoirs of Childhood and Youth, *trans. by Kurt Bergel and Alice R. Bergel [Syracuse: Syracuse Univ. Press, 1997], 3–41). This book of reminiscences of experiences early in life is based upon Schweitzer's sessions, in 1923, with the psychologist and pastor Oscar Pfister in Zurich. The reminiscences indicate that as a young person Schweitzer may well have already been sensitive to the pains and sufferings of other living beings, both humans and animals, although they may also reflect his adult values being projected back upon his prior experiences.*

I was born on January 14, 1875, in little Kaysersberg in Upper Alsace in the house with the turret, on the left side as you leave town. My father was the pastor and teacher of the small Protestant congregation of Kaysersberg, which was mainly Catholic. When Alsace became French, the small vicarage ceased to exist. The little house with the turret has now become the police station. I was the second child, following a sister who was my elder by a year.

The famous medieval preacher Geiler von Kaysersberg (1445–1510), who used to give sermons at Strasbourg Cathedral, took his name from this town. Born in Schaffhausen in Switzerland, he grew up in the house of his grandfather in Kaysersberg after the death of his father.

The vintage of 1875 was excellent. As a boy I took great pride in having been born in Geiler von Kaysersberg's hometown in a year famous for its wines.

Half a year after my birth, my father moved to Günsbach in the Münster Valley to be its pastor. My mother hailed from this region; she was the daughter of Pastor Schillinger in Mühlbach, farther back in the valley. When we came to Günsbach, I was a very weak child. On the day my father was inaugurated as pastor, my mother decked me out as best she could in a little white dress with colored ribbons. Despite her efforts none of the neighboring pastors' wives who had come for the celebration dared compliment her on the scrawny baby with the little yellow face. They took refuge in embarrassed commonplaces. At that point my mother—she often told me this—could no longer control herself; she fled with me to the bedroom and shed hot tears over me. At one time they even thought I was dead, but the milk of the neighbor Leopold's cow and the good Günsbach air worked wonders on me. From my second year on, I became healthy and grew up a strong boy. In the parsonage of Günsbach I spent a happy childhood with three sisters and a brother. A sixth child, a girl named Emma, was taken from my parents by an early death.

My earliest recollection is of seeing the Devil. When I was three or four years old, I was allowed to go along to church every Sunday. I looked forward to that all week. I still feel our maid's cotton glove on my lips when she put her hand over my mouth to stifle my yawn or when I sang along too loud. Every Sunday I saw in a shiny frame up on the side of the organ a shaggy face moving back and forth and looking down into the church. It became visible when the organ was played and the singing began, disappeared as my father prayed at the altar, returned with the organ playing and singing, disappeared once again when my father was preaching, and later reappeared once more with organ playing and singing. "This is the Devil looking into the church," I told myself. "When your father preaches the word of God, he has to make himself scarce." This theology, which I experienced every Sunday, shaped my childlike piety. Only much later, when I had been going to school for quite some time, did it become clear to me that the shaggy face which so strangely appeared and disappeared was that of Father Iltis, the organist. It appeared in a mirror which was mounted on the organ so the organist could see when my father stepped to the altar or went up to the pulpit.

Another event I remember from my earliest childhood is the moment when I felt consciously ashamed of myself for the first time. I was still wearing a little skirt and was sitting on a small stool in the yard while my father was busying himself about the beehives in the garden. Soon, a pretty little creature landed on my hand. I was delighted to watch it crawling back and forth. But suddenly I began to scream. The little creature was a bee, which was justifiably angry that the pastor was taking full honeycombs from the beehive. In revenge it stung the pastor's little son. Upon my screams the whole household came rushing out. Everyone commiserated with me. The maid took me in her arms and tried to console me with kisses. My mother reproached my father for working at the beehive without first putting me in a safe place. Since my misfortune made me so interesting, I kept crying with satisfaction until I suddenly became aware that I was shedding tears without feeling pain any longer. My conscience told me to stop now; but in order to remain the center of attention, I continued my lamentation and went on accepting consolations which I no longer needed. In doing so I felt so despicable that I was unhappy for days. How often has the memory of this experience restrained me when, as a grown-up, I felt tempted to make a fuss about something that happened to me.

The terror of my early childhood was the sacristan and gravedigger Jägle. On Sunday mornings after the first ringing of the bells, he came to the parsonage to pick up the numbers of the hymns that were to be sung and the baptismal vessels. He used to touch my forehead and say, "The horns are growing." I worried about the horns because I had rather pronounced bumps on my forehead. These caused me a great deal of anxiety since I had seen in the Bible a picture of Moses with horns. I don't know how the sacristan found out about my worries, but he did know them and he fueled them. When he wiped his feet in front of the door before ringing the doorbell on Sundays, I felt like running away. But he had me in his power as the snake does the rabbit. I could not help but face him, feel his hand on my forehead, and accept his damning pronouncement. After having carried the anguish about with me for a year or so, I brought Moses' horns up in a conversation with my father and learned from him that Moses had been the only human who ever had horns. Therefore, I had nothing to fear.

When the sacristan noticed that I was escaping him, he devised something new. He talked to me about soldiering. "Now we are Prussian," he would say, "and with Prussians everybody has to be a soldier. And the soldiers wear iron uniforms. In a few years you must be fitted with an iron uniform by the blacksmith up the street." From then on I sought every opportunity to stop in front of the blacksmith's shop and see whether some soldier was coming to be fitted for such a uniform. But only horses and donkeys showed up to be shod. On a later occasion, as my mother and I were looking at a picture of a cuirassier, I asked her about the iron uniforms of soldiers. To my relief I found out that ordinary soldiers wore uniforms made of cloth and that I would be a common soldier.

The sacristan, an old soldier who had fought in the Crimean War, was one of those dry jokers of whom there has never been a lack in Günsbach. He wanted to teach me how to take a joke. But he was somewhat too hard a taskmaster for me. As sacristan and gravedigger he was extremely dignified. He strode through the church with a majestic bearing, but otherwise he was known for being a bit odd. One morning in the haying season he was about to go off to the fields with a rake when a man stopped him to report the death of his father and to order a grave dug. The sacristan reacted with the words, "Why, anybody could come along and say his father had died." Once we passed by his house on a Sunday evening in midsummer. He came up to my father almost in tears and confided to him the story of his calf. He had raised a fine calf which followed him around like a dog. In the beginning of the summer, he had taken it out to graze in the hills and that Sunday he had gone to visit it. The calf did not recognize him. It acted as if he were a man like any other. This ingratitude hurt him deeply. The calf was not allowed back into its stable. He sold it right away.

I did not look forward to school. When, on a beautiful October day, my father first put the slate under my arm and took me to the teacher, I cried all the way. I had an inkling that this meant the end of my dreaming and my glorious freedom. Since then, I have never allowed my expectations to be dazzled by the beautiful aura which clothes the new. I have always stepped into the unknown without illusions.

The first visit of the school inspector made a deep impression on me. This was not just because the teacher's hands trembled with excitement as she offered him the class register, and Father Iltis—who ordinarily looked so stern—kept smiling and bowing. No, what moved me so deeply was that I saw for the first time, face to face, a man who had written a book. It was his name—he was called Steinert—which appeared on the covers of the yellow intermediate reader and the green upper-grade one. And now I saw before me in the flesh the author of these two books, which to me came right after the Bible. He did not look imposing. He was short, bald, had a red nose and a little potbelly, and was wedged in a gray suit. To me, though, he wore a halo, for he was a man who had written a book! It seemed incomprehensible to me that the schoolmaster and mistress were talking to him as with an ordinary mortal.

That first meeting with a writer of books was soon followed by a second even more significant experience. Mausche, a Jew from a neighboring village, who dealt in cattle and land, occasionally passed through Günsbach with his donkey cart. Since there were then no Jews living in our village, this was an event for the local boys each time. They ran after him and made fun of him. In order to advertise that I was beginning to feel grown-up, I felt compelled to join in one day, even though I did not really know what it was all about. So I followed him and his donkey with the other boys, shouting "Mausche, Mausche!" like them. The most courageous of us folded the corner of their apron or jacket to look like a pig's ear and jumped with it to him as close as possible. In this manner we pursued him beyond the village down to the bridge. Mausche, however, with his freckles and gray beard, continued on his way as unperturbed as his donkey. Only now and then did he turn around and look at us with an embarrassed, good-natured smile. This smile overwhelmed me. From Mausche I learned for the first time what it means to be silent in the face of persecution. He became a great educator for me. From that time on, I got accustomed to shaking hands with him and accompanying him a little way. But he never knew what he meant to me. There was a rumor that he was a usurer and unscrupulous real estate shark. I never investigated that. To me he remains Mausche with the forgiving smile, who even now forces me to be patient when I feel like fuming and raging.

I did not look for fights, but I loved to match bodily strength with others in friendly scuffles. One day on my way home from school, I wrestled with George Nitschelm—he now rests beneath the earth—who was taller and considered stronger than I, and I beat him. As he was lying there under me, he hissed, "Darn it, if I got soup with meat twice a week as you do, I would be as strong as you are!" Shaken by this outcome of the game, I staggered home. George Nitschelm had expressed with shocking clarity what I had already come to feel on other occasions. The village boys did not fully accept me as one of their own. To them I was one who was better off than they, the parson's son, the gentleman's boy. I suffered because of this, for I did not want to be different from them or to be better off. The meat soup became loathsome to me. Whenever it was steaming on the table, I heard George Nitschelm's voice.

From then on I anxiously tried not to distinguish myself from the others in any way. For the winter I had been given an overcoat made out of an old one of my father's. But no village boy wore an overcoat. When the tailor tried it on me and said, "My goodness, Albert, you'll soon be a monsieur!" I could hardly hold back my tears. On the day I was to wear it for the first time—it was on a Sunday morning for church—I refused. There ensued an ugly scene. My father slapped my face. To no avail. They had to take me along without an overcoat. After that each time I was supposed to wear the coat, the same thing happened. How many blows I received on account of that piece of clothing! But I stood my ground.

That same winter my mother took me with her to Strasbourg to visit an elderly relative. On that occasion she wanted to buy me a cap. In a fine store they had me try on a few. In the end, my mother and the saleswoman settled for a nice sailor's cap, which I was to wear immediately. But they had reckoned without their host. The cap was unacceptable to me because none of the village boys wore a sailor's cap. When they urged me to take it or another of the ones I had tried on, I made such a scene that everyone in the store rushed up to me. "Well, what kind of cap do you want, you silly boy?" the saleswoman snapped. "I don't want any of your new-fangled ones, I want one like the ones the village boys wear." So they sent a salesgirl to get me a brown cap that could be pulled down over the ears, from the unsalable stock. Beaming with joy, I put it on while my poor mother had to endure a few "nice" remarks and scornful glances on account of her oaf.

It pained me that she felt ashamed before the city folk because of me. Still, she did not scold me. She must have had an inkling that something serious lay behind my behavior.

This hard struggle continued as long as I attended the village school and embittered not only my life but also that of my father. I wanted to wear mittens exclusively because the village boys did not wear any other kind of glove. On weekdays I wanted to walk only in clogs because they wore leather shoes only on Sundays. Every visitor who came rekindled the conflict, for I was supposed to present myself in clothes "befitting our social position." While at home, I gave in to all demands; but whenever I was told to go for a walk with the visitor dressed as a "gentleman's boy," I became again the obstreperous fellow who infuriated his father—the courageous hero who endured being slapped and locked in the cellar. Nevertheless, I suffered badly from rebelling against my parents. My sister Louise, who was a year older than I, understood what I was going through and was touchingly sympathetic. The village boys did not know the cross I bore because of them. They coolly accepted all my efforts not to differ from them, but would, when the least quarrel occurred, wound me again with the terrible words "gentleman's boy."

At the beginning of my school years, I had to cope with one of the hardest lessons that life teaches us—a friend betrayed me. This is how it happened. When I first heard the word "cripple," I did not know what it meant. It seemed to me to express a particularly strong dislike. One newly arrived teacher, Miss Goguel, had not yet earned my favor, so I bestowed the mysterious word upon her. When I was guarding the cows with my best friend, I confided to him in a secretive manner, "The teacher is a cripple, but don't you tell anybody!" He promised.

On the way to school a short time afterward, we had a falling out. Then he whispered to me on the stairs, "O.K., I'm going to tell the teacher that you called her a cripple." I did not take the threat seriously, for I did not think such a betrayal possible. But during the break he really did go up to the teacher's desk and announced, "Miss, Albert said that you are a cripple." Nothing came of it, for the teacher did not understand what the statement was supposed to mean. I, however, could not grasp the horror of it. This first experience of betrayal smashed to pieces everything that I had thought and expected of life. It took me weeks to get over the shock. I had lost my innocence about life. I bore within me the painful wound which life inflicts on us all and which it reopens again and again with new blows. Some of the blows I have received since then were harder than that first one, but none has hurt more.

Even before I started school, my father had begun to instruct me in music on an old square piano. I did not play much sheet music. Rather, it was my delight to improvise and play songs and chorale melodies with accompaniments of my own invention. When the teacher in singing class repeatedly played the chorale one note at a time without accompaniment, I thought it lacked beauty, so I asked her during the break why she didn't play it correctly with accompaniment. In my zeal I sat down at the harmonium and played from memory both melody and accompaniment for her as best as I could. Thereupon she became very friendly toward me and looked at me in a strange way. Still, she continued to pick out the chorale with one finger. Then it dawned upon me that I could do something she was unable to do, and I was ashamed for having shown off my skill, which I considered something quite natural. Usually, though, I was a quiet pupil who did not learn to read or write without effort.

I remember one more thing from my first school year. Before I went to school, my father had already told me many Bible stories, among them the one about the Flood. Once when we had a very rainy summer, I assailed him, observing, "It has rained here about forty days and forty nights, yet the water has not even touched the houses, much less risen above the mountains.""Well, at that time," he answered, "in the beginning of the world, the rain didn't just come down in drops as it does now, it came down in bucketfuls." This explanation made sense to me.

Later, when the teacher at school told the story of the Flood, I waited for her to draw the distinction between rain at that time and that of ours, but she didn't. At last I could not longer control myself. "Teacher," I called out from my seat, "you must tell the story correctly." Not allowing her to silence me, I continued, "You must say that at that time rain did not come down in drops, but in bucketfuls."

When I was eight years old, my father gave me, at my request, a New Testament, which I read eagerly. One of the stories that occupied my mind most was that of the Wise Men from the East. What did Jesus' parents do with the gold and precious things that they received from these men? I wondered how they could later have been poor again. It was completely incomprehensible to me that the Wise Men from the East never bothered about the Christ child later on at all. I was also offended that there is no report about the shepherds of Bethlehem having become disciples of Jesus.

In my second year of school, we had lessons in penmanship twice a week with the teacher who gave singing lessons to the older children just before. Sometimes we came over from the elementary school too early and had to wait in front of the older children's classroom. When the two-part song "Down by the Mill I Was Sitting in Sweet Peace" or "Who Planted Thee, O Beautiful Forest?" began, I had to hold onto the wall to keep from falling down. The delight of the two-part music made my skin tingle and surged through my whole body. Also, when I heard brass music for the first time, I almost fainted. The violin did not sound beautiful to me, though, and I got used to it only little by little.

While at the village school, I witnessed the introduction of the bicycle. We had heard several times about the carters getting angry with people who dashed about on high wheels frightening the horses. Then one morning, as we were playing in the schoolyard during the break, we learned that a "speed runner" had stopped at the inn on the other side of the street. We forgot school and everything else and ran over to gape at the "high wheel" which had been left outside. Many grown-ups showed up as well and waited with us while the rider drank his pint of wine. At last he came out. Everybody laughed at the grown man wearing short pants. He mounted his bicycle and, lo, was gone.

In addition to the high wheels, the ones of medium height—the so-called kangaroos—were introduced in the mid-eighties. Soon thereafter the first low-wheeled bicycles appeared. The first bicyclists were taunted for not having the courage to get up on high wheels.

In my second to last year of high school, I myself acquired a bicycle, which I had fervently desired for a long time. It had taken me a year and a half to earn the money for it by tutoring students who lagged behind in mathematics. It was a second-hand bicycle which cost 230 marks. At that time, however, it was still considered unseemly for the son of a pastor to ride a bicycle. Fortunately, my father disregarded these prejudices. There was no shortage of those who found fault with the "arrogant" conduct of his son.

The well-known orientalist and theologian Eduard Reuss, in Strasbourg, did not want theology students to ride bicycles. When, as a student of theology, I moved into the St. Thomas Institute with my bicycle in 1893, the director, Erichson, remarked that he could permit this only because Professor Reuss was dead.

Today's youth cannot imagine what the coming of the bicycle meant to us. It opened up undreamed-of opportunities for getting out into nature. I used it abundantly and with delight.

I remember the first tomatoes just as I do the first bicycle. I may have been six years old when our neighbor Leopold brought us, as a great novelty, some of those red things which he had planted in his garden. The gift created some embarrassment for my mother, for she did not know how to prepare them. When the red sauce made its appearance on the table, it received such little appreciation that most of it went into the garbage. It was not until the end of the eighties that the tomato was generally accepted in Alsace.

My father's study was a very uncanny place to me. Only when I absolutely had to did I set foot in it. The smell of books that pervaded it took my breath away. It seemed terribly unnatural to me that my father was always sitting at the table, studying and writing. I could not understand how he could endure it and vowed to myself never to become a person like him who was forever studying and writing. I began to understand my father's literary efforts a little better when I was old enough to sense the charm of his village stories, which appeared in the Church Messenger and in calendars. His model was Jeremias Gotthelf, a Swiss pastor known for his writing. However, my father was more considerate; he avoided sketching the people who served as models for the characters in his stories so accurately that they could be identified.

Once a year, alas, I had to spend a day in my father's study. That was between Christmas and New Year's when Father declared after breakfast, "Today the letters are to be written! You accept the Christmas presents, but when the time for writing thank-you letters comes, you are too lazy. So, get to work! And I don't want to see any sullen faces!"

Oh, those hours sitting with my sisters in the study, breathing the bookish air, hearing the scratching of my father's pen, while in my mind's eye I was with my friends gliding down the road behind the church on their sleds . . . and I had to write letters to uncles, aunts, godparents, and other givers of

Christmas presents! And what kind of letters! In a lifetime of writing I have never again faced anything as difficult as that. As a matter of course, all the letters had three parts and the same content:

1. Thanks for the present given by the addressee, accompanied by the assurance that it had afforded me the greatest pleasure of all my presents.

2. Enumeration of all gifts received.

3. New Year's wishes.

Although they all had the same content, each letter was supposed to be different from all the others! And in each letter I was faced with the enormous difficulty of finding a good transition from the Christmas presents to the New Year's wishes. I won't even mention the challenge of finding the courteous concluding phrase suitable to the addressee for each letter.

Each one had to be drafted and presented to my father. Then it had to be corrected, reworked, and finally copied on a neat sheet of paper, without any mistakes or ink spots. Often it got to be time for lunch and I hadn't even roughed out one of the six or seven necessary letters.

For years I salted the meals between Christmas and New Year's with my tears! Once I even started crying right after receiving the presents on Christmas Day thinking of the letters that had now become unavoidable. My sister Louise managed to write each letter differently and to find ever-new transitions from the presents to the good wishes for the New Year. No one has ever again impressed me as much as she did with her literary dexterity.

The disgust with studies and letter writing which I acquired in my childhood because of these thank-you and New Year's letters remained with me for years. Although I have been forced by the conditions of my life to keep up an extraordinarily voluminous correspondence, I have still not learned to write letters which end nicely with New Year's wishes. Therefore, whenever I give Christmas presents as uncle or godfather, I always forbid the recipients to write me thank-you letters. They shall not salt their soup as I used to at that time of the year. To this day I do not feel comfortable in my father's study.

The week after Christmas was the only one in which our father was strict with us. At all other times he allowed us as much freedom as children can handle. We appreciated his kindness and were deeply grateful for it. During summer vacations he took us to the mountains two or three times a week for whole days. Thus we grew up like wild roses.

In my third year of school, I was promoted to the school for older children where Father Iltis taught us. He was a very competent teacher. Without putting in much effort, I learned a lot from him.

Throughout my life I have been glad that I started my education in the village school. It was good for me to compete with the village boys and to discover that they were at least as clever as I. I never shared the arrogance shown by so many boys who start in the *gymnasium* and think that the children of the educated are by nature more gifted than those who walk about in patched pants and wooden shoes. Even today, when I run into my former classmates in the village or the fields, I immediately remember where their abilities exceeded mine. This one was better in mental arithmetic, that one made fewer mistakes in dictation, a third always knew the historical dates, and still another was first in geography. One—I mean you, Fritz Schöppeler—had a better handwriting than the teacher himself. To this day I recall each one as superior to me in some subject.

At age nine I was sent to the secondary school in Münster. Mornings and evenings I had to walk three kilometers beside the hills. My delight was to walk alone, without the classmates who took the same route, and to indulge my thought. How deeply I experienced autumn, winter, spring, and summer in those years. When, during the vacation of 1885, it was decided that I should attend the gymnasium in Mulhouse in Upper Alsace, I cried secretly for hours. I felt that I would be cut off from nature.

I tried to put my enthusiasm for the beauty of nature as I experienced it on my walks to Münster into poems; but I never got beyond the first two or three rhymes. Several times I also tried to sketch the mountain with its old castle on the other side of the road. However, I also failed at that. From then on I resigned myself to enjoying beauty simply by looking at it without attempting to translate it into art. I never again tried to draw anything or render it in verse. Only in improvising music have I been creative.

At the secondary school in Münster it was Pastor Schäffer who taught religion. He was a distinguished religious personality and, in his way, an excellent speaker. The way he told the Bible stories took our breath away. I still remember how he cried at the teacher's desk and we sobbed on our benches as Joseph revealed himself to his brothers. He nicknamed me Isaak, which means "he who laughs," for I was easily provoked to laugh, a weakness which my classmates exploited mercilessly in school. Quite often the class register read: "Schweitzer laughs." Yet I was not cheerful, but rather shy and reserved.

I had inherited this reserved temperament from my mother. We lacked the gift of expressing in words the love we felt for each other. I can count on my fingers the times when we really had heart-to-heart talks, but we understood each other without words.

I also had inherited from my mother a deeply passionate nature, which she in turn had inherited from her father—who was very kind, but at the same time very irascible. I became aware of my passionate disposition when playing games. I took every game very seriously and got angry when others did not play with similar devotion. When I was nine or ten, I once struck my sister Adele because she played a game carelessly and let me win an easy victory. From that time on I became afraid of my passion and gradually gave up all games. I never dared touch a playing card. I also stopped smoking on January 1, 1899, because it had become an addiction.

I had to fight hard against my hot temper. I remember many events of my childhood which still humiliate me and keep me watchful in this struggle.

My grandfather Schillinger, who died before I was born, had been a zealous worker for enlightenment—a man quite filled with the spirit of the eighteenth century. After the service he used to inform his congregation, who waited for him outside, of the political news and also acquainted them with the latest discoveries of the human mind. When there was something special to see in the sky, he set up a telescope in front of his house in the evening and let everyone look through it.

Since the Catholic priest was also inspired by the spirit of the eighteenth century and its open-mindedness, the two clergymen lived in brotherly harmony in their neighboring vicarages. If one of them had more guests than he had space for, he would put them up in the other's parsonage. If one of them went on a trip, his colleague would occasionally visit the sick of the other denomination so they would not lack spiritual comfort. On Easter morning when the Catholic priest was hurrying from mass to his Easter meal, my grandfather would open his window and call out to him his congratulations on the end of Lent.

One night there was a great fire in the village. When the Protestant vicarage seemed threatened, it was evacuated and the contents stored in the

Catholic one. That was how my grandmother's hoop skirt came to be in the priest's bedroom and had to be taken back into the other parsonage the next morning.

My grandfather prepared his sermons meticulously. On Saturdays his house had to be very quiet. No visitor was admitted. When his son was a college student, he even had to plan to arrive for vacation on some day other than Saturday.

He seems to have been an autocrat, the good Pastor Schillinger. He kept people in awe. If a person wanted to talk to the pastor, he had to appear at the parsonage in a black coat and a tall hat. Numerous anecdotes about him still make the rounds back in the valley.

Two of these deal with the *Turt,* the classical meat pie of the Münster Valley. As pastor, he had to cut these at the wedding and baptismal meals over which he presided. Once he is said to have asked whether it mattered where he cut the pie. When he was told it did not matter, he said, "In that case I will cut it at home."

Another time he cut one piece too few by mistake. When the platter returned without a piece for him he said, "I don't like it that much anyway, you know," even though everybody knew how fond of it he was.

These and other stories about Pastor Schillinger are still told and still evoke the customary laughter at wedding and baptismal meals in our valley.

The parsonage in which he lived and the church in which he preached are no more. Bombs have shattered them. A big trench was cut through the middle of the church, but the old pastor's grave beside it remained intact as if by a miracle.

When I was still so small that I hardly understood what was said to me, my mother told me I was called Albert in memory of her late brother. This brother—really a half-brother from the first marriage of my grandfather—had been the pastor of the Church of St. Nicolai in Strasbourg.

In 1870, after the Battle of Weissenburg, he was sent to Paris to get medical supplies in preparation for the expected siege of Strasbourg. There, instead of receiving the medicines urgently requested by the Strasbourg physicians, he was given the runaround. When he finally started home with a small portion of what had been requested, the fortress was already completely surrounded. General von Werder, the commander of the German besieging army, allowed the medical supplies to get through to Strasbourg but made my uncle prisoner of war. Living through the siege among the besiegers, he worried that his congregation would think he had left them in the lurch in those difficult times of his own free will. Because he had a heart ailment, he never got over the stress of those months. In the summer of 1872 he collapsed and died, surrounded by his friends, in Strasbourg.

The idea of continuing the existence of a person who had been so dear to my mother gave me a lot to think about, especially since I was told so much about his kindness. When for a while milk was very scarce after the siege of Strasbourg, he took his milk to a poor old woman every morning. After his death, this woman told my mother how she had gotten her morning milk at that time.

As far back as I can remember, I have suffered because of the misery I saw in the world. I never really knew lighthearted, youthful enjoyment of life, and I believe this is true of many children, even though they seem quite cheerful and carefree.

What especially saddened me was that the poor animals had to suffer so much pain and misery. The sight of a limping old horse being dragged to the slaughterhouse in Colmar by one man while another beat it with a stick haunted me for weeks.

Already before I started school it seemed quite incomprehensible to me that my evening prayers were supposed to be limited to human beings. Therefore, when my mother had prayed with me and kissed me goodnight, I secretly added another prayer which I had made up myself for all living beings. It went like this: "Dear God, protect and bless all beings that breathe, keep all evil from them, and let them sleep in peace."

I had an experience during my seventh or eighth year which made a deep impression on me. Heinrich Bräsch and I had made ourselves rubber band slingshots with which we could shoot small pebbles. One spring Sunday during Lent he said to me, "Come on, let's go up the Rebberg and shoot birds." I hated this idea, but I did not contradict him for fear he might laugh at me. We approached a leafless tree in which birds, apparently unafraid of us, were singing sweetly in the morning air. Crouching like an Indian hunter, my friend put a pebble in his slingshot and took aim. Obeying his look of command, I did the same with terrible pangs of conscience and vowing to myself to miss. At that very moment the church bells began to ring out into the sunshine, mingling their chimes with the song of the birds. It was the warning bell, half an hour before the main bell ringing. For me, it was a voice from heaven. I put the slingshot aside, shooed the birds away so that they were safe from my friend, and ran home. Ever since then, when the bells of Passiontide ring out into the sunshine and the naked trees, I remember, deeply moved and grateful, how on that day they rang into my heart the commandment "Thou shalt not kill."

From that day on I have dared to free myself from the fear of men, and when my innermost conviction was at stake, I have considered the opinions of others less important than before. I began to overcome my fear of being laughed at by my classmates. The way in which the commandment not to kill and torture worked on me is the great experience of my childhood and youth. Next to it, all others pale.

Before I began attending school, we had a yellow dog named Phylax. Like many dogs, he could not stand uniforms and always attacked the mailman. Therefore, I was given the job of restraining Phylax when the mailman was due, for Phylax was apt to bite and had once assaulted a policeman. Wielding a switch, I used to drive Phylax into a corner of the yard and keep him there until the mailman had left. What a proud feeling it was to stand in front of the barking, snarling dog like a lion tamer and master him with blows when he wanted to break out of the corner! That proud feeling did not last, however. When we were later sitting together again as friends, I reproached myself for having beaten him. I knew I could keep him away from the mailman by holding his collar and stroking him. Nevertheless, when the critical hour approached, I yielded again to the intoxication of playing a tamer of wild beasts.

During vacations I was allowed to play the coachman for our next-door neighbor. His brown horse was already somewhat old and short-winded. He was not supposed to trot much. Nevertheless, in my driver's passion I again and again let myself be carried away. I forced him into trotting even when I knew and felt he was tired. The pride of controlling a trotting horse bewitched me. The neighbor allowed it "in order not to spoil my fun." What became of the fun, though, when I unharnessed the horse at home and saw how hard he was breathing, which I had not noticed from the seat on the wagon? What good was it to look into his tired eyes and ask him silently for forgiveness?

Once, when I was in high school and home for Christmas vacation, I drove a sleigh. The neighbor's dog, Löscher, who was known to be vicious, came out of the house and lunged, yelping, at the horse. I thought I was within my rights when I gave him a well-aimed blow with my whip, although it was clear that he was only attacking the sleigh playfully. Alas, I had aimed all too well. Hit in the eye, he howled and wallowed in the snow. His wailing haunted me. I could not free myself from it for weeks.

Twice I went fishing with other boys. Then, horrified by the maltreatment of the skewered worms and the tearing of the fishes' mouths, I did not go along with them any longer and even found the courage to prevent others from fishing.

From such experiences, which moved my heart and often put me to shame, there slowly arose in me the unshakable conviction that we may inflict death and suffering on another living being only when there is an inescapable necessity for it and that we must all feel the horror of thoughtlessly killing and causing pain. This conviction has driven me ever more powerfully. I have become more and more certain that in the depths of our hearts we all feel this. We do not dare admit it and act accordingly because we are afraid of being smiled at condescendingly by others who would consider us as "sentimental." We allow our feelings to be blunted. I, however, vowed to myself never to become emotionally blunted and never to fear the reproach of sentimentality.

CHAPTER 7

Out of My Life and Thought

Albert Schweitzer

In 1931 Albert Schweitzer wrote this epilogue for his major autobiographical volume, Out of My Life and Thought *(trans. Antje Bultmann Lemke [Baltimore: Johns Hopkins University, 2000], 223–45). A dominant theme of this epilogue is the ethical principle of reverence for life. In his discussion Schweitzer suggests, "The ethic of reverence for life is the ethic of love widened into universality. It is the ethic of Jesus, now recognized as a logical consequence of thought." The epilogue is reproduced here (modified slightly for style) with the permission of Rhena Schweitzer Miller and the translator of the epilogue, Antje Bultmann Lemke.*

Two observations have cast their shadows over my life. One is the realization that the world is inexplicably mysterious and full of suffering, the other that I have been born in a period of spiritual decline for humanity.

I myself found the basis and the direction for my life at the moment I discovered the principle of reverence for life, which contains life's ethical affirmation. I therefore want to work in this world to help people to think more deeply and more independently. I am in complete disagreement with the spirit of our age, because it is filled with contempt for thought. We have come to doubt whether thinking will ever be capable of answering questions about the universe and our relationship to it in a way that would give meaning and substance to our lives.

Today, in addition to that neglect of thought, there is also a mistrust of it. The organized political, social, and religious associations of our time are at work convincing the individual not to develop his or her convictions through his or her own thinking, but to assimilate the ideas they present. Anyone who thinks for himself is to them inconvenient and even ominous. He does not offer sufficient guarantees that he will merge into the organization.

Corporate bodies do not look for their strength in ideas and in the values of the people for whom they are responsible. They try to achieve the greatest possible power, offensive as well as defensive.

Hence the spirit of the age, instead of deploring the fact that thought seems to be unequal to its task, rejoices in it and gives it no credit for what, in spite of its imperfections, it has already accomplished. Against all evidence it refuses to admit that human progress up until today has come about through the efforts of thought. It will not recognize that thought may in the future accomplish what it has not yet achieved. The spirit of the age ignores such considerations. Its only concern is to discredit individual thought in every way possible.

A person today is exposed throughout his life to influences that try to rob him of all confidence in his own thinking. He lives in an atmosphere of intellectual dependence, which surrounds him and manifests itself in everything he hears or reads. It is in the people whom he meets every day; it is in the political parties and associations that have claimed him as their own; it pervades all the circumstances of his life.

From every side and in the most varied ways it is hammered into him that the truths and convictions that he needs for life must be taken away from the associations that have rights over him. The spirit of the age never lets him find himself. Over and over again, convictions are forced upon him just as he is exposed, in big cities, to glaring neon signs of companies that are rich enough to install them and enjoin him at every step to give preference to one or another shoe polish or soup mix.

By the spirit of the age, the person of today is forced into skepticism about his own thinking, so that he may become receptive to what he receives from authority. He cannot resist this influence because he is overworked, distracted, and incapable of concentrating. Moreover, the material dependence that is his lot has an effect on his mind, so he finally believes that he is not qualified to come to his own conclusions.

A person's self-confidence is also affected by the prodigious developments in knowledge. He cannot comprehend or assimilate the new discoveries. He is forced to accept them as givens, although he does not understand them. As a result of this attitude toward scientific truth he begins to doubt his own judgment in other spheres of thought.

Thus the circumstances of the age do their best to deliver us to the spirit of the age. The seed of skepticism has germinated. In fact, the modern person no longer has any confidence in himself. Behind a self-assured exterior he conceals an inner lack of confidence. In spite of his great technological achievements and material possessions, he is an altogether stunted being, because he makes no use of his capacity for thinking. It will always remain incomprehensible that our generation, which has shown itself so great by its discoveries and inventions, could fall so low in the realms of thought.

◆　　◆　　◆

In a period that ridicules as antiquated and without value whatever seems akin to rational or independent thought, and which even mocks the inalienable human rights proclaimed in the eighteenth century, I declare myself to be one who places all his confidence in rational thinking. I venture to tell our generation that it is not at the end of rationalism just because past rationalism first gave way to romanticism and later to a pretended realism that reigned in intellectual as well as material life. When we have passed through all the follies of the so-called universal realpolitik, and because of it suffered spiritual misery, there will be no other choice but to turn to a new rationalism more profound and more effective than that of the past. To renounce thinking is to declare mental bankruptcy.

When we give up the conviction that we can arrive at the truth through thinking, skepticism appears. Those who work toward greater skepticism in our age expect that by denouncing all hope of self-discovered truth, people will come to accept as true whatever is forced up on them by authority and by propaganda.

But their calculations are mistaken. Whoever opens the sluices to let a flood of skepticism pour over the land cannot assume that later he can stem the flood. Only a few of those who give up the search for truth will be so docile as to submit once and for all to official doctrine. The mass of people will remain skeptical. They lose all desire for truth, finding themselves quite comfortable in a life without thought, driven now here, now there, from one opinion to another.

But merely accepting authoritarian truth, even if that truth has some virtue, does not bring skepticism to an end. Blindly to accept a truth one has never reflected upon retards the advance of reason. Our world rots in deceit. Our very attempt to manipulate truth itself brings us to the brink of disaster.

Truth based on a skepticism that has become belief has not the spiritual qualities of truth that originated in thought. It is superficial and inflexible. It exerts an influence over man, but it cannot reach his inner being. Living truth is only that which has its origin in thought.

Just as a tree bears the same fruit year after year and at the same time fruit that is new each year, so must all permanently valuable ideas be continually created anew in thought. But our age pretends to make a sterile tree bear fruit by tying fruits of truth onto its branches.

Only when we gain confidence that we can find the truth through our own individual thought will we be able to arrive at living truth. Independent thought, provided it is profound, never degenerates into subjectivity. What is true in our tradition will be brought to light through deep thought, and it can become the force of reason in us. The will to sincerity must be as strong as the will to truth. Only an age that has the courage of conviction can possess truth that works as a force of spirit and of reason.

Sincerity is the foundation of the life of the mind and spirit. With its disdain for thinking, our generation has lost its feeling for sincerity. It can therefore be helped only by reviving the voice of thought.

◆　　◆　　◆

Because I have this certainty, I oppose the spirit of the age and accept with confidence the responsibility for contributing to the rekindling of the fire of thought.

The concept of reverence for life is by its very nature especially well qualified to take up the struggle against skepticism. It is elemental.

Elemental thinking starts from fundamental questions about the relationship of humankind to the universe, about the meaning of life, and about the nature of what is good. It is directly linked to the thought that motivates all people. It penetrates our thought, enlarges and deepens it, and makes it more profound.

We find such elemental thinking in Stoicism. When as a student I began to study the history of philosophy, I found it difficult to tear myself away from Stoicism and to make my way through the utterly different thinking that succeeded it. It is true that the results of Stoic thought did not satisfy me, but I had the feeling that this simple kind of philosophizing was the right one. I could not understand how people had come to abandon it.

Stoicism seemed to me great in that it goes straight for its goal, is universally intelligible and at the same time profound. It makes the best of what it recognizes as truth, even if it is not completely satisfying. It puts life into that truth by seriously devoting itself to it. It possesses the spirit of sincerity and urges people to gather their thoughts and to become more inward. It arouses in them a sense of responsibility. It also seemed to me that the fundamental tenet of Stoicism is correct, namely that a person must bring himself into a spiritual relation with the world and become one with it. In its essence, Stoicism is a natural philosophy that ends in mysticism.

Just as I felt Stoicism to be elemental, so I felt that the thought of Lao-tse was the same when I became acquainted with his *Tao Te Ching.* For him, too, it is important that someone come, by simple thought, into a spiritual relation with the world and prove his unity with it by his life.

There is, therefore, an essential relationship between Greek Stoicism and Chinese philosophy. The difference between them is that the first had its origin in well-developed, logical thinking, the second in intuitive thinking that was undeveloped yet marvelously profound.

This elemental thinking, however, which emerges in European as in Far Eastern philosophy, has not been able to maintain the position of leadership that it should occupy within systems of thought. It is unsuccessful because its conclusions do not satisfy our needs.

Stoic thought neglects the impulse that leads to ethical acts that manifest themselves in the will to live as it evolved with the intellectual and spiritual development of man. Hence Greek Stoicism goes no further than the ideal of resignation, Lao-tse no further than the benign passivity that to us Europeans seems so curious and paradoxical.

The history of philosophy documents that the thoughts of ethical affir-

mation of life, which are natural to people, cannot be content with the results of simple logical thinking about a person and his relationship to the
universe. They cannot integrate themselves. Logical thought is forced to
take detours via which it hopes to arrive at its goal. The detours logic has to
take lead primarily to an interpretation of the universe in which ethical action has meaning and purpose.

In the late Stoicism of Epictetus, of Marcus Aurelius, and of Seneca, in
the rationalism of the eighteenth century, and in that of Cong-tse (Confucius), Meng-tse (Mencius), Mi-tse (Micius), and other Chinese thinkers,
philosophy starts from the fundamental problem of the relationship of humankind to the universe and reaches an ethical affirmation of life and of the
world. This philosophy traces the course of world events back to a world
will with ethical aims and claims people for service to it.

In the thinking of Brahmanism and of the Buddha, in the Indian systems
generally, and in the philosophy of Schopenhauer, the opposite explanation
of the world is put forward, namely that the life that runs its course in space
and time is purposeless and must be brought to an end. The sensible attitude
of people to the world is therefore to renounce the world and life.

Side by side with the kind of thought that is concerned with elemental
issues, another kind has emerged, especially in European philosophy. I call it
"secondary" because it does not focus on the relationship between humankind and the universe. It is concerned with the problem of the nature of
knowledge, with logical speculation, with natural science, with psychology,
with sociology, and with other things, as if philosophy were really concerned with the answers to all these questions for their own sake, or as if it
consisted merely in sifting and systematizing the results of various sciences.
Instead of urging a person toward constant meditation about himself and his
relationship to the world, this philosophy presents him with the results of
epistemology, of logical deduction, of natural science, of psychology, or of
sociology, as if it could, with the help of these disciplines, arrive at a concept
of his relation with the universe.

On all these issues this "secondary" philosophy discourses with him as if
he were, not a being who is in the world and lives his life in it, but one who
is stationed near it and contemplates it from the outside.

Because it approaches the problem of the relationship of humankind to the universe from some arbitrarily chosen standpoint, or perhaps it bypasses it altogether, this nonelemental European philosophy lacks unity and cohesion. It appears more or less restless, artificial, eccentric, and fragmentary. At the same time, it is the richest and most universal. In its systems, half-systems, and nonsystems, which succeed and interpenetrate each other, it is able to contemplate the problem of philosophy of civilization from every side and every possible perspective. It is also the most practical in that it deals with the natural sciences, history, and ethical questions more profoundly than the others do.

The world philosophy of the future will not result in efforts to reconcile European and non-European thought but rather in the confrontation between elemental and nonelemental thinking.

Mysticism is not part of intellectual life today. By its nature, it is a kind of elemental thought that attempts to establish a spiritual relationship between humankind and the universe. Mysticism does not believe that logical reasoning can achieve this unity, and it therefore retreats into intuition, where imagination has free reign. In a certain sense, then, mysticism goes back to a mode of thinking that takes roundabout routes.

Since we only accept knowledge that is based on truth attained through logical reasoning, the convictions on which mysticism is founded cannot become our own. Moreover, they are not satisfying in themselves. Of all the mysticism of the past it must be said that its ethical content is slight. It puts people on the road of inwardness, but not on that of a viable ethic. The truth of philosophy is not proved until it has led us to experience the relationship between our being and that of the universe, an experience that makes us genuine human beings, guided by an active ethic.

Against the spiritual void of our age, neither nonelemental thought with its long-winded interpretations of the world nor the intuition of mysticism can do anything effective.

The great German philosophical systems of the early nineteenth century were greeted with enthusiasm, yet they prepared the ground on which skepticism developed.

In order to become thinking beings again, people must rediscover their ability to think, so they can attain the knowledge and wisdom they need to truly live. The thinking that starts from reverence for life is a renewal of elemental thinking. The stream that has been flowing for a long distance underground resurfaces again.

♦   ♦   ♦

The belief that elemental thought can lead us today to an affirmative ethic of life and the world, for which it has searched in the past in vain, is no illusion.

The world does not consist of phenomena only; it is also alive. I must establish a relationship with my life in this world, insofar as it is within my reach, one that is not only passive but active. In dedicating myself to the service of whatever lives, I find an activity that has meaning and purpose.

The idea of reverence for life offers itself as the realistic answer to the realistic question of how humankind and the universe are related to each other. Of the universe, a person knows only that everything that exists is, like himself, a manifestation of the will to live. With this universe, he stands in both a passive and an active relationship. On the one hand he is subject to the flow of world events; on the other hand he is able to preserve and build, or to injure and destroy, the life that surrounds him.

The only possible way of giving meaning to his existence is to raise his physical relationship to the world to a spiritual one. If he remains a passive being, through resignation he enters into a spiritual relationship with the world. True resignation is this: that someone, feeling his subordination to the course of world events, makes his way toward inward freedom from the fate that shapes his external existence. Inward freedom gives him the strength to triumph over the difficulties of everyday life and to become a deeper and more inward person, calm and peaceful. Resignation, therefore, is the spiritual and ethical affirmation of one's own existence. Only one who has gone through the trial of resignation is capable of accepting the world.

By playing an active role, a person enters into a spiritual relationship with this world that is quite different: he does not see his existence in isolation. On the contrary, he is united with the lives that surround him; he experiences the destinies of others as his own. He helps as much as he can and realizes that there is no greater happiness than to participate in the development and protection of life.

Once someone begins to think about the mystery of his life and the links connecting him with the life that fills the world, he cannot but accept, for his own life and all other life that surrounds him, the principle of reverence for life. He will act according to this principle of the ethical affirmation of life in everything he does. His life will become in every respect more difficult than if he lived for himself, but at the same time it will be richer, more beautiful, and happier. It will become, instead of mere living, a genuine experience of life.

Beginning to think about life and the world leads us directly and almost irresistibly to reverence for life. No other conclusions make any sense.

If someone who has begun to think wishes to persist in merely vegetating, he can do so only by submitting to a life devoid of thought. If he perseveres in his thinking he will arrive at reverence for life.

Any thought that claims to lead to skepticism or life without ethical ideals is not genuine thought but thoughtlessness disguised as thinking. This is manifested by the absence of any interest in the mystery of life and the world.

♦   ♦   ♦

Reverence for life in itself contains resignation, an affirmative attitude toward the world, and ethics. These are the three essential and inseparable elements of a worldview that is the result (or fruit) of thinking.

Because it has its origin in realistic thinking, the ethic of reverence for life is realistic, and leads a person to a realistic and clear confrontation with reality.

It may look, at first glance, as if reverence for life were something too general and too lifeless to provide the content for a living ethic. But thinking need not worry about whether its expressions sound lively, so long as they hit the mark and have life in them. Anyone who comes under the influence of the ethic of reverence for life will very soon be able to detect, thanks to what that ethic demands from him, the fire that glows in the seemingly abstract expression. The ethic of reverence for life is the ethic of love widened into universality. It is the ethic of Jesus, now recognized as a logical consequence of thought.

Some object that this ethic sets too high a value on natural life. To this one can respond that the mistake made by all previous ethical systems has been the failure to recognize that life as such is the mysterious value with which they have to deal. Reverence for life, therefore, is applied to natural life, and the life of the mind alike. In the parable of Jesus, the shepherd saves not merely the soul of the lost sheep but the whole animal. The stronger the reverence for natural life, the stronger also that for spiritual life.

The ethic of reverence for life is judged particularly strange because it establishes no dividing line between higher and lower, between more valuable and less valuable life. It has its reasons for this omission.

To undertake to establish universally valid distinctions of value between different kinds of life will end in judging them by the greater or lesser distance at which they stand from us human beings. Our own judgment is, however, a purely subjective criterion. Who among us knows what significance any other kind of life has in itself, as a part of the universe?

From this distinction comes the view that there can be life that is worthless, which can be willfully destroyed. Then in the category of worthless life we may classify various kinds of insects, or primitive peoples, according to circumstances.

To the person who is truly ethical all life is sacred, including that which from the human point of view seems lower. A person makes distinctions only as each case comes before him, and under the pressure of necessity, as, for example, when it falls to him to decide which of two lives he must sacrifice in order to preserve the other. But all through this series of decisions he is conscious of acting on subjective grounds and arbitrarily, and he knows that he bears the responsibility for the life that is sacrificed.

I rejoice over the new remedies for sleeping sickness, which enable me to preserve life, where once I could only witness the progress of a painful disease. But every time I put the germs that cause the disease under the microscope I cannot but reflect that I have to sacrifice this life in order to save another.

I bought from some villagers a young osprey they had caught on a sandbank, in order to rescue it from their cruel hands. But then I had to decide whether I should let it starve or kill a number of small fishes every day in order to keep it alive. I decided on the latter course, but every day the responsibility to sacrifice one life for another caused me pain.

Standing, as all living beings are, before this dilemma of the will to live, a person is constantly forced to preserve his own life and life in general only at the cost of other life. If he has been touched by the ethic of reverence for life, he injures and destroys life only under a necessity he cannot avoid, and never from thoughtlessness.

Devoted as I was from boyhood to the cause of protecting animal life, it is a special joy to me that the universal ethic of reverence for life shows such sympathy with animals—so often represented as sentimentality—to be an obligation no thinking person can escape. Past ethics faced the problem of the relationship between a human being and an animal either without sensitivity or as being incomprehensible. Even when there was sympathy with animal creation, it could not be brought within the scope of ethics because ethics focused solely on the behavior of human being to human being.

Will the time ever come when public opinion will no longer tolerate popular amusements that depend on the maltreatment of animals!

The ethic, then, that originates in thinking is not "rational," but irrational and enthusiastic. It does not draw a circle of well-defined tasks around me, but charges each individual with responsibility for all life within his reach and forces him to devote himself to helping that life.

◆   ◆   ◆

Any profound view of the universe is mystic in that it brings people into spiritual relationship with the Infinite. The concept of reverence for life is ethical mysticism. It allows union with the Infinite to be realized by ethical action. This ethical mysticism originates in logical thinking. If our will to live begins to meditate about itself and the universe, we will become sensitive to life around us and will then, insofar as it is possible, dedicate through our actions our own will to live to that of the infinite will to live. Rational thinking, if it goes deep, ends of necessity in the irrational realm of mysticism. It has, of course, to deal with life and the world, both of which are nonrational entities.

In the universe the infinite will to live reveals itself to us as will to create, and this is filled with dark and painful riddles for us. It manifests itself in us as the will to love, which resolves the riddles through our actions. The concept of reverence for life therefore has a religious character. The one who adopts and acts upon this belief is motivated by a piety that is elemental.

◆   ◆   ◆

With its active ethic of love, and through its spirituality, the concept of the world that is based on respect for life is in essence related to Christianity and to all religions that profess the ethic of love. Now we can establish a lively relationship between Christianity and thought that we never before had in our spiritual life.

In the eighteenth century Christianity in the time of rationalism entered into an alliance with thought. It was able to do so because at that time it encountered an enthusiastic ethic that was religious in character. Thought itself had not produced this ethic, however, but had unwittingly taken it over from Christianity. When, later on, it had to depend solely upon its own ethic, this proved to have little life and so little religion that it had not much in common with Christian ethics. As a consequence, the bonds between Christianity and active thought were loosened. Today Christianity has withdrawn into itself and is occupied with the propagation of its own ideas in agreement with thought, but prefers to regard them as something altogether outside of, and superior to, rational thought. Christianity thereby loses its connection with the elemental spirit of the times and the possibility of exercising any real influence over it.

The philosophy of reverence for life once again poses the question of whether Christianity will or will not join hands with a form of thought that is both ethical and religious in character.

To become aware of its real self, Christianity needs thought. For centuries it treasured the great commandments of love and mercy as traditional truths without opposing slavery, witch burning, torture, and all the other ancient and medieval forms of inhumanity committed in its name. Only when it experienced the influence of the thinking of the Enlightenment was Christianity stirred up to enter the struggle for humanitarian principles. This remembrance ought to keep it forever from assuming any air of arrogance vis-à-vis thought.

Many people find pleasure today in recalling how "superficial" Christianity became in the Enlightenment. It is, however, only fair to acknowledge to what degree this "superficial" character was balanced by the services Christianity rendered in this period.

Today torture has been reestablished. In many countries the system of justice quietly tolerates torture being applied before and simultaneously with the regular proceedings of police and prison officials in order to extract confessions from those accused. The amount of suffering thus caused every hour surpasses imagination. To this renewal of torture Christianity today offers no opposition even in words, much less in deeds.

Because Christianity hardly acts on its spiritual or ethical principles, it deceives itself with the delusion that its position as a church becomes stronger every year. It is accommodating itself to the spirit of the age by adopting a kind of modern worldliness. Like other organized bodies it tries to prove itself by becoming an ever stronger and more uniform organization, justified and recognized through its role in history and its institutions. But as it gains external power, it loses in spiritual power.

Christianity cannot take the place of thinking, but it must be founded on it. In and by itself it is not capable of overcoming thoughtlessness and skepticism. Only an age that draws its strength from thought and from an elemental piety can recognize the imperishable character of Christianity.

Just as a stream is kept from gradually drying up because it flows along above underground water, so Christianity needs the underground water of elemental piety that issues from thinking. It can only attain real spiritual power when people no longer find the road from thought to religion barred.

I know that I myself owe it to thought that I was able to retain my faith in religion.

The thinking person stands up more freely in the face of traditional religious truth than the nonthinking person and feels the intrinsic, profound, and imperishable elements much more strongly.

Anyone who has recognized that the idea of love is the spiritual ray of light that reaches us from the Infinite ceases to demand from religion that it offer him complete knowledge of the metaphysical. He ponders, indeed, the great questions: What is the meaning of evil in the world? How in God, the source of being, are the will to create and the will to love one? In what relation do the spiritual life and the material life stand to one another? And in what way is our existence transitory and yet eternal? But he is able to leave these questions unanswered, however painful that may be. In the knowledge of his spiritual union with God through love he possesses all that is necessary.

"Love never fails: but whether there be knowledge it shall be done away," says Paul.

The deeper is piety, the humbler are its claims with regard to knowledge of the metaphysical. It is like a path that winds between the hills instead of running over them.

The fear that a Christianity that sees the origin of piety in thought will sink into pantheism is without foundation. All living Christianity is pantheistic, since it regards everything that exists as having its origin in the source of all being. But at the same time all ethical piety is superior to any pantheistic mysticism, in that it does not find the God of love in nature, but knows about him only from the fact that he announces himself in us as the will to love. The First Cause of Being, as he manifests himself in nature, is to us always impersonal. To the First Cause of Being that is revealed to us in the will to love, however, we relate as to an ethical personality.

The belief that the Christianity that has been influenced by rational thought has lost its ability to appeal to someone's conscience, to his sinfulness, is unfounded. We cannot see that sin has diminished where it has been much talked about. There is not much about it in the Sermon on the Mount. But thanks to the longing for deliverance from sin and for purity of heart that Jesus has included in the Beatitudes, these form the great call to repentance that is unceasingly working on people.

If Christianity, for the sake of any tradition or for any considerations whatever, refuses to let itself be interpreted in terms of ethical religious thinking, it will be a misfortune for itself and for humankind. Christianity needs to be filled with the spirit of Jesus, and in the strength of that shall spiritualize itself into the living religion of inwardness and love that is its destiny. Only then can it become the leaven in the spiritual life of humankind.

What has been presented as Christianity during these nineteen centuries is merely a beginning, full of mistakes, not a full-grown Christianity springing from the spirit of Jesus.

Because I am deeply devoted to Christianity, I am trying to serve it with loyalty and sincerity. I do not attempt to defend it with the fragile and ambiguous arguments of Christian apologetics. I demand from Christianity that it reform itself in the spirit of sincerity and with thoughtfulness, so it may become conscious of its true nature.

◆　　◆　　◆

To the question of whether I am a pessimist or an optimist, I answer that my knowledge is pessimistic, but my willing and hoping are optimistic.

I am pessimistic because I feel the full weight of what we conceive to be the absence of purpose in the course of world events. Only at rare moments have I felt really glad to be alive. I cannot help but feel the suffering all around me, not only of humanity but of the whole creation.

I have never tried to withdraw myself from this community of suffering. It seemed to me a matter of course that we should all take our share of the burden of pain that lies upon the world. Even while I was a boy at school it was clear to me that no explanation of the evil in the world could ever satisfy me; all explanations, I felt, ended in sophistries, and at the bottom had no other object than to minimize our sensitivity to the misery around us. That a thinker like Leibniz could reach the miserable conclusion that though this world is, indeed, not good, it is the best that is possible, I have never been able to understand.

But however concerned I was with the suffering in the world, I never let myself become lost in brooding over it. I always held firmly to the thought that each one of us can do a little to bring some portion of it to an end. Thus I gradually came to the conclusion that all we can understand about the problem is that we must follow our own way as those who want to bring about deliverance.

I am also pessimistic about the current world situation. I cannot persuade myself that it is better than it appears to be. I feel that we are on a fatal road, that if we continue to follow it, it will bring us into a new "Dark Ages." I see before me, in all its dimensions, the spiritual and material misery to which mankind has surrendered because it has renounced thinking and the ideals that thought engenders.

And yet I remain optimistic. One belief from my childhood I have preserved with a certainty I can never lose: belief in truth. I am confident that the spirit generated by truth is stronger than the force of circumstances. In my view no other destiny awaits humanity than that which, through its mental and spiritual disposition, it prepares for itself. Therefore I do not believe that it will have to tread the road to ruin right to the end.

If people can be found who revolt against the spirit of thoughtlessness and are sincere and profound enough to spread the ideals of ethical progress, we will witness the emergence of a new spiritual force strong enough to evoke a new spirit in humanity.

Because I have confidence in the power of truth and of the spirit, I believe in the future of humanity. Ethical acceptance of the world contains within itself an optimistic willing and hoping that can never be lost. It is, therefore, never afraid to face the somber reality as it really is.

In my own life, I had times in which anxiety, trouble, and sorrow were so overwhelming that, had my nerves not been so strong, I might have broken down under the weight. Heavy is the burden of fatigue and responsibility that has lain upon me without break for years. I have not had much of my life for myself. But I have had blessings too: that I am allowed to work in the service of compassion; that my work has been successful; that I receive from other people affection and kindness in abundance; that I have loyal helpers who consider my work as their own; that I enjoy health that allows me to undertake the most exhausting work; that I have a well-balanced temperament, which varies little, and an energy that can be exerted with calm and deliberation; and that I can recognize whatever happiness I feel and accept it as a gift.

I am also deeply grateful that I can work in freedom at a time when an oppressive dependence is the fate of so many. Though my immediate work is practical, I also have opportunities to pursue my spiritual and intellectual interests.

That the circumstances of my life have provided such favorable conditions for my work, I accept as a blessing for which I hope to prove worthy.

How much of the work I have planned shall I be able to complete?

My hair is beginning to turn gray. My body is beginning to show signs of the exertions I have demanded of it and of the passage of the years.

I look back with gratitude to the time when, without having to husband my strength, I could pursue my physical and mental activities without interruption.

I look forward to the future with calmness and humility so that I may be prepared for renunciation if it be required of me. Whether we are active or suffering, we must find the courage of those who have struggled to achieve the peace that passes all understanding.

CHAPTER 8

The Ethics of Reverence for Life

Albert Schweitzer

In 1936 Albert Schweitzer published this article in the periodical Christendom *(1 [1936]: 225–39), as a general discussion of the ethics of reverence for life. The article rehearses many familiar aspects of Schweitzer's ethic. Particularly noteworthy in this article are Schweitzer's suggestions about how ethics is rooted in physical life and his anecdotes about ethical geese, monkeys, and sparrows. Also reprinted in Henry Clark,* The Ethical Mysticism of Albert Schweitzer *(Boston: Beacon Press, 1962), 180–94, the article is reproduced here (modified slightly for style) with the permission of the World Council of Churches.*

In the history of world thought we seem to be met by a confusion of antagonistic systems. But if we look closely, we see that certain essential laws of thought are to be discerned. And as we trace them, we see a certain definite progress in this bewildering history. In fact, there emerge two main classes of problems. To begin with, we see certain facade problems, important looking, but not really connected with the main structure. Questions as to the reality of the world and the problem of knowledge belong here. Kant tried in vain to solve the essential questions by busying himself with these scientific, facade problems. Admittedly they are intriguing, but they are not the real, elementary matters.

We are concerned with the other problems, the essential ones. As we know life in ourselves, we want to understand life in the universe, in order to enter into harmony with it. Physically we are always trying to do this. But that is not the primary matter; for the great issue is that we shall achieve a spiritual harmony. Just to recognize this fact is to have begun to see a part of life clearly.

There is in each of us the will-to-live, which is based on the mystery of what we call "taking an interest." We cannot live alone. Though someone is an egoist, he or she is never completely so. He *must* always have some interest in life about him. If for no other reason, he must do so in order to make his own life more perfect. Thus it happens that we want to devote ourselves; we want to take our part in perfecting our ideal of progress; we want to give meaning to the life in the world. This is the basis of our striving for harmony with the spiritual element.

The effort for harmony, however, never succeeds. Events cannot be harmonized with our activities. Working purposefully toward certain ends, we assume that the Creative Force in the world is doing likewise. Yet, when we try to define its goal, we cannot do so. It tends toward developing a type of existence, but there is no coordinated, definite end to be observed, even though we think there should be. We like to imagine that humankind is nature's goal; but facts do not support that belief.

Indeed, when we consider the immensity of the universe, we must confess that humankind is insignificant. The world began, as it were, yesterday. It may end tomorrow. Life has existed in the universe but a brief second. And certainly human life can hardly be considered the goal of the universe. Its margin of existence is always precarious. Study of the geologic periods shows that. So does the battle against disease. When one has seen whole populations annihilated by sleeping sickness, as I have, one ceases to imagine that human life is nature's goal. In fact, the Creative Force does not concern itself about preserving life. It simultaneously creates and destroys. Therefore, the will-to-live is not to be understood within the circle of Creative Force. Philosophy and religion have repeatedly sought the solution by this road; they have projected our will to perfection into nature at large, expecting to see its counterpart there. But in all honesty we must confess that to cling to such a belief is to delude ourselves.

As a result of the failure to find ethics reflected in the natural order, the disillusioned cry has been raised that ethics can therefore have no ultimate validity. In the world of human thought and action today, humanitarianism is definitely on the wane. Brutality and trust in force are in the ascendant. What, then, is to become of that vigorous ethics which we inherited from our parents?

Knowledge may have failed us, but we do not abandon the ideals. Though they are shaken, we do not turn from them to sheer skepticism. In spite of being unable to prove them by rational argumentation, we nevertheless believe that there is a proof and defense for them within themselves. We are, so to speak, immunized against skepticism. Indeed, the classical skepticisms were, after all, puerile. That a truth cannot be proved by argument is no reason why it should be utterly abandoned, so long as it is in itself possessed of value. Kant, trying to escape from skepticism, is a preindication of this immunity. In intent, his philosophy is great and eternal. He said that truth is one of two kinds: scientific and spiritual. Let us look to the bottom of this; not by Kant's method, however, since he was often content with naïve reflections on very deep questions. We shall avoid his way of seeking abstract solutions and distinctions between material and immaterial. Instead, let us see that truths which are not provable in knowledge are given to us in our will-to-live.

Kant sought to give equal value to practical and theoretical reason. More, he felt the demand for a more absolute ethic. It would, he thought, give new authority to spiritual and religious truth, thus making up for the loss involved in not being able to verify these truths by knowledge. This is the very heart of Kant's gospel, being much more important than anything he taught about space and time. But he did not know where to find the new ethic. He only gave a new, more handsome, and more impressive facade to the old. By his failure to point out the new ethic, he missed the new rationalism. His thought was on too narrow a basis.

1

The essential thing to realize about ethics is that it is the very manifestation of our will-to-live. All our thoughts are given in that will-to-live, and we but give them expression and form in words. To analyze reason fully would be to analyze the will-to-live. The philosophy that abandons the old rationalism must begin by meditating on itself. Thus, if we ask, "What is the immediate fact of my consciousness? What do I self-consciously know of myself, making abstractions of all else, from childhood to old age? To what do I always return?" we find the simple fact of consciousness is this, *I will to live.* Through every stage of life, this is the one thing I know about myself. I do not say, "I am life," for life continues to be a mystery too great to understand. I only know that I cling to it. I fear its cessation—death. I dread its diminution—pain. I seek its enlargement—joy.

Descartes started on this basis. But he built an artificial structure by presuming a person knows nothing and doubts all, whether outside himself or within. And in order to end doubt, he fell back on the fact of consciousness: *I think.* Surely, however, that is the stupidest primary assumption in all philosophy! Who can establish the fact that he thinks, except in relation to thinking *something?* And what that something is, is the important matter. When I seek the first fact of consciousness, it is not to know that I think, but to get hold of myself. Descartes would have a person think once, just long enough to establish certainty of being, and then give over any further need of meditation. Yet meditation is the very thing I must not cease. I *must* ascertain whether my thoughts are in harmony with my will-to-live.

Bergson's admirable philosophy also starts from such a beginning. But he arrives at the sense of time. The fact of immediate consciousness, however, is much more important than the sense of time. So Bergson misses the real issue.

Instinct, thought, the capacity for divination, all these are fused in the will-to-live. And when it reflects upon itself, what path does it follow? When my will-to-live begins to think, it sees life as a mystery in which I remain by thought. I cling to life because of my reverence for life. For, when it begins to think, the will-to-live realizes that it is free. It is free to leave life. It is free to choose whether or not to live. This fact is of particular significance for us in this modern age, when there are abundant possibilities for abandoning life, painlessly and without agony.

Moreover, we are all closer to the possibility of this choice than we may guess of one another. The question which haunts men and women today is whether life is worth living. Perhaps each of us has had the experience of talking with a friend one day, finding that person bright, happy, apparently in the full joy of life; and then the next day we find that he has taken his own life! Stoicism has brought us to this point, by driving out the fear of death; for, by inference it suggests that we are free to choose whether to live or not. But if we entertain such a possibility, we do so by ignoring the melody of the will–to–live, which compels us to face the mystery, the value, the high trust committed to us in life. We may not understand it, but we begin to appreciate its great value. Therefore, when we find those who relinquish life, while we may not condemn them, we do pity them for having ceased to be in possession of themselves. Ultimately, the issue is not whether we do or do not fear death. The real issue is that of reverence for life.

Here, then, is the first spiritual act in someone's experience: reverence for life. The consequence of it is that one comes to realize his dependence upon events quite beyond his control. Therefore he becomes resigned. And this is the second spiritual act: resignation.

What happens is that one realizes that he is but a speck of dust, a plaything of events outside his reach. Nevertheless, he may at the same time discover that he has a certain liberty, as long as he lives. Sometime or another all of us must have found that happy events have not been able to make us happy, nor unhappy events to make us unhappy. There is within each of us a modulation, an inner exaltation, which lifts us above the buffetings with which events assail us. Likewise, it lifts us above dependence upon the gifts of events for our joy. Hence, our dependence upon events is not absolute; it is qualified by our spiritual freedom. Therefore, when we speak of resignation it is not sadness to which we refer, but the triumph of our will–to–live over whatever happens to us. And to become ourselves, to be spiritually alive, we must have passed beyond this point of resignation.

The great defect of modern philosophy is that it neglects this essential fact. It does not ask someone to think deeply on himself. It hounds him into activity, bidding him find escape thus. In that respect it falls far below the philosophy of Greece, which taught people better the true depth of life.

I have said that resignation is the very basis of ethics. Starting from this position, the will–to–live comes first to veracity as the primary ground of virtue. If I am faithful to my will–to–live, I cannot disguise this fact, even though such disguise or evasion might seem to my advantage. Reverence for my will–to–live leads me to the necessity of being sincere with myself. And out of this fidelity to my own nature grows all my faithfulness. Thus, sincerity is the first ethical quality which appears. However lacking one may be in other respects, sincerity is the one thing which he must possess. Nor is this point of view to be found only among people of complex social life. Primitive cultures show the fact to be equally true there. Resignation to the will-to-live leads directly to this first virtue: sincerity.

2

Having reached this point, then, I am in a position to look at the world. I ask knowledge what it can tell me of life. Knowledge replies that what it can tell me is little, yet immense. Whence this universe came, or whither it is bound, or how it happens to be at all, knowledge cannot tell me. Only this: that the will-to-live is everywhere present, even as in me. I do not need science to tell me this; but it cannot tell me anything more essential. Profound and marvelous as chemistry is, for example, it is like all science in the fact that it can lead me only to the mystery of life, which is essentially in me, however near or far away it may be observed.

What shall be my attitude toward this other life? It can only be of a piece with my attitude toward my own life. If I am a thinking being, I must regard other life than my own with equal reverence. For I shall know that it longs for fullness and development as deeply as I do myself. Therefore, I see that evil is what annihilates, hampers, or hinders life. And this holds good whether I regard it physically or spiritually. Goodness, by the same token, is the saving or helping of life, the enabling of whatever life I can to attain its highest development.

This is the absolute and reasonable ethic. Whether such-and-such a person arrives at this principle, I may not know. But I know that it is given inherently in the will-to-live. Whatever is reasonable is good. This we have been told by all the great thinkers. But it reaches its best only in the light of this universal ethic, the ethic of reverence for life, to which we come as we meditate upon the will-to-live. And since it is important that we recognize to the best of our ability the full significance of this ethic, let us now devote our attention to some commentaries upon it.

Our first commentary: the primary characteristic of this ethic is that it is rational, having been developed as a result of thought upon life.

We may say that anyone who truly explores the depths of thought must arrive at this point. In other words, to be truly rational is to become ethical. (How pleased Socrates would be with us for saying this!) But if it is so simple a matter of rationality, why has it not long since been achieved? It has, indeed, been long on the way, while in every land thought has been seeking to deepen ethics. Actually, whenever love and devotion are glimpsed, reverence for life is not far off, since one grows from the other. But the truth of the matter is that thought fears such an ethic. What it wants is to impose regulations and order that can be duly systematized. This ethic is not subject to such bounding. Therefore, when modern thought considers such an ethic it fears it, and tries to discredit it by calling it irrational. In this way its development has been long delayed.

Again, it may be asked if this sort of meditation is not definitely that of civilized rather than primitive people. The primitive person, it may be argued, knows no such reverence for life. To this I must agree, having associated with primitive people in my work in Africa. Nevertheless, it remains true that the primitive person who begins to meditate must proceed along this same path. He must start with his own will-to-live, and that is certain to bring him in this direction. If he does not reach a point as far along the way as we do, that is because we can profit by the meditations of our predecessors. There are many great souls who have blazed sections of the trail for us. Proceeding along that way, I have led you to this conclusion: that rational processes, properly pursued, must lead to the true ethic.

Another commentary: What of this ethic? Is it absolute?

Kant defines absolute ethics as that which is not concerned with whether it can be achieved. The distinction is not one of *absolute* as opposed to *relative,* but *absolute* as distinct from *practicable* in the ethical field. An absolute ethic calls for the creating of perfection in this life. It cannot be completely achieved; but that fact does not really matter. In this sense, reverence for life is an absolute ethic. It does not lay down specific rules for each possible situation. It simply tells us that we are responsible for the lives about us. It does not set either minimum or maximum limits to what we must do.

In point of fact, every ethic has something of the absolute about it, just as soon as it ceases to be mere social law. It demands of one what is actually beyond his strength. Take the question of one's duty to his neighbor. The ethic cannot be fully carried out, without involving the possibility of complete sacrifice of self. Yet, philosophy has never bothered to take due notice of the distinction. It has simply tried to ignore absolute ethics, because such ethics cannot be fitted into tabulated rules and regulations. Indeed, the history of world teachings on the subject may be summarized in the motto "Avoid absolute ethics, and thus keep within the realm of the possible."

We have already noted that Kant did postulate and demand an absolute ethics as the foundation for a spiritual ethics. He knew it must be more profound than what is just and reasonable. But he did not succeed in establishing what it was. All he did was label ordinary ethics "absolute." Consequently, he ended in a muddle of abstraction. As Descartes said, "Think," without telling what to think, so Kant demanded, "Observe absolute ethics," without elucidating what the term involved. The ethics he proposed could not be called absolute in matter of content. His "practical ethics" proved to be simply the good old utilitarian ethics of his own day, adorned with the label "absolute." He failed by not thinking far enough. To justify the name, absolute ethics must be so not only in authority, but in matter of content as well.

Another commentary: reverence for life is a universal ethic.

We do not say this because of its absolute nature, but because of the boundlessness of its domain. Ordinary ethics seeks to find limits within the sphere of human life and relationships. But the absolute ethics of the will-to-live must reverence every form of life, seeking so far as possible to refrain from destroying any life, regardless of its particular type. It says of no instance of life, "This has no value." It cannot make any such exceptions, for it is built upon reverence for life as such. It knows that the mystery of life is always too profound for us, and that its value is beyond our capacity to estimate. We happen to believe that human life is more important than any other form of which we know. But we cannot prove any such comparison of value from what we know of the world's development. True, in practice we are forced to choose. At times we have to decide arbitrarily which forms of life, and even which particular individuals, we shall save, and which we shall destroy. But the principle of reverence for life is nonetheless universal.

Ordinary ethics has never known what to do with this problem. Not realizing that the domain of ethics must be boundless, it has tried to ignore any absolute ethic. But when its boundlessness is realized, then its absoluteness is more plain. Indian thought recognizes this, but it limits its effectiveness by making ethics negative. The characteristic attitude of Indian thought is less a positive reverence for life than a negative duty to refrain from destroying. This comes about through a failure to appreciate the essentially illusory nature of an ethic of inaction. Nor has European thought been free from that same illusion. The great works on philosophy and ethics in recent years have all tried to avoid absolute ethics by concentrating on a type which should apply only socially. But when reason travels its proper course, it moves in the direction of a universally applicable ethic.

Another commentary: a universal ethic has great spiritual significance.

Ordinary ethics is too narrow and shallow for spiritual development. Our thought seeks ever to attain harmony with the mysterious Spirit of the Universe. To be complete, such harmony must be both active and passive. That is to say, we seek harmony both in deed and in thought. I want to understand my ethical activity as being at the service of the Universal Spirit.

Spinoza, Hegel, and the Stoics show us that the harmony of peace is a passive harmony, to which true philosophy leads us, and toward which religion tries to lead us. But this does not suffice, since we want to be at one in activity as well. Philosophy fails us here because of too narrow an ethical basis. It may seek to put me in relation to society, and even to humanity at large (although contemporary philosophies are in some instances directed only toward the relationship to a nation or a race). In any case, no philosophy puts me in relationship to the universe on an ethical basis. Instead, the attempt is made to take me there by knowledge, through understanding. Fichte and Hegel present such an intellectual philosophy. But it is an impossible path. Such philosophies are bankrupt. Ethics alone can put me in true relationship with the universe by my serving it, cooperating with it, not by trying to understand it. This is why Kant is so profound when he speaks of practical reason. Only by serving every kind of life do I enter the service of that Creative Will whence all life emanates. I do not understand it; but I do know (and it is sufficient to live by) that by serving life, I serve the Creative Will. It is through community of life, not community of thought, that I abide in harmony with that Will. This is the mystical significance of ethics.

Every philosophy has its mystical aspects, and every profound thought is mystical. But mysticism has always stopped with the passive, on an insufficient basis, in regard to ethics. Indian, Stoic, medieval—all the great mysticisms—have aimed at achieving union through passivity. Yet every true mysticism has instincts of activity, aspiring to an ethical character. This fact explains the development of Indian mysticism from the detachment of Brahminism to modern Hindu mysticism. Medieval mysticism, in the same way, comes in its great exponent, Eckehart, to the point where it longs to comprehend true ethics. Failing to find the universal ethic, it has commonly been content to exist with none. But in the universal ethic of reverence for life, mystical union with the Universal Spirit is actually and fully achieved. Thus it is proved to be indeed the true ethic. For it must be plain that an ethic which only commands is incomplete, while one which lets me live in communion with the Creative Will is a true and complete ethic.

3

In what sense is this a natural ethic, and how does it stand in relation to other explanations of the origin of ethics?

There have been three general classifications of ethical origins. The first is a spiritual interpretation. We find in Plato, Kant, and many others the assertion that ethics comes out of an inherent, insubstantial, given sense of duty, which has its source in our own power of reason. Through it, we are told, we see ourselves bound to the immaterial world. The exponents of this view believed that they had thus given great dignity to ethics. But there are difficulties in the way of accepting this view. It bears little resemblance to our own ethical sense; and we cannot see how it can be carried into our lives in this world in which we live.

The second classification comprises the intellectual theories of ethics. Here we find such philosophies as those of the Stoics and Lao-tse. This group claims to see ethics in the natural world, and concludes thereby that whoever is in harmony with the universe is by that fact ethical. Now, this is a grand theory, and it is based on a profound realization that one who is truly in such harmony must be ethical. But the fact remains that we do not in deed understand the Spirit of the Universe. Therefore, we cannot draw any ethics from such understanding. Consequently, these theories of ethics are pallid and lacking in vigor. What they really amount to is a negative quietism, which has been tinged with ethics.

The third classification consists of three kinds of natural ethics. There is, to start with, the suggestion that ethics exists within our very natures, waiting to be developed. It is argued that we are primarily composed of egoism, but that we nevertheless have an inherent selflessness. Altruism, as we know it, is thus simply exalted egoism. A person is assumed to get his greatest fulfillment in society; wherefore, he must serve it, sacrificing his own wishes temporarily. But such an explanation is childish.

Next comes the sort of natural ethics which is said to exist in human nature, but is incapable of being developed by the individual himself. Society, so the theory runs, has worked out a system of ethics in order to subject the individual to its will. Centuries of such exalting of society have had beneficial results, but it is mere delusion to imagine that that is native to us which has actually been created by society. But observe how childish this is also. I grant that society has its place in ethics, but the fact remains that I have individual as well as social relationships, and society simply cannot be responsible for the ethic which determines my dealings in the individual sphere.

The third type of natural ethics was expounded by Hume. It admits that ethics is a matter of sentiment, but explains that it is given in the nature of a human being, for the sake of preserving his life. Thus, in the late eighteenth century came Hume's teaching that ethics is natural, while in the same period came Kant's realization that it must be absolute.

To explain that ethics is a matter of feeling, prompted by our own hearts, Hume called it sympathy. The capacity to understand and live others' lives in our own is, he said, what makes us developed individuals. In this, he was joined by George Adam Smith. They were headed in the right direction, too. If they had properly explored sympathy, they would have reached the universal ethic of reverence for life. But they stopped on the very threshold of their great opportunity, because they were dominated by the contemporary dogma that ethics is concerned only with the relationship of human being to human being. Therefore, they twisted sympathy to mean only a relationship between like kinds. Spencer and Darwin did the same thing in their time, putting ethics on the basis of the herd. This brought them to the explanation of nonegoistic action as arising from herd instinct. What Darwin failed to see is that the herd relationship is more than this superficial sort of instinct. He did, it is true, catch a glimpse of the possibility of sympathy extending beyond the range of humankind and society. But he concluded that it was just a high development of the herd instinct!

It is only when we break loose from such traditions that we find sympathy to be natural for any type of life, without any restrictions, so long as we are capable of imagining in such life the characteristic which we find in our own. That is dread of extinction, fear of pain, and desire for happiness. In short, the adequate explanation of sympathy is to be found rooted back in reverence for life.

But let us inquire into this sympathy more closely. On what foundations does it exist? What is its natural explanation? To answer these questions, let us ask ourselves how we can live the life of another being in our own lives. In part, we depend upon the knowledge received through our senses. We see others; we hear them; we may touch them or be touched by them. And we may then engage in activities to help them. In other words, there is a natural, physical aspect to the matter which anyone must recognize. But what *compels* all this?

The important thing is that we are part of life. We are born of other lives; we possess the capacities to bring still other lives into existence. In the same way, if we look into a microscope we see cell producing cell. So nature compels us to recognize the fact of mutual dependence, each life necessarily helping the other lives which are linked to it. In the very fibers of our being, we bear within ourselves the fact of the solidarity of life. Our recognition of it expands with thought. Seeing its presence in ourselves, we realize how closely we are linked with others of our kind. We might like to stop here, but we cannot. Life demands that we see through to the solidarity of all life which we can in any degree recognize as having some similarity to the life that is in us.

No doubt you are beginning to ask whether we can seriously mean that such a privilege extends to other creatures besides human beings. Are they, too, compelled by ethics? I cannot say that the evidence is always apparent as it may be in human instances. But this I can say, that wherever we find the love and sacrificial care of parents for offspring (for instance) we find this ethical power. Indeed, any instance of creatures giving aid to one another reveals it. Moreover, there are probably more proofs than we might at first think. Let me tell you of three instances which have been brought to my attention.

The first example was told to me by someone from Scotland. It happened in a park where a flock of wild geese had settled to rest on a pond. One of the flock had been captured by a gardener, who had clipped its wings before releasing it. When the geese started to resume their flight, this one tried, frantically but vainly, to lift itself into the air. The others, observing his struggles, flew about in obvious efforts to encourage him; but it was no use. Thereupon, the entire flock settled back on the pond and waited, even though the urge to go on was strong within them. For several days they waited until the damaged feathers had grown sufficiently to permit the goose to fly. Meanwhile, the unethical gardener, having been converted by the ethical geese, gladly watched them as they finally rose together and all resumed their long flight.

My second example is from my hospital in Lambaréné. I have the virtue of caring for all stray monkeys that come to our gate. (If you have had any experience with large numbers of monkeys, you know why I say it is a virtue thus to take care of all comers until they are old enough or strong enough to be turned loose, several together, in the forest—a great occasion for them— and for me!) Sometimes there will come to our monkey colony a wee baby monkey whose mother has been killed, leaving this orphaned infant. I must find one of the older monkeys to adopt and care for the baby. I never have any difficulty about it, except to decide which candidate shall be given the responsibility. Many a time it happens that the seemingly worst-tempered monkeys are most insistent upon having this sudden burden of foster-parenthood given to them.

My third example was given to me by a friend in Hanover, who owned a small café. He would daily throw out crumbs for the sparrows in the neighborhood. He noticed that one sparrow was injured, so that it had difficulty getting about. But he was interested to discover that the other sparrows, apparently by mutual agreement, would leave the crumbs which lay nearest to their crippled comrade, so that he could get his share, undisturbed.

So much, then, for this question of the natural origin of the ethic of reverence for life. It does not need to make any pretensions to high titles or noble-sounding theories to explain its existence. Quite simply, it has the courage to admit that it comes about through physiological makeup. It is given physically. But the point is that it arrives at the noblest spirituality. God does not rest content with commanding ethics. He gives it to us in our very hearts.

This, then, is the nature and origin of ethics. We have dared to say that it is born of physical life, out of the linking of life with life. It is therefore the result of our recognizing the solidarity of life which nature gives us. And as it grows more profound, it teaches us sympathy with *all* life. Yet, the extremes touch, for this material-born ethic becomes engraved upon our hearts, and culminates in spiritual union and harmony with the Creative Will which is in and through all.

PART THREE

Assessing Reverence for Life

CHAPTER 9

Albert Schweitzer's Reverence for Life

Kurt Bergel

Kurt Bergel, codirector of the Chapman University Albert Schweitzer Institute until his death, published this article (here modified slightly for style) in The Humanist *(6 [1946]: 31–34) in the spring of 1946, just after the conclusion of World War II. The reference to "the recent war" thus calls to mind the death and destruction of that devastating war, but the article speaks equally to war, peace, and ethical issues in our time.*

Those who caused the recent war by their contempt for human dignity and human life, as well as those who have killed in order that these basic human values might be preserved, must now readjust themselves to a world at peace. The very things they have been taught to do in wartime will now again be considered crimes. In war life is no longer a value in itself. The soldier has been conditioned to desire the death of his enemy as much as the preservation of the life of his compatriot and ally. When the categories of friend and foe alone determine the value of life, a cynicism toward it will often become the permanent attitude of many people after the war. This will be especially true with persons who are mentally not well balanced or who are not rooted in a philosophy or religion which places a definite value on life. Needed, therefore, is not only a psychological readjustment, but a more general reevaluation and reaffirmation—and for many it will be a first realization—of basic human attitudes and philosophies.

It seems that on the threshold of peace Albert Schweitzer, the great missionary-physician, theologian, philosopher, and musician, can very well be-

141

come a guide to those who are able and willing to reexamine ethical fundamentals. Ever since the boy Schweitzer at the age of eight realized that *Thou shalt not kill* applied also to the birds he was just about to kill, Schweitzer has meditated on ethical principles and has tried to live a life in accordance with the precepts at which he had arrived. Ever since that experience, the question of life and death, which is so much in the forefront of our own minds, has been to him like the test problem of ethical philosophizing.

Schweitzer's presentation of his own ethics in his book *Civilization and Ethics* (1923) follows a comprehensive survey and criticism of ethical thinking from Socrates to Bergson. He shows how and why no thinker of the past has offered a workable system of ethics. He finds the classical systems either too formal or too narrowly utilitarian. His criticism of Kant and others for limiting their systems of ethics to the relations between man and man instead of working out those between man and life as such indicates the central position which *life* has in his thinking.

Schweitzer's ethics starts with a great *non possumus.* We cannot base ethics and a philosophy of life on knowledge of the essence and meaning of the world. We do not have this knowledge. "In the world we can discover nothing of any purposive evolution in which our activities can acquire a meaning." However, we do not depend on knowledge of the world in erecting a structure of ethics. Schweitzer finds the cornerstone of this structure in the universal will-to-live which manifests itself in the world. A person is conscious of himself as "will-to-live in the midst of will-to-live." *Reverence for life* is the greatest demand of ethics. "Ethics is in its unqualified form extended responsibility with regard to everything that has life."

Schweitzer's ethics is essentially religious. His language is theistic, but his emphasis is humanistic, concerned with the fulfillment of life here and now. In experiencing the universal will-to-live he recognizes God's creative will in the world. "Reverence for life means to be in the grasp of the infinite, inexplicable, forward-urging Will in which all Being is grounded." In merging our own with the universal will-to-live and in trying to reconcile the universal will with itself we think and act in the spirit of ethical mysticism. Schweitzer certainly does not mean that the "will" is transcendent; it is immanent. The "will" is, of course, impersonal, and the term is used in a way similar to Schopenhauer's use of the term; in Schweitzer it is almost synonymous with "drive."

It is one of Schweitzer's great achievements that he includes the treatment of plants and animals in his system of ethics. We have merely to compare this with the role animals play in Descartes's and Kant's philosophies to appreciate the widening of ethical responsibility which our modern minds cannot help considering a progress. The individual, making decisions in his relations to plants and animals, is well guided by a remark of Schweitzer's which connects ethical responsibility and realism most admirably:

> The farmer who has mown down a thousand flowers in his meadow to feed his cows must be careful on his way home not to strike off in thoughtless pastime the head of a single flower by the roadside, for he thereby commits a wrong against life without being under the pressure of necessity.

What this "pressure of necessity" demands of us in our concrete relations with other people is a harder problem. Our scale of values generally places animal life above plant life, and human life above both. But what about the conflict between human lives? The ethics of reverence for life requires someone to respect and further life in others as well as in himself. The principle of equality is thereby founded in ethics. Yet only with a scale of values can the individual settle conflicting claims: the physician when deciding whether he should save the child's or the mother's life, a person when deciding whether he should save his attacker's life or his own. And what about conflicts between life and truth? Schweitzer does not give a theory or scale of values. His is an ethics for mature individuals who can shoulder the responsibility of making decisions.

This strong sense of *individual* ethical responsibility which we find in Schweitzer is needed today. There is a good deal of pseudo-individualism which finds its expression in phrases like "I don't care . . ." and which does not conceal the growing collectivization of behavior patterns into which modern mass production and consumption has forced humankind. By confronting the individual with ethical problems without solving them for him, a system of ethics like Schweitzer's is bound to perform an important task in the process of individuation. The future of civilization, I believe, depends upon the success of this process.

While working by day in his hospital on the edge of the jungle, Schweitzer has been writing by night the third and fourth volumes of his ethics, which will presumably apply the ethics of reverence for life to the civilized state. When life in all its forms is respected, all nations must have an equal right to live their lives. Schweitzer, born in Alsace, was reared in the atmosphere of a binational culture; his background and convictions have never allowed him to become submerged in narrow nationalism. Aggressive nationalism is possible only on a level on which one possessed of a national will-to-live has not yet become ethically aware of others like him. The timeliness of these ideas today does not have to be demonstrated.

The ethics of reverence for life corresponds to and dissociates itself from natural life in a significant manner. By making it an ethical precept to further the natural will-to-live, the ethical thinker affirms the positive value of creation in spite of all evil, just as in Jesus' love of humanity an element of optimism militates against early Christian eschatological pessimism. But in the fight of all against all which pervades all nature, we find the universal will-to-live in conflict with itself. At this point, humankind, in Schweitzer's ethics, dissociates itself from nature. "In me the will-to-live has come to know about other wills-to-live. There is in it a longing to arrive at unity with itself, to become universal."

Schweitzer holds a double position of cooperating with the creative will without accepting the destructive will. In this respect his teaching is clearly distinguished from that of other philosophers who developed a philosophy of life and who, by upholding the right of "superior" life, arrived at a philosophy that sacrifices biologically inferior life to the "fittest," to a superman's will to power or to a master race.

Life in Schweitzer's thought is conceived primarily as a biological category. In the biological sphere life conflicts with life. Yet human beings transcend this sphere, and in them life becomes conscious of other life and thus of conflicting wills-to-live. By recognizing each other as parts of the same universal will-to-live, they become reconciled in the ethical precept of reverence for life.

The Christian attitude, according to Schweitzer, is "to live and act within the world as one who is different from the world." Christianity, as interpreted and actually lived by Schweitzer, is devoid of the otherworldliness and defeatism of much that now passes for Christianity. Also, it lacks the authoritarian spirit of some Christian creeds, placing the center and responsibility for ethical thinking and living in the here and now in the inner autonomous individual rather than on the compulsions of external authority. It seems to me that a reaffirmation of this position, a true balance of spirit and nature (or ethical responsibility and realism, as we called it above), is exactly what is needed today. Racism and power politics have betrayed the spirit, whereas utopians, naïve democrats, and all sorts of people of good will have comfortably ignored the nature of man and nature in man. Only if we achieve a unity of idealism and realism can we hope to rebuild Western civilization. Schweitzer's philosophy as well as his life of service as a physician among the people of French Equatorial Africa can serve as a guide in achieving this unity.

CHAPTER 10

The Assessment of the Life
and Thought of Albert Schweitzer
in Germany and Africa

Sylvère Mbondobari

Sylvère Mbondobari is a scholar from Gabon who is doing research in Germany on Albert Schweitzer. Here he examines and evaluates assessments of Schweitzer and his work, especially the reception of Schweitzer in Gabon, where Schweitzer lived and worked for half a century. Mbondobari's study focuses upon novels that present aspects of the life and thought of Schweitzer and the points of view of the various novelists.

Many people—philosophers, critics, scholars—around the world know Albert Schweitzer, his work, and his ideals. For each of them, however, he means something different. Some people admire the philosopher and the author of the two volumes *The Decay and the Restoration of Civilization* and *Civilization and Ethics*. Others appreciate the great interpreter of the organ music of Bach or the brilliant theologian and scholar writing on the life of Jesus. But most of the people just know the Nobel Prize winner as the man who, in 1913, left Europe and went to Africa with his wife to set up a medical mission at Lambaréné.

The impact of Schweitzer's work in Gabon can be examined on two different levels. First, most of the Gabonese people belong to this last group mentioned above. In fact, most of them just know the "grand docteur" who founded a medical mission at Lambaréné and see in him "a vision and a promise; a white man who was interested in them as human beings; who as-suaged their bitter pain, who healed their wounds." [1] In spite of the fact that nowadays Gabon has the means to pay for its own health care (Gabon has the highest average income per person in black Africa), Schweitzer's hospital still plays an important part in the Gabonese health system. As in the past, peo-ple come in greater numbers to this hospital than to the government hospi-tals or other private clinics. This is not only because of better facilities and competent medical personnel but also because of the Schweitzer hospital's reputation.

The second level to consider Schweitzer's work is the literary impact. Schweitzer contributed to the discussion about Africa with his report from Africa, *On the Edge of the Primeval Forest* (*Zwischen Wasser und Urwald,* 1921), and his autobiographical book *Out of My Life and Thought* (*Aus meinem Leben und Denken,* 1931). Schweitzer stands astride several traditional discussions. First is his discussion of successors to the (Protestant) Christian Mission in Africa, European doctors who came with colonizers and served as their le-gitimization. Second, he participated in the tradition of European colonial discussion on the concepts of "civilization" and "primitivism," as well as in discussions on the need for education in the new ethic of reverence for life. In this sense it is interesting to analyze the point of view of Africans to this literature. The focus here is to situate the works in the context in which they were written and to explore the intended effect. The main goal is to de-scribe and explain the processes of the critical reception of Schweitzer.

In this study I would like to focus on the reception of Schweitzer in Gabon in particular, but I also will make some comments on his reception in Germany. My primary intention is not to add to our factual knowledge about Schweitzer, but to assemble carefully the existing material in an at-tempt to gain a critical perspective on both the details and the full panorama of his long life.

Albert Schweitzer in Germany

German scholars have a long tradition of dealing with Schweitzer's ideals and work. His conception of religion, his criticism of civilization, and his ethic of reverence for life have often been discussed in German academic circles during the first half of the twentieth century. In the 1920s, newspapers frequently reported on his work in Lambaréné. His travelogue *On the Edge of the Primeval Forest* and his autobiographical book *Out of My Life and Thought* were both best-sellers.

In the postwar period, the story of Schweitzer the doctor, the philosopher, and the theologian provided the material for a multiform treatment both in fiction and in the media. In the service of ethical and humanist reflection, Schweitzer found his way into numerous youth novels and assumed an important didactic function, especially in Germany. Germany, just a few years after the Second World War, had more than one reason to look for a role model with an international standing. Schweitzer, the selfless humanist and German-speaking Alsatian, readily met those expectations. On German soil, during the years of reconstruction of the country and its new orientation, he became the ideal embodiment of a culture influenced by Christianity and humanism. As a result, many institutions were founded, numerous biographies written, and in this way a collective symbolism created.

In the late 1940s and 1950s, the story of Schweitzer inspired a considerable number of literary works, mainly novels, fictional biographies, and light fiction for young people. Here are some examples:

Rolf Italiaander, *Der weiße Oganga Albert Schweitzer: Eine Erzählung aus Äquatorialafrika*. Hanover, 1954.

Kurt Vethake, *Das weiße Haus im Dschungel*. Kiel, 1955.

Bernhard Goetz, *Albert Schweitzer: Ein Mann der guten Tat*. Göttingen, 1955.

Luise Maria Schmied, *An den Ufern des Ogowe*. Berlin, 1956.

M. Z. Thomas, *Unser großer Freund Albert Schweitzer*. Munich, 1960.

From 1949 to 1959 about ten fictional biographies and several essays were published in Germany. Most authors were familiar with Schweitzer's biography and his philosophical ideas. It can be taken for granted that these authors were basically influenced by Schweitzer's own works. When one considers everything that was written on Schweitzer's life story, one realizes immediately that in spite of the extent of material and the diversity of characters, there are a number of occurrences that appear in many of the accounts in the same or in a transformed form. Most of the authors were content to report on the story of Albert Schweitzer from different standpoints. The analysis of most of the biographical accounts shows how closely connected they all are in terms of content. The German accounts can be understood as coherent works on the basis of their reference to Schweitzer's philosophy of culture and experiences in Africa. These common features are not just to be found in geographical facts (all novels take Lambaréné as the setting) or in the presence of Schweitzer as the main protagonist, but they mainly have to do with the presence of recurring essential features. The first such feature is the selection of certain passages from Schweitzer's life. This is, first, the oft-commented-upon decision by Albert Schweitzer to migrate to Africa as a doctor; second, the famous arrival in Lambaréné; third, the return home as prisoner of war; and finally, the second trip back to Lambaréné after the First World War. The second feature is the moral and spiritual picture one or more characters in the respective works produce of the bush doctor. The picture projects not only the experiences of the respective author in his confrontation with the "genius of humanism" (Churchill) but also the collective memory of a whole people. The third feature consists of the stylization of Dr. Schweitzer, in which special moral and ethical qualities are attributed to him.

The recurrence of certain types of novels, which often insist on the relevance of Schweitzer's ethic of reverence for life for the postwar period and on his character as a "hero without weapons" (*Held ohne Waffe*) or as a "genius of the human spirit" (*Genie der Menschlichkeit*), expresses the malaise of the German postwar generation. The literary environment in Germany only concentrated on Schweitzer's role as a model for the youth. His work in Lambaréné or his writings in cultural philosophy were interpreted accordingly and perceived only from this perspective. The aim of this reflection for Schweitzer's experience is the production of a discourse and of a field of cultural symbolism in which what the reader, especially the young German reader, should know is fixed. The authors see Schweitzer not just as a model, but also as a man who in spite of an increasingly loud critique in the 1950s and 1960s guarantees an immediate recognition value.[2]

The White Oganga

Rolf Italiaander's account, *Der weiße Oganga* (1954), is from the point of view of a theme no different from the rest of the narratives in which Schweitzer is placed at the center of the story. Stylistically, however, Italiaander's book is impressive because of its originality: while most authors simply retell the life history of Schweitzer, Italiaander seeks to work out his own history. Italiaander's narrative is fundamentally a mixture of a travel diary and a novel with a subjective way of presentation, which successfully mixes realistic details and fiction. In his narrative, an intensive blending of sources plays a central role, which he binds together with his literary imagination and personal interpretation. The quality of Italiaander's narrative should not be measured by what his main character says but by how it is said: on the one hand the reader is guided in the traditional way by an omniscient perspective. However, at another level of the novel, the story is told from the perspective of the young character Robert, thus creating opportunities for the young to identify with it.

Italiaander tells the story of a young man named Robert who, after learning about the work of the white doctor Schweitzer (also known as white Oganga), decides to stay with his uncle, André Gorrik, a lumberjack, in the vicinity of Lambaréné. He hopes to meet the bush doctor Schweitzer personally. Robert's paternal grandparents come from around Strasbourg and his family has had personal contacts with Schweitzer for two generations. Already during this time Robert's grandparents were particularly impressed by the young vicar from St. Nicolai's Church in Strasbourg.

Robert reports on his travels from "Europe's heart to Africa's heart." Parallel to descriptions of everyday life in the tropical rainforests of central Africa, Robert's conversation, in particular with his uncle Gorrik on Schweitzer and his work, catches the attention of the reader. The aim of the narrative is to replace the man of the people, Albert Schweitzer, with a mythological heroic character. His ordinary name and his legacy depend largely on this perspective, that is, the country of origin, the cultural and historical background, and the generation of the observer. In the literature, Schweitzer became an "elastic figure" who could be borrowed, used, processed, and made to fit different ends. He could be adjusted to fit any perspective and interest. He has also been used to communicate messages that correspond to the author's feelings and thoughts rather than to the real image of Schweitzer. Schweitzer's name is exchanged in the novel for exotic names, such as "white Oganga" or "bush doctor," and is replaced by descriptions, such as "healer of body and soul." In the narrative the work of the bush doctor in Lambaréné takes up a great deal of space and is described in detail.

The narrative is linked to Schweitzer's works through quotes and a whole range of references. Moreover, the point is to put across perspectives that are deemed "specific to Schweitzer," particularly his ethic of reverence for life and selfless brotherly love. Just like his role model Schweitzer, Robert cannot simply have ideals but also must put them into practice. As long as he is able to achieve his aim, he does not care about what his bodily pain and his psychic and financial efforts bring forth. The main character comes across as a young idealist, and in this way the identification with Schweitzer is made easier. He plays the role of a mediator between Schweitzer and the European youth.

The White Oganga and the other novels have in fact didactic and metaphysical dimensions that go beyond their main topic and can be measured by the profound malaise to which they bear testimony. It seems evident that this humanist ethic has influenced a vast majority of the postwar world traumatized by Nazism. Reimar Hollman speaks about "ein willkommenes Alibi einer inhumanen Welt" (a welcome alibi of an inhumane world, "Zum 100. Geburtstag Albert Schweitzers," *Neue Hannoversche Zeitung,* January 1975). Schweitzer served in Germany as an example of courage, generosity, human brotherhood, and respect for life. The act of writing forces the postwar generation to voyage into its own history. It is a form of introspection. Even today, Schweitzer is present in the collective memory of Germans as a symbol of humanitarian compassion and commitment to peace.

Albert Schweitzer in Africa: The Emergence of a New Symbolism

Research in Gabon, Germany, and France demonstrates that very few articles appeared in Gabonese newspapers about Schweitzer, his work, and his thought. To understand this, we have first to consider the historical background. Before, during, and after the colonial rule, the standard of education in Gabon remained low. We also need to consider that Schweitzer's books were first published in German and quickly translated into English, Dutch, and Scandinavian languages, but it was often years before they appeared in French. For example, his autobiography *Out of My Life and Thought,* published in German in 1931, Dutch in 1932, and English in 1933, did not appear in French until 1959. This means that few French readers had access to Schweitzer's books.

Africans began to come to terms with the Schweitzer materials in the 1960s, just after Gabon's independence. Seen from this perspective, this coming to terms can be regarded as a critique of colonialism. One result of this is not only a new, original "retelling" of Schweitzer's life and work, but also a way of bringing his image into a new perspective. In spite of all the commotion, it retains its efficacy to date.

It is important to note that the African critics of Schweitzer's work focus on just one dimension, the relationship between Schweitzer and Africans, and the criticism concentrates mainly on the hospital in Lambaréné.

Chronologically, the first article about Schweitzer published by an African newspaper was a satirical tract, "Le scandale de Lambaréné" (The scandal of Lambaréné), written by Jane Rouch in 1962. Two years after the independence of the majority of African countries, an article appeared in the weekly *Jeune Afrique* on Albert Schweitzer and his hospital in Lambaréné, and the article caused mayhem in Europe. The introductory note makes it clear that the magazine *Jeune Afrique* sets out to "swallow the bitter pill" and bring down the legend surrounding the patriarch of Lambaréné: "Documents à l'appui, 'Jeune Afrique' a donc décidé de 'manger le morceau' " (As documents in support, *Jeune Afrique* has decided to swallow the pill, *Jeune Afrique* [1962]: 14).

The author of "The Scandal of Lambaréné" describes and notes the deficiencies of Schweitzer's hospital and his contempt for Africans (they are children, he said). On the one hand, this is a deconstruction of the form of presentation noted so far. On the other hand, this breaks with Europe's monopolization of discourse. This marked the new political arrangement and the new power relationships in the production of discourse. The symbolism that accompanies this "event" is interesting in this connection. As the writer puts it, "The new wind which blows across Africa does not stop before the mahogany forest around Lambaréné."

The symbolism of the wind, which is quite common in the language of journalism and politics, expresses the political and social renewal in Africa after 1960. In this sense it deals above all with the independence of most African countries and the official end of the colonial system. The logical implication of political change is the rejection of all symbols of European presence. One of the most powerful symbols of this system (which is presented as mahogany) is Schweitzer. From the point of view of syntactic construction this symbolism forms a rigid dichotomous structure. The wind paradigm of "modernity," "progress," and "right to self-determination" contrasts with the mahogany-Lambaréné paradigm of "conservatism," "backwardness," and "political oppression." The opposition is taken up in the text and brought to bear on further distinguishing marks of the different positions.

Photographs present only patients living in dire straits: everywhere there is misery, poverty, and dirt. With the choice of particularly nasty pictures the reporter wants, on the one hand, to live up to his own ideas and to meet the expectations of his African readership and, on the other hand, to shock European readers. There is, in fact, according to *Jeune Afrique,* an exaggerated mystification of the bush doctor: "Le monde entier imagine que Lambaréné est le seul coin où l'on puisse se soigner en Afrique, alors que l'hôpital du Dr. Schweitzer soigne plus mal que partout ailleurs en Afrique" (The entire world imagines that Lambaréné is the only place in Africa where one can obtain medical service, yet the hospital of Dr. Schweitzer serves patients more inadequately than anywhere else in Africa, *Jeune Afrique* [1962]: 14). From such descriptions, the choice of subject matter and theme is affected by the need to express a suppressed viewpoint. I believe that it manifests itself in such expressive maneuvers as "writing back" (Salman Rushdie) to the center or reclaiming for the margin that which has been elided by the center.

The Representation of Schweitzer in Gabonese Literature

The only book on Albert Schweitzer written by an African is the novel *The Trial of a Nobel Prize Winner*, published in 1983 by the Gabonese writer and lawyer Séraphin Ndaot. Ndaot is writing from a predominantly postcolonial perspective. The writer uses the biography of Schweitzer and the factual history as background in his novel. Ndaot's approach vacillates between the representation in the German literature as described above and the radical position of *Jeune Afrique,* without clearly adhering to one or the other. I would like to examine the novel from two related angles: first, to look at Ndaot's radical version of Schweitzer's life and work in Africa against the backdrop of those versions produced by the dominant ideology, and second, to examine his "manipulation" of certain facts in terms of his aesthetic and ideological aims. An adequate reading of the text *Le procès d'un prix Nobel* seems to be possible only if the text is seen simultaneously as an individual and as a collective confrontation with the history of colonialism, neocolonialism, and today's African society in the form of "micro-text within a macro-text," that is, as part of a wide-ranging journalistic and literary production on Albert Schweitzer in the past fifteen years.

The Trial of a Nobel Prize Winner is a fictitious trial of the medical doctor André Seller from a fictitious country, "Relande." The protagonist at eighty is a practicing doctor, a widower, a philosopher, a Nobel laureate, and a recipient of many honorary degrees. He is charged with having performed experiments with fatal consequences for the native population and with having tested self-concocted medicine on his patients in Galemba, a fictitious country in equatorial Africa. The presiding judge accuses Dr. André Seller of having no concern for the individual fate of the native population. He is only concerned with his ambition to be famous in the world:

> Ce don't il rêvait depuis toujours, c'était du triomphe, le triomphe mondial, tel que l'avaient connu ses idoles: Bach et Beethoven. Il aspirait sans doute à cette notoriété qui cristallise l'exploit quel qu'il soit. . . . Mais il s'était aussi souvenu que Bach ne connut la célébrité qu'au XIXe siècle et la consécration qu'au début du XXe siècle. Un succès posthume ne satisfaisait pas ses aspirations. (8–9)

[Fame, world fame, that is what had always been his dream, the kind that had come to his idols, Bach and Beethoven. No doubt, he aspired toward the fame that great achievement brings. . . . But he also remembered that Bach became famous only in the nineteenth century and that he was consecrated at the beginning of the twentieth. A posthumous fame did not satisfy his ambitions.]

The major criticism was that Schweitzer was a relic of nineteenth-century colonialism, with no sympathy for the movement of black independence sweeping across Africa. The intellectuals of 1960 said Schweitzer was merely a petty bush autocrat who did not care for Africans, and who ran his hospital, out of respect for "all life," with no regard for modern hygiene. The doctor was, Ndaot writes, an anachronism, stubbornly living in the Africa of 1913:

Mais vous voulez savoir quel était l'état de nos rapports personnels? Eh bien, c'étaient les mêmes rapports que ceux qui peuvent exister entre un nostalgique de la colonisation, fortement attaché au passé, et un adepte du progrès, résolument tourné vers l'avenir. Le choc est inévitable, l'humeur incompatible. (201)

[But you wish to know what the status was of our personal relationship? Well, it was a relationship between someone who lives with a longing for the past time of colonialism and someone who is a disciple of progress, firmly oriented toward the future. The conflict is unavoidable, it is an incompatible relationship.]

The charge of the prosecutor, that Dr. Seller was a vulgar cheat and a criminal, cannot be proven, however. The author exploits this doubtful situation to reflect upon justice and its relation to politics. This discussion in turn represents a change of topic or transition in the novel, which develops into a critique of Galemban society. Seller is not prosecuted in the end. Although he could have been saved, he dies of a heart attack. He had given the last "Selleryine"—a medication against heart disease that he had developed—to the prosecutor, who also suffered from heart disease. Prior to this, the prosecutor had the laboratory in which Selleryine was produced shut down. The novel ends with this generous and worthy gesture from Dr. Seller.

The novel itself implicitly invites an intertextual approach. By writing this book Ndaot seems to have the Schweitzer autobiography *Out of My Life and Thought* in mind. His purpose is clearly to attack the mythical figure. His choice of irony and parody expresses exactly the intention of the author. The main action of the novel takes place in the law court of Galemba. Structurally, it is divided into two parts: a long presentation of Dr. André Seller and his work in Galemba (these detailed descriptions of Seller's early life, his experiences, his family, and his passions are imaginatively recreated and are part of the fictional elements in the novel) and the trial. Thus, the narrative moves in a linear progression over several days: from the beginning of the trial until the death of Dr. André Seller. But the novel is not completely chronological. There is a series of flashbacks that reconstruct Seller's early life. The method the author adopts is to treat each statement and each day in a separate section.

One of the problems with the novel is its structure. The novel is rather episodic; the story is developed somewhat erratically, and events are only loosely tied together. It may be argued that Ndaot is dealing with a biography and a disjointed series of events. This argument is not satisfactory because Ndaot devotes long passages to narrating the past history of André Seller, and these passages do not advance the action of the novel or really do anything to improve our understanding of the hero. It is not even a question of one part not being properly connected to succeeding or preceding parts. It is simply that within each part of the novel there is not sufficient coherent development. The flashback technique, instead of serving as a source of illumination, becomes more or less a digression. I believe that Ndaot's problem is how to blend artistically the biographical and historical realities and the imaginative elements in a work of fiction. However, his attempt to give imaginative treatment to biographical and historical facts has not been wholly successful. But few readers could deny its specificity as the expression of a Gabonese point of view.

Despite all the precautions taken and all the narrative strategies employed, the text is easily recognizable as a roman à clef. Many biographical and historical details, such as the humanist discourse and the many talents of

Dr. André Seller (he is a doctor, a musician, an author, a philosopher, and a theologian), make quite clear that the novel is really about Dr. Albert Schweitzer. In fact, *Le procès d'un prix Nobel* is not one book but many. It oscillates from style to style and from theme to theme: colonialism, neocolonialism, and criticism of the postcolonial society and the elite (Ndaot uses this opportunity to examine various perspectives on justice and democracy in Galemba).

Ndaot's *Le procés d'un prix Nobel,* I would argue, must be placed in a postcolonial context. In this sense the novel is a kind of active reappropriation and rewriting of Schweitzer's biography. It is a counterdiscourse that has its specificity. Behind this strategy of appropriation, there is the recognition that the success of colonial oppression was not only on account of colonialism's direct assault on property and life, but was also based on the control of the means of communication. The way of expressing the situation contrasts in a fundamental way with the known image of the bush hospital, where "the healing of the body goes hand in hand with the healing of the soul." Lambaréné as a symbol of healing and humanity now turns into a symbol of death and racism. The aim of this type of description is surely not only the presentation of "another truth," but also the demythologization of Schweitzer. In the novel Dr. Seller appears as a representative symbol of colonialism and as a metaphor for paternalism, primitivism, and anachronism:"Le docteur est un homme du passé, aveuglement attaché au passé et qui ne souhaite pas l'évolution de ce pays" (The doctor is a man of the past, blindly attached to the past, a man who does not welcome the evolution of this country, 31). What emerges above all from a comparison of Schweitzer's own biography with Ndaot's fictional version is the extent to which Ndaot's text concurs with the data the sources include, and how this agreement in choice of detail only serves to underscore the fundamental ideological differences.

The end of the novel therefore demonstrates the dilemma of the postindependence generations in Gabon and the nature of disagreement when it comes to discussing Schweitzer. It demonstrates also that we cannot reduce the complexity of Schweitzer's life and thought to easy slogans.

Conclusion

Created and nourished by popular imagination after the Second World War, the image of Schweitzer as "the greatest man in the world" has survived decades of social and political change, managing to adapt with remarkable pliability and success. The reception of Schweitzer and the collective symbolism associated with him and his legacy depend largely on the perspective, that is, the country of origin, the cultural and historical background, and the generation of the observer. In the literature, Schweitzer became an "elastic figure" who could be borrowed, used, processed, and made to fit different ends. He could be adjusted to fit any perspective and interest. He has also been used to put across messages that correspond to the author's feelings and thought rather than to the real image of Schweitzer.

My analysis has revealed that writing about Schweitzer could be an act of introspection or self-criticism, an act of colonial criticism and "writing back to the center," and an act of criticizing one's own society.

CHAPTER II

The Significance of Reverence for Life Today

Erich Gräßer

Erich Gräßer is professor emeritus at the University of Bonn and a well-known scholar on the life and ethic of Albert Schweitzer. In this essay Gräßer addresses some of the most significant of contemporary ethical challenges, and he explains why the ethic of reverence for life needs to be taken seriously, today more than ever. He concludes, "Indeed, whether the world has a future and what kind of a future this may be will crucially depend on the capability of the power of love, justice, and peace to put the powers of evil, exploitation, and destruction of nature in their place."

In 1963, two years before his death, Albert Schweitzer wrote, "I am able to observe that the ethic of reverence for life is beginning to make its way in the world. This encourages me beyond everything with which they could reproach or hurt me."[1] So Schweitzer died after a long, self-sacrificing life with the conviction that his ethic of reverence for life would be acknowledged, and acknowledged everywhere. He believed that his ethic would turn us all into better human beings:"Through reverence for life we become devout in a fundamental, deep, and living way."[2]

It seems, however, as if Schweitzer took this deceptive hope to the grave with him. Not reverence for life, but irreverence for life is advancing! The most significant feature of this is the incomparably brutal recklessness with which the potentiality of modern technology is carried through at the expense of the life interests of the nonhuman creation and partly even at the expense of humanity itself. For quite some time the big industrial nations

159

have not been living on the interest of the rich, natural capital to finance their prosperity and wastefulness: they have been living on the capital itself. The demand for more and more growth and prosperity could turn out to be a suicidal program that is irreversible.[3] "We rejoice over the fire we lit, we gaze in wonder at the beautiful flames, but we still don't see that they are consuming us," writes a critical contemporary in view of the atomic piles which make us pay a price for our energy consumption that eventually nobody will be able to pay.[4] Suffering from the shock of numerous catastrophes and the now-impending climatic disaster, we have become aware of the fact that the relationship between humanity and nature has entered a new phase. The attitudes have changed: "We have to protect the oceans more from us than us from the oceans. We have become more dangerous to nature than it has ever been to us," said Hans Jonas,[5] a philosopher of religion, for whom the progressive industrial societies of the West are the "cardinal sinners against the earth."[6] In short: with his admirably big and often helpful technology humanity turns out to be the "planetary villain number one."[7]

The "total crisis" in which we find ourselves isn't just based on misuse.[8] The German philosopher Robert Spaemann determines a certain type of science and technology as the cause of the crisis. He says, "The specific focus of modern science is the radical hypostatization of the world."[9] It has turned man into master and owner of nature with the serious consequences we are already aware of. Amery states, "By 'hominizing' the world, which means turning it into the exclusive raw material for one single species, we dehumanized it."[10] Wherever it is not helpful to economic interests, we dispute the right of our co-creatures from the animal and plant kingdoms to live on this planet earth. We exterminate elephants and butterflies, we overfish the seas, and we wipe out wild animals while turning tame ones into animal machines—not to mention worse things, such as the millions of victims of fur-farming, seal-hunting, or unnecessary animal experimentation.[11] But even we are threatened by this. The mechanistic-materialistic scientific medicine, for example, is turning "more and more from the original 'art of healing' into a spare-part-repair-medicine" for which a human being is in the first place not part of an entirety, but a biological machine, "every now and then in need of repair, every now and then to be provided with spare-parts and every now and then stricken by pathogens like iron by rust."[12] And whether the peaceful use of nuclear energy and nuclear power stations as energy sources for human beings are a blessing or a curse has been an open question since the reactor accident in Chernobyl, Russia. As of yet nobody knows where and how the atomic waste, which will be toxic for thousands of years, can be stored safely.

The new government we elected in September 1998 in Germany has decided to eliminate nuclear energy. Now members of this government are having violent arguments about it. I am surprised that the questions of economic viability, protection of jobs, and profitability dominate this controversy, while the ethical problem fades into the background completely. This happens even though we know from Albert Schweitzer that nothing can be appropriate when it is not ethical.

After Albert Schweitzer had occupied himself for months with the question What is radioactivity? and had become convinced that it is a threat to human beings, especially to our descendants, he addressed the public in 1957 and 1958 on Radio Oslo with three appeals. He said, among other things:

> The fact that nature holds radioactive elements made by people is an incomprehensible occurrence in the history of the earth and of humankind. Refraining from dealing with its significance and its consequences is a foolishness which will cost humankind dearly. We stroll around in thoughtlessness. It must not be that we will not pull ourselves together in good time and summon up the reason, the seriousness, and the courage to renounce it and concern ourselves with reality.[13]

All of these observations suggest that the qualitative leap of our technological power and "the victories of civilization over nature," as Hans Jonas calls it,[14] have become a general threat. Not only nature, "but humankind itself has become one of the objects of technology."[15] The "completion of his power" can mean the overpowering of man himself,[16] as "The victory which is too great endangers the winner himself."[17]

♦   ♦   ♦

It is an unavoidable logical conclusion that a qualitatively changed power demands a qualitatively changed ethic. That is why Hans Jonas, together with many others, has started searching for a new ethic for the new situation. He missed the fact that Albert Schweitzer, who had already foreseen the decay of culture at the beginning of the twentieth century, had long ago found it. Hence, it is necessary to revisit Schweitzer's ethic of reverence for life, because it could be an anchor of hope for us. It could put a stop to the unrestrained exploitation of nature and to the boundless profit-increase in many parts of the world. Many ethicists today know that an ethic will no longer be appropriate without self-restriction of our freedom, without relinquishment, without asceticism. Modesty is becoming the main virtue in every ethic of responsibility. So far everybody agrees. But now Hans Jonas thinks that because of the novelty of our situation, not only is the doctrine outdated, but also the theory of every previous ethic, which always had in view the well-being of people.[18]

As far as Albert Schweitzer is concerned, this focus only upon the well-being of people has to be denied. Hans Jonas is admittedly right when he says, "None of the previous ethics had to consider the global conditions of human life and the distant future, or the existence of the species."[19] And genetic manipulation, by which the creature slips into the role of the creator and thus may exceed a limit beyond which it is not permitted to go, is the only case that drifts beyond *every* previous ethic, and in doing so reveals itself as the impossible possibility. But apart from that, one has to deny with regard to Albert Schweitzer's ethics of reverence for life that the new situation requires a "rethinking in the foundation of ethics" as well.[20] No, not at all! It is the nature of an ethic primarily based on reverence, as presented to the public by Albert Schweitzer in a Strasbourg sermon for the first time on February 16, 1919,[21] that it cannot be restricted to brotherly love. It refers to anything living, and it asks us to be aware of the whole realm of the living.

From the beginning Albert Schweitzer rejected the anthropocentrism of traditional ethics as "semi-ethics of European philosophy" and contrasted it with the "deep and complete ethic" that alone is capable "of creating an ethical culture."[22] What Hans Jonas is looking for was already found by Albert Schweitzer. It was never "futile to him to ask whether the condition of the non-human nature, the biosphere as a whole and in its parts, which is now subjected to our power, has thereby been given to us for safekeeping and has something like a moral claim on us, not for our sake but for its own sake and in its own right."[23] Of course, the biosphere is of value for its own sake! For Albert Schweitzer "the love for any creature, the reverence for any being . . . however different it may outwardly be from ourselves, is the beginning and foundation of any morality."[24]

In my opinion Hans Jonas is not right in saying that it was only the impending danger of decline—the "heuristic of fear," as he calls it—that gave us the idea of looking for an ethic of responsibility for the whole.[25] Responsibility for the whole has been something natural for Schweitzer. His expression "reverence for life" includes "all living creatures," that is, plants, animals, and human beings—in other words, nature as a whole. That is what makes the ethic "complete and true and lively."[26] For him this ethic is the "epistemologically necessary and absolutely basic principle of any morality."[27] And this ethic was meant to be understandable not only for Christians, but for all thinking human beings. Therefore it was not based on theological but on elemental thinking, which makes no difference for Schweitzer, however, because for him Christianity "as the deepest religion" is at the same time "the deepest philosophy."[28] In his *Philosophy of Civilization* (1923) Schweitzer developed his ethic of reverence into an *absolute* ethic. It "does not accept any relative ethic. It only regards the preservation and promotion of life as good. It calls evil any way of destroying and damaging life, under whatever circumstances it may happen."[29] This conception of ethics is based on the epistemological claim of the philosopher Immanuel Kant, on Jesus' Sermon on the Mount (in regard to content), and on Arthur Schopenhauer's empirical foundation of ethics.

◆　　◆　　◆

Albert Schweitzer succeeded in constructing a great vision of ethics, and he was ahead of his time. When he developed his ethic of reverence for life at the beginning of the twentieth century, he did so against the background of the decline of culture, which was the same to him as the decline of anything human. He saw the main reason for this as an imbalance of material and cultural development: the latter did not keep up with the former. "Nowadays planes take people through the air across a world where starvation and bands of thieves strike terror into people's hearts."[30] Schweitzer chose this example in 1923 to show clearly what kind of progress he would call "grotesque." And today the grotesque nature of this progress becomes even clearer to us. We explore space, fly to the moon and to Mars, send a probe to Jupiter and Venus, but still thousands of people die of starvation in developing nations. Schweitzer could only regard a technical culture dissociated from ethics as a disastrous "non-culture," because he was convinced that "in the end the useful could only be realized by ethics."[31]

In our present time it becomes obvious how right Schweitzer was. The fact that what is technically possible is not necessarily technically responsible, that an economy may be dissociated from ecology, has resulted in a kind of progress which now has a stranglehold on us. It covers the world with ecological disasters of apocalyptic extent and only leaves us with the alternative "end or change." That is, the counterforce Schweitzer displayed with the example of his life and thinking against the disaster of a nonethical conception of culture ought no longer to remain ineffective. And indeed, a process of rethinking has started in the meantime, which gives us hope. By breaking down the anthropological reduction of traditional ethics, Schweitzer made way for a global ethic of responsibility, which was convincingly demanded by Hans Jonas fourteen years after Schweitzer's death. The theory Jonas's critique is based on has been found by Albert Schweitzer. It is reverence for life. And one should not forget that this always meant reverence for *every* life. What gives us reason to believe that the formula's success is gradually being realized is the fact that it has found its way into two German federal constitutions: the constitution of Mecklenburg-Western Pomerania (article 15.4) and Saxony (article 101.1).

Today more than ever reverence for life is an indispensable guiding principle for an ethic that is meant to instruct people how to act in view of a total crisis looming on the horizon. Therefore, the following words of Albert Schweitzer are especially valid now: "Today, being humane is of great significance in world history."[32] For Schweitzer, who has never ceased being a theologian, this means "What is at stake for humanity today is to realize the kingdom of God or else to decline,"[33] "kingdom of God" meaning "the power of love in the world and in ourselves."[34] Indeed, whether the world has a future and what kind of future this may be will crucially depend on the capability of the power of love, justice, and peace to put the powers of evil, exploitation, and destruction of nature in their place.

Albert Schweitzer's life and thought shine as a bright light in the darkness of our world. To cite a saying of Jesus from his Sermon on the Mount: we should not hide this light under a bushel, meaning that we should not put any vessel over it but should put it on a candlestick, so that it may shine for everybody in the house.

CHAPTER 12

Rethinking Reverence for Life

Mike W. Martin

Mike W. Martin, professor of philosophy at Chapman University, here considers the ethic of reverence for life by proposing four problematical issues in Schweitzer's presentation of the ethic. He suggests that when aspects of Schweitzer's metaphysical framework are eliminated, key features of the ethic may be retained without the unpalatable elements: unity of life without pantheism, empathy with life without anthropomorphism, moral guidance rather than arbitrariness, and responsibility without guilt mongering. This article was published in 1993 in the periodical Between the Species *(9 [1993]: 204–13) and is reproduced here with the permission of the author.*

Albert Schweitzer's ethics of reverence for life is more complex and interesting than first appears. It contains themes relevant to contemporary environmental ethics, including a virtue-ethics approach that emphasizes personal responsibility and tolerance, empathy for living organisms, and the fundamental unity of life. Not surprising, then, Schweitzer has recently been acknowledged for pioneering a biocentric (life-centered) ethical theory.[1]

At the same time, Schweitzer's ethic has four unpalatable features: pantheism, anthropomorphism, excessive subjectivity, and guilt mongering. I trace these features to the metaphysical framework in which Schweitzer develops his ideal of reverence for life. I also show how the framework can be set aside while retaining much of the spirit and substance of his ethics. My aim is not to defend his ethics, but to interpret it and show its contemporary relevance.

1. Unity of Life (Without Pantheism)

Theories of environmental ethics differ according to their conceptions of what things have *inherent worth,* that is, value in themselves independent of human desires and appraisals.[2] According to human-centered (anthropocentric) ethics, only humans have inherent worth. Other natural objects have value only because humans value them, whether instrumentally or intrinsically. Things have *instrumental value* when they are useful to humans. For example, drinkable water, breathable air, and natural medicines have instrumental value because they contribute to the further good of health. Things have *intrinsic value* when they are pleasing because of their aesthetic or symbolic properties, as when we value wilderness areas and bald eagles because of their beauty and community significance.

Nonhuman-centered ethics locates inherent worth in natural things in addition to humans. In particular, biocentric ethics locates inherent worth in living things. Although Schweitzer did not explicitly use the distinction between inherent worth versus intrinsic value, it is clear he defended a biocentric ethics that locates inherent value in all living things: all life is "sacred" and "something possessing value in itself" (C 57).[3]

Theories of environmental ethics also differ according to whether they are individualistic or holistic in approach. Thus, biocentric theories are individualistic when they locate inherent worth in particular organisms. They are holistic when they locate inherent worth in communities of life (ecosystems), in types of life (species), or in the environment as a whole. Schweitzer bridges the dichotomy between individualistic and holistic bioethics. He insists that each living organism has inherent worth, yet at the same time his primary theme is the unity of life. This moral and spiritual unity is ultimately unfathomable, which is why he calls his theory *ethical mysticism.* This is an "active mysticism" that inspires commitments to further life, in contrast to "passive mysticism," which is centered on emotional experiences of identity with God or nature (C 79).

Schweitzer renounced metaphysics in the sense of a search for an ultimate purpose of the universe that gives meaning to humanity (C 73). The meaning of our lives is created through personal commitments, not discovered through cosmic speculation. Nevertheless, Schweitzer did hold a metaphysical theory in the sense of a view of ultimate reality, and that theory forms the framework in which he develops his theme of life's unity. He maintained a faith in a universal, infinite, and creative will-to-live (C 79). Much of the time this faith remained in the background, but it surfaced periodically, as in this passage: "Reverence for life means to be in the grasp of the infinite, inexplicable, forward-urging Will in which all Being is grounded" (C 283).[4]

Schweitzer was influenced by Arthur Schopenhauer's voluntarist metaphysics, according to which ultimate reality is *will*. "Behind all phenomena" there is will-to-live, and each organism constitutes part of that will—a will both to survive and to develop according to its natural tendencies (C 308, 282). Unlike Schopenhauer, Schweitzer was deeply religious, though his religious convictions were highly unorthodox. They hovered somewhere near pantheism but were closer to *biotheism*—the view that God is manifested in and constituted by all life.[5] By the time he wrote *The Philosophy of Civilization* Schweitzer was most likely an agnostic concerning supernatural beings (God, angels, souls), even though he continued to use conventional religious language when speaking as a minister and theologian. The divine is immanent in nature rather than transcendent to it: "The Essence of Being, the Absolute, the Spirit of the Universe, and all similar expressions denote nothing actual. . . . The only reality is the Being which manifests itself in phenomena"(C 304).

Schweizer's metaphysics has some interest. It shares a kinship with the worldviews of Spinoza, Hinduism, Buddhism, and Native American religions. Perhaps its greatest value lies in bridging Christian orthodoxy and naturalistic worldviews. Even so, I wish to set the metaphysics aside, at least the part of it which suggests there is a cosmic and semideified Will-to-live that can be said to *act* creatively in the universe. What then remains of the theme of life's moral unity?

Abandoning Schweitzer's metaphysics need not mean rejecting his ethics.[6] I offer three preliminary observations. First, Schweitzer is the first to remind us that the core of a moral outlook can survive intact after being freed from the worldview in which it was first developed. In *The Quest of the Historical Jesus* he argues that Jesus held a false eschatology which anticipated the end of the world during his lifetime. That eschatology led to some unjustified value judgments, including a pessimistic renunciation of human society as a mere overture to the approaching kingdom of God. Nevertheless, Schweitzer embraces Jesus as a moral paragon whose ideal of love can be transplanted from the metaphysics in which it was initially formulated. I suggest the same is true of Schweitzer's ideal of reverence for life.

Second, Schweitzer insists that ethics cannot be inferred from metaphysics. In particular, the ideal of reverence for life cannot be derived from observing nature's spectacle of killing. Schweitzer prides himself on being "absolutely skeptical" about cosmic purposes while maintaining an optimistic and life-affirming attitude (C 76). As I have suggested, he is not as metaphysically skeptical as he claims, since he continues to assume there is a unified and universal Will-to-live manifested in all life. Nevertheless, setting aside his metaphysics is consistent with the spirit of his largely empirically oriented "natural ethic" (L 235).

Third, Schweitzer's metaphysics distorts some of his most important ideas. For example, in the next section I show how his central argument for the ideal of reverence for life is cogent only when freed from its metaphysical moorings. Even the central theme of the unity of life is better appreciated without relying on metaphysical speculations. When Schweitzer urged in his sermons "Wherever you see life—that is yourself!" he evoked responses that were not dependent on his parishioners being pantheists (R 115).

We might understand the unity-of-life theme as drawing together a rich variety of familiar experiences and facts, including the following.

1. Compassion is a natural response to the suffering of other people and animals, a response which Schweitzer felt in extraordinary degrees from childhood on.[7] He was ahead of his time in calling for humane treatment of animals in medical experiments and food production (C 318).

2. We have benefited in many ways from animals, including the suffering inflicted on animals in medical experiments. Because of this a "new and special relation of solidarity has been established between them and us" (C 318).

3. Caring in the animal world is often strikingly analogous to human

caring, and both have a biological origin. Just as humans care for their children, many species of animals care for their offspring and even for animals outside their kinship groups. In citing such examples Schweitzer anticipates the insights of sociobiologists about the genetic basis for human and nonhuman caring (L 237–39, C 224–26).

4. With many individual animals we can enter into reciprocal caring relationships, indeed "friendship with animals." [8]

5. Plants, animals, and humans interact in complex chains of interdependency. We are united with nature in that our very survival depends on those interdependencies being sustained (L 237).

6. We experience moments of awe in which we marvel at the sheer existence of life and the infinite diversity of living creatures (R 114–15).

7. We also experience moments of humility when we understand that humanity is but one of millions of fragile life-forms and not the final goal of the universe (L 226).

8. The competition and killing defining the food chain are not the only significant aspects of nature. Equally noteworthy are the cooperation and tolerance which have evolved as part of the shared struggle to survive (C 260).

The moral implications of these experiences need to be sorted out and considered separately. Nevertheless, they have a cumulative impact in moving us toward a sense of oneness with nature of a sort aptly conveyed in the phrase "reverence for life"—reverence for life as a whole, as well as for particular organisms.

2. Empathy with Life (Without Anthropomorphism)

An adequate ethical theory, according to Schweitzer, meets several general criteria.

1. It provides a unifying perspective on moral values (C 105).

2. It focuses on self-perfection, where complete self-perfection implies bringing our lives into a positive relationship with the universe and with life as a whole (C 57, 296).

3. It is optimistic in the sense of evoking positive commitments on behalf of civilization, which consists in progress of all kinds, and it evokes

steady and enthusiastic commitment by tapping into our most basic sources of motivation (C xiii, 107).

4. It avoids metaphysical assumptions about the ultimate purposes of the universe (C 76).

Surveying the history of ethics, Schweitzer argues that the ethic of reverence for life meets these criteria better than competing theories. His arguments, however, turn substantially on personal factors about how the idea of reverence for life brings self-fulfillment through service to others (C 255). Alternative moral theories generate greater motivation and self-fulfillment for some individuals, and from a modern pluralistic point of view it is misguided to call for a "single ideal of civilized man" (C 47). In any case, something more is needed to justify reverence for life than the four general criteria.

That "something more" is Schweitzer's famous *will-to-live argument* (C 308–11, O 155–58, L 227–29). The argument is easily ridiculed because it seems to depend on attributing human features to all living things. Anthropomorphic attributions permeate Schweitzer's writings, such as when he says that all organisms suffer,[9] that a beetle is capable of "rejoicing in the sun like you" (R 115), and that each organism "strives" to achieve its highest perfection (C 282). But anthropomorphism is especially prominent in the will-to-live argument, and it makes the argument seem utterly naïve, as the following summary indicates.

I am a will-to-live, with desire for self-preservation, self-perfection, pleasure, happiness, and avoiding pain. All other organisms have these same desires, feelings, and aspirations: "As in my own will-to-live there is a longing for wider life and for . . . pleasure, with dread of annihilation and . . . pain; so is it also in the will-to-live all around me" (C 309). Therefore, since I value my life I must (in consistency) value all other life, "for I shall know that it longs for fullness and development as deeply as I do myself" (L 230).

The obvious rejoinder is that most organisms do not have desires like mine, whether for gaining pleasure and avoiding pain or for self-survival and self-perfection. Pleasure and pain are conscious states, and plants and protozoa lack the neurological structures for having or desiring conscious states. Moreover, desiring self-survival and self-perfection implies having a conception of oneself, a *self*-consciousness, that plants and most animals lack. Even ascribing a will-to-live to plants and lower animals seems anthropomorphic insofar as a "will," at least in one literal sense, implies conscious intentions, desires, and beliefs.

How can we explain Schweitzer's seemingly naïve anthropomorphism? As a physician and scientist, he was well aware that plants and lower animals lack the required neurological structures for consciousness. Clearly he was influenced by Goethe and other Romantics who in their poetry personified nature, but how could a well-trained scientist be so apparently credulous in responding to that influence?[10]

Much of the explanation is his metaphysics. If each organism is literally part of a universal will-to-live, and if the basic features of that universal will are uniform in all living organisms, then anthropomorphism is virtually inevitable, especially if we begin by reflecting on our own will-to-live. This tendency to anthropomorphize, however, is blocked once we set aside the metaphysics. There is little temptation to make literal ascriptions of human properties to algae and protozoa if they are no longer regarded as instantiations of a universal and personified will-to-live.

Another part of the explanation, however, is that Schweitzer may not have been as naïvely anthropomorphic as first appears.[11] We can construe his anthropomorphic images as metaphors designed to evoke empathy with other life, rather than as literal ascriptions of human features to nonhuman organisms. Whether or not this was his primary intention, it invites a more serious examination of the will-to-live argument. Let us strip away the anthropomorphic images, retaining only the idea of a will-to-live understood as a literal reference to genetically driven instincts to survive and develop. The following argument emerges (O 155–58).

1. Will-to-live thesis:"I am life that wills to live in the midst of life that wills to live."

2. Definition: My will-to-live is defined by instinctive tendencies to survive and develop.

3. Self-affirmation thesis: When I am healthy and sincere toward myself, I feel reverence for my will-to-live. I affirm my will-to-live, as defined in (2), as having inherent worth, and I devote myself to its expression, preservation, and development.

4. Analogy: All other organisms have similar tendencies to survive and develop.

5. Empathy thesis: I experience empathy with other life as I reflect honestly, dwelling on its similarity to my own life.

6. Life-affirmation thesis: My empathy generates sympathy, caring, and a "compulsion" (a strong desire and felt obligation) to approach other life with the same reverence I feel for my life.

7. Conclusion: Reverence for life is a fundamental virtue that consists in "preserving life, promoting life, developing all life that is capable of development to its highest possible value" and in not "destroying life, injuring life, repressing life that is capable of development."

This argument is phenomenological or experience based. It proceeds by reflecting on our experiences of our instincts to survive and develop, our affirmation of our lives inherent in those instincts, and our experience and knowledge of those same instincts in other life. Notice also that the conclusion is a statement about a virtue, not a rule of conduct. To be sure, reverence for life is a mandatory virtue, a virtue that we ought to cultivate and that embodies obligations. But it is a character trait, a desirable attitude and disposition, rather than a principle of action per se.

This interpretation captures Schweitzer's insistence that ethics is a product of reasoning that reveals how our attitudes toward all life should be "of a piece with" attitudes toward ourselves (L 230). It also captures his conviction that reverence for life is a natural expression of our will-to-live: "I can do nothing but hold to the fact that the will-to-live in me manifests itself as will-to-live which desires to become one with other will-to-live" (C 312). Our inclination to contribute to other living things expresses our desires for self-fulfillment. We achieve "self-perfection through self-devotion": self-fulfillment through exercising and expanding our natural capacities for empathy and sympathy for other life (C 255).

The crux of the argument is the experience of empathy of a kind that inspires sympathetic concern for other life. This appeal does not make Schweitzer's ethics human centered. Empathy is a response to other life as like us, but just as much a response that we are like other life, at the fundamental level of shared drives to survive and develop.

Schweitzer does not use the word "empathy" as frequently as "sympathy," but he does use various phrases to convey the idea. Reverence for other life begins when one experiences that life "in" one's own life, "feeling as one's own all the circumstances and all the aspirations of the will-to-live" (O 157, C 311). Empathy does not imply sharing the feelings and desires of the organisms we empathize with, and hence it is not based on anthropomorphic ascriptions of feelings and desires to all life. It is also broader than compassion, which is a sympathetic response to the suffering of sentient creatures (C 311). Empathy means identifying with other life, at least at the level of shared tendencies to survive and develop within the range of possibilities made possible by circumstances and genetic inheritance. But the identification must involve a degree of concern sufficient to develop naturally into sympathy and caring.

Is the will-to-live argument sound? Not in the sense of providing a knockdown proof. Nevertheless, the argument is far from being silly. It is provocative and relevant to contemporary environmental ethics. Here are some of the problems which need to be confronted in assessing the argument.

Contrary to premise five, not all of us experience empathy for all life-forms. What then? Schweitzer can only try to generate, intensify, and expand empathy. One way is by asking us to reflect further on similarities between our will-to-live and other organisms' instincts to survive and develop. Another way is to urge us to recall occasions when we felt moments of union and kinship with nature (of the sort listed earlier). Still another way is to use anthropomorphic metaphors to evoke empathy and sympathy.

Even if we do come to the point where we experience a "compulsion" to feel empathy with all other life, as premise six suggests, perhaps that compulsion should be resisted. Desires and feelings of obligations can be misguided. Just because they are natural does not mean that they are justified. Thus, even if premise six states a fact, there is a contestable move to the value statement in premise seven about a worthy ideal of character. The move involves an "is-ought" gap: If there is a compulsion to feel reverence for life, how does that establish that we *ought* to cultivate it, or that it is the most fundamental virtue? Still, if we do come naturally to experience a strong desire to revere life, this experience is certainly relevant to the conclusion. It bears on matters of personal identity, integrity, and fidelity to our experiences of unity with life.

Questions about personal identity return us to premises one and two: Does our will to survive and develop define us in some basic way? Schweitzer insists the most "elemental" (basic, immediate) discovery is of ourselves and other life as sharing a will-to-live whose essence is to survive and develop. He chastises Descartes for beginning with an empty abstraction: "I think, therefore I am." "To think means to think something," and the most primordial thought to emerge from introspection is that I am a will-to-live amidst other wills-to-live (O 156). Yet, introspection can only uncover what our conceptual schemas predispose us to uncover. Descartes's conceptual framework predisposed him to discover a thinking substance, whereas Schweitzer's metaphysical framework predisposed him to discern a will-to-live among other such wills. At the same time, perhaps premises one and two will survive in some form within a contemporary sociobiological framework that does not rely on Schweitzer's metaphysics.

Is premise three true? Does sincerity toward ourselves lead us to affirm our will-to-live at the "elemental" level indicated? "Sincerity" implies honesty with oneself, but it also implies being "true to oneself" and maintaining "fidelity with oneself" (C 78, 282; L 230). It implies a fundamental self-affirmation by bringing to consciousness an instinctive desire to survive and develop (O 157). The deepest level of self-affirmation does seem to be an outgrowth of instinctive will-to-live. This bedrock affirmation is not based on specific features of ourselves, nor even our general capacities as humans. If it is as primordial as Schweitzer suggests then it gives some cogency to the will-to-live argument.

The will-to-live argument omits, however, that we value ourselves and other humans for additional reasons beyond our instinctive will-to-live. We affirm ourselves at many levels, including the level of specific relationships (our interests, accomplishments, relationships, virtues, etc.) and generic properties (our general human capacities). In these respects we are not comparable to all other life, and our full worth turns on things beyond the instinctive drives we share with all life. That is relevant in understanding how to act when confronted with conflicts between our lives and others, or between killing one life to save another, topics to which I turn next.

In short, there are difficulties with the will-to-live argument, but nevertheless the argument carries some force, especially when its appeal to empathy is combined with the unity-of-life experiences mentioned earlier. It may turn out that we do discover within us an empathetic desire to identify with and care for other life, a desire that is as natural ("healthy," "sincere") and deeply rooted ("elemental") as our self-affirmation. If so, it seems likely that empathy will be a key ingredient in any nonhuman-centered ethics.[12]

3. Moral Guidance (Versus Arbitrariness)

In saying that all life deserves reverence, Schweitzer did not claim that all life has an equal value, and he was usually careful not to assert moral equality among all living things (whatever that would mean). At the same time, he consistently refused to rank the value of different species and types of life. The ethical person, he tells us, "does not ask how far this or that life deserves one's sympathy as being valuable, nor, beyond that, whether and to what degree it is capable of feeling. Life as such is sacred to him" (C 310). Yet, as Schweitzer also emphasizes, we cannot live outside nature's cycle of killing. Even to breathe or to take a walk is to kill microorganisms, and often we must save one life by destroying others. What guidance, then, does he offer about killing versus preserving life?

Schweitzer tells us we must kill only when "necessary" and that determining when killing is necessary involves "subjective" and "arbitrary" decisions (O 236, L 233). As it stands, the idea of arbitrary decisions about killing is a dead end (no pun intended). What led to this impasse?

Schweitzer offers two reasons against ranking life-forms, each of which is interesting but inconclusive (O 235). First, ranking encourages abuses and callousness, such as dismissing some forms of life, whether "primitive peoples" or endangered species, as being worthless and destroyable at whim. This is a genuine problem, but it can be resolved by exercising good moral judgment based on sound reasoning and caring. Second, he insists that ranking cannot be justified in terms of differential roles of life-forms in the universe, since we lack knowledge of any such cosmic roles. Perhaps, however, we might justify at least rough guidelines about the differential treatment of life-forms by reapplying Schweitzer's own appeals to empathy, as I will suggest in a moment.

I believe that the real reason why Schweitzer refuses to rank life-forms or offer priority rules is his metaphysics. If all organisms are a sacred part of a universal and semideified Will-to-live, then it would seem blasphemous to grade or rank them, either as individuals or as members of a species. It would also follow that killing any life is sacrilegious. If we set aside the metaphysics, are there perhaps other aspects of Schweitzer's ethics that provide some guidance about when killing is justified?

Schweitzer boldly set forth a virtue (or character) ethics before it became fashionable to do so. Now, according to long-standing objections, virtue ethics is too vague and provides insufficient guidance; it encourages subjectivity and even arbitrariness. Aristotelians offer a twofold reply. First, the virtues do provide significant guidance, especially when they are carefully sorted out and applied. Aristotle sorted the virtues according to particular areas of conduct and feeling where they function as a reasonable guide between excess and defect. Contemporary virtue ethicists have developed more subtle approaches to clarifying the meaning and application of specific virtues. Second, while rules play a role in moral conduct, they are not enough. The essential factor in difficult situations is good judgment—practical wisdom. Good judgment is a product of proper upbringing, breadth of experience, and nuanced moral sensitivity, rather than a mechanical application of rules.

Because Schweitzer does not openly follow Aristotle's lead, he is especially vulnerable to the charge of being excessively subjective or even vacuous.[13] He fails to make prominent a conception of good judgment in making decisions, and at least at first glance, he tries to reduce all virtues to one: reverence for life. In doing so his ethics may gain inspirational force, but it loses the fine-tuning of Aristotelian approaches.

In reply, we can note that the surface simplicity of Schweitzer's ethics belies an underlying complexity. He is not trying to reduce all virtues to one. Instead, like most virtue-ethicists, he seeks an organizing framework for the virtues. Ethics needs a focus in a central idea of character, since "the mere giving of a list of virtues and duties is like striking notes at random on the piano and thinking it is music" (C 105). But nor do all virtues dissolve into one grand virtue of reverence for life. On the contrary, the ideal of reverence for life yokes together (without blurring) specific virtues, including forgiveness, self-control, tolerance, justice, and especially compassion, gratitude, and sincerity with oneself (honesty with and fidelity to oneself).[14]

These virtues can and do conflict, creating familiar moral dilemmas whose resolution requires good judgment. Indeed, any one of these virtues can point in different directions. Compassion requires supporting sentient life, but it can also require ending it: "In many ways it may happen that by slavish adherence to the commandment not to kill compassion is less served than by breaking it. When the suffering of a living creature cannot be alleviated, it is more ethical to end its life by killing it mercifully than it is to stand aloof." [15] Passages like this imply a conception of good moral judgment in exercising the virtues, even though that judgment cannot be neatly encapsulated in rules.

While Schweitzer sometimes claimed that reverence for life is a comprehensive moral principle, in other places he denied it. His theory is primarily about individual rather than social ethics (C 245). Thus he could write: "My idea of reverence for life is not meant to guide the African in striving for his own and his nation's freedom. It is meant to get him to deal with more than himself in the spiritual world." [16] This is a revealing statement. Reverence for life implies a deepened respect for human rights (C 328), but understanding the complex interplay of rights in international affairs will require an exploration of more specific moral principles than his ideal of reverence for life can provide by itself. [17] Similarly, we might think of reverence for life as the primary ideal for individuals in morally relating themselves to life while acknowledging that matters of public policy concerning the environment need to involve more focused rules.

Why did Schweitzer leave so much leeway for individual interpretations in applying the ideal of reverence for life? Although he claims to have uncovered the ultimate foundation for ethics, we can view him as responding to the needs of a particular time—though a time not altogether unlike our own. Writing in the aftermath of World War I, he saw a crisis in Western civilization. The crisis was manifested in the devaluation of human life but rooted in the forces of mass society. Most people, he charged, are "lost in the mass" and prevented from working out their own convictions, whether due to overwork, overspecialization, or control by governments, corporations, and churches (C 17). To counterbalance these forces, each of us must engage in personal reflection on moral values and respect the similar efforts of others. Accordingly, an adequate ethics must be flexible, open, and tolerant. It will be individualistic and overcome traditional ethicists' "downright fear of what cannot be subjected to rules and regulations" (C 291). A creative ethics of altruism will have a "fluid indefiniteness" that embraces innumerable avenues for caring (C 166, 320).

This spirit of flexibility is attractive, but can an environmental ethic reasonably forgo all rankings of life-forms? I do not see how. Perhaps we should heed Schweitzer's advice to avoid abstract cosmological rankings, but we do and must implicitly use rankings when we make decisions about differential treatment of species in cases of conflicting interests. Indeed, Schweitzer himself sometimes implies there are good reasons for valuing organisms differentially according to the forms of life possible for them. He clearly implies that sentient creatures have a moral status unlike that of plants and nonsentient animals. He devotes special attention to arguing against killing sentient creatures for pleasure: bull fighting, cock fighting, and hunting for sport.[18] And he inveighs against misuse of sentient animals in medical experiments and in teaching science. No similar pronouncements are made about experiments on plants. Even if we avoid saying sentient animals have greater inherent worth than other animals, clearly the implication is that sentient animals make special claims on us (as do humans).

Does Schweitzer's ethical theory leave any room for making the rankings he disavows? Return to the first premise in the will-to-live argument: "I am life which wills to live, in the midst of life which wills to live." Even if we grant that the most basic form of self-affirmation is affirmation of our will-to-live, and even if we agree that at this level we share a kinship with all life, we also discover dissimilarities between our will-to-live and other organisms once we turn from introspection to inspection of the world. Depending on the organism, the dissimilarities will be striking (as with plants and lower animals) or less striking (as with higher mammals). Rarely will they justify eradication of a species (as with the polio and AIDS viruses), but they will justify the commonsense conviction that humans have greater inherent worth than algae. They will also justify cherishing chimpanzees more highly than chiton, because of the former's more sophisticated mental and social life.

Does reverence for life permit eating sentient animals or does it require vegetarianism? The refusal to make differential judgments about life-forms prevents us from grasping this question as urgent in the way that Schweitzer himself did toward the end of his life.[19] If cows and cabbage are equally sacred, why should eating one raise greater moral qualms than eating the other? Once we recognize moral differences between sentient and nonsentient life, especially as we attend to the suffering inflicted on sentient creatures in modern meat production, the issue becomes important within an ethics of reverence for life, even though that ethic does not by itself settle the issue.

Also consider Schweitzer's conduct. He helped a wounded osprey by choosing to kill a fish to feed it. Although he insisted that such choices are arbitrary, most of us see a good reason in the unique features of the osprey and in its rarity, compared to the abundance of fish. We justify special efforts to preserve endangered species, rather than treating each living organism as on par with every other. Even if we share Schweitzer's hesitation to make abstract rankings of life-forms, we can understand his stories about saving one animal by sacrificing others as parables of good judgment in "necessary" killing.

What, after all, is necessary killing? Schweitzer suggests we can kill non-human life

1. in self defense,

2. as an inevitable part of legitimate activities, such as when we crush microorganisms by going for a walk, and

3. in order to save other human lives, as when a physician kills dangerous microorganisms (C 316).

These pronouncements qualify as moral rules, however rough.[20] As such they call for justification, presumably in terms of greater value of a human life compared with dangerous microorganisms.

Rethought along these lines, Schweitzer's ideal of reverence for life remains somewhat vague (or creatively open), but hardly vacuous. After setting aside his metaphysics, we can maintain the spirit of flexibility and personal discretion in his ethics while taking into account the forms of life possible for them. Schweitzer repeatedly insisted that we must stop killing thoughtlessly, that we must think before we kill. He should have insisted that we think *well,* that we exercise good moral judgment—but he implied as much.

4. Responsibility (Without Guilt Mongering)

Contemporary ethics is preoccupied with complex moral dilemmas. Schweitzer, by contrast, was preoccupied with motivation and with finding an ethics that inspires moral commitment and enthusiasm (C 229). Reverence for life is an ideal of character that "penetrates unceasingly and in all directions a man's observation, reflection, and resolutions" in devotion to life (C 316). It is absolute in the sense that it can never be fully achieved, given that to be alive is to participate in some killing (L 232). Yet that very absoluteness evokes a higher moral pitch in everyday emotion and conduct.

This emphasis on high moral aspiration was distorted by his occasional preoccupation with guilt. I am guilty, he says, each time I kill any living thing, no matter what my motive: "Whenever I in any way sacrifice or injure life, I am not within the sphere of the ethical, but I become guilty, whether it be egoistically guilty for the sake of maintaining my own existence or welfare, or unegoistically guilty for the sake of maintaining a greater number of other existences or their welfare" (C 325). For Schweitzer, then, "necessary" killing does not mean justified killing. Nor does it mean killing which is wrong but excusable, so as to remove guilt. To kill is to be culpable. We are "murderers" when we kill a mosquito and "mass murderers" when we kill bacteria (C 316–17).

These are extraordinary claims! Admittedly, they have a certain authenticity insofar as they flow from Schweitzer's metaphysics.[21] If each organism is sacred, then killing it is tantamount to desecrating the sacred, rendering one guilty. But the consistency is one thing; cogency is another. Schweitzer's metaphysics is a recipe for guilt mongering, which is my final reason for setting it aside.

Does setting the metaphysics aside diminish the high demands contained in reverence for life? There is some danger, of course, that the demands may be too great. Schweitzer placed enormous pressure on himself and seemed to find his feelings of guilt a helpful source of motivation.[22] Most people, however, would be crushed by comparable feelings of guilt.

Surely we can respond to a call for greater responsibility for life without being drawn into excessive guilt. In its core meaning, responsibility means trying to act responsibly and being morally accountable, that is, susceptible to being called to account for our conduct in terms of good moral reasons.[23] When those reasons are sound and sufficient, killing is justified and (at least often) no guilt is involved. In particular, there is no guilt—none whatsoever—when a physician like Schweitzer killed bacteria by sterilizing surgical instruments or when patients take antibiotics. Nor is there guilt when we eat vegetables and nonsentient animals (leaving aside the controversy over eating sentient animals).

That does not mean that we should never feel bad when we justifiably participate in killing. *Regret* is often appropriate. Regret is the appropriate emotion when we reasonably wish we did not have to take a life, in contrast with guilt for unjustified killing. Regret can be mild or intense, and it can be accompanied by strong feelings of sadness, grief, and even horror. (Think of euthanizing a beloved pet whose suffering from cancer can no longer be lessened in other ways.) In addition to being focused on specific acts of killing, regret can be a general response to our immersion in the cycle of killing.

If we reassert common sense in justifying "necessary" killing, have we abandoned the spirit of reverence for life? Surely not. Reverence for life includes reverence for our own lives, as manifested in justifiable self-defense. Understandably and admirably, Schweitzer wanted to avoid an ethic of expediency in which human concerns automatically override the interests of other life-forms. But in doing so he established a misleading dichotomy between "ethical and necessary," such that taking life is unethical even when necessary to protect other life (C 325). This dichotomy is inconsistent with his own insistence that the ethical includes reverence for oneself as manifested in self-defense and self-development. It is also inconsistent with his belief that devotion to other life sometimes requires killing for its sake. To be consistent, Schweitzer should say that the ethical includes necessary killing, not contrasts with it.

To conclude, Schweitzer's metaphysical vision contributed to the boldness with which he set forth a biocentric ethics over a half a century before most philosophers began to struggle with his issues. That metaphysics distorts some of his central ideas, and the key elements in his ethics survive intact after his metaphysics is set aside. Those elements include unity of life, empathy for other living organisms based on shared instincts, a flexible, virtue-guided perspective focused in a (complex) ideal of reverence for life, and responsible commitment to furthering life while being sensitive to differences among life forms.[24]

CHAPTER 13

Jainism and Ethics

Ronald M. Huntington

Ronald Huntington, former professor of religion at Chapman University and codirector of the Chapman University Albert Schweitzer Institute, was preparing a textbook on world religions at the time of his death. A chapter of the textbook was to introduce Jainism and the ethical principle of ahimsa as a way of life. On account of the probable influence of Jainism upon Schweitzer and his ethic of reverence for life, the essay prepared by Huntington is published here. This chapter may also function as an introduction to the more detailed study of Schweitzer and Jainism in Ara Paul Barsam's essay, which follows.

At the beginning of the twentieth century Lord Curzon, the British viceroy of India, estimated that half the mercantile wealth of India passed through the hands of Jains. The statement is remarkable when we consider that less than .5 percent of Indians profess this little-known religion. It is even more remarkable to discover such apparent worldly success in a community whose doctrines advocate a more thoroughgoing asceticism than those of any other religion. Mahatma Gandhi was born in a part of India where Jainism is widespread and admitted that he was strongly influenced by its followers. Perhaps we may find a clue here to Gandhi's paradoxical life of practical political involvement coupled with an equally intense saintly detachment. We may also find a clue here to the form of the ethic of Albert Schweitzer, who studied the Jains as he was developing his ethic of reverence for life.

Jainism is sometimes presented as one of the two great "heresies" from Hinduism, along with Buddhism. While in the strict sense this is not wholly inaccurate, since Jainism does not acknowledge the authority of the Vedas, it is better to emphasize its numerous similarities with Hinduism than to posit it as a kind of rebellion against it. If it were not for the altogether obscure beginnings of the Jain religion, which may precede Hinduism in some of its concepts, we might even characterize it as a reformation movement within the parent religion.

The Pathfinders

Jains regard their religion, like the universe, as having existed eternally—without ultimate beginning or ending. Like a giant cosmic respiration process extending over inconceivably lengthy eons, the universe has its alternating cycles of moral decline and ascent. If one pictures a clock with the twelve representing the peak of ethical achievement and the six being the lowest ebb, Jains would place our present age at the number five.

As goodness declines, so also is there a need for religion to be restored periodically. Thus in each ascending and each descending cycle twenty-four humans are born whose work is to remind the world once more by their lives and teaching of the forgotten truth and the life of goodness. Such a figure is called a *jina,* a victor or conqueror, and a Jain is therefore a follower or "son" of the one who has achieved victory over the ceaseless round of universal history. More vivid is the synonymous term *tirthankara,* which literally means "ford-finder." This comes from a time when India, vivisected by rivers, was without bridges, and it was often necessary to explore for hundreds of miles in order to find a shallow spot to cross. The *tirthankara* is one who has discovered for all humans the place to ford the stream—the stream of unending striving, suffering, and reincarnation.

In our particular cycle the last of the twenty-four *tirthankaras* was Mahavira, an elder contemporary of the Buddha. Born in the sixth century B.C.E., both men entered an age in which there was a need for religious revitalization among the masses. Hinduism had increasingly become a matter of complex sacrificial offerings and rituals under the control of the Brahmin priesthood or, under the influence of the Upanishads, an inward withdrawal into a world of meditation and rarefied metaphysics. With such fertile ground for the growth of a new religion, it is not surprising that Buddhism began at such a time nor that Mahavira was until recently regarded as the founder of Jainism by those outside the faith. Now it is recognized that the preceding *tirthankara,* Parshva, was also a historical figure who lived some 250 years earlier. While there is nothing to prove that Parshva was the real founder of Jainism, we may be forgiven some skepticism about the historicity of earlier *tirthankaras* in view of the fabulous life spans and physical dimensions attributed to them by Jain tradition.

Older Than Methuselah

According to a twelfth-century Jain account Arishtanemi, the twenty-second *tirthankara,* lived eighty-four thousand years before Parshva, was sixty feet tall, and died at the age of one thousand years. Compared to Rishabha, the first *tirthankara* of this cycle, Arishtanemi must be regarded as something of a dwarf who died in infancy, for Rishabha was no less than three thousand feet tall and lived for more than seventy trillion years! Comparable claims, though varying greatly in degree, are found in most of the world's religions. Needless to say, many Jains take such astronomical figures no more seriously than many Jews, Christians, and Muslims faced with the lesser but still incredible ages of patriarchs such as Methuselah, Noah, Abraham, and others.

It is not enough to dismiss these assertions as the idle fantasies of naïve minds. Although they defy any ultimate historical verification (or absolute disproof!), the appropriate questions to ask concern why such claims were made and what worldview underlies them. The headwaters from which flow the answers to these questions are the two general themes of the meaning of death and the meaning of history.

The ancient assumption is still widespread that there is a connection between morality and longevity. The perverse proverb that "the good die young" has never gained acceptance, despite its shallow utility when a specific instance temporarily disturbs our more deeply held—and more desirable—view. Death, the ultimate disease of humankind, is a punishment for some failure, and conversely, old age is a valued reward. From this point the rivers of explanation run a variety of courses, depending on the definition of "the good" and the intellectual sophistication of an age or culture. A long life may be held to be the result of acceptable sacrifices to the gods, obedience to divine commands, vegetarianism, jogging, or the pursuit of wisdom. The list is suggestive, not exhaustive, for each modern centenarian improvises some response to the reporter's inevitable question.

If we add to this the frequently encountered belief that the stream of history has run a downward course from some remote golden age, the conclusion is inescapable that people lived longer in "the good old days." The determinants of the actual ages assigned to the legendary heroes vary. Numbers regarded as symbolically auspicious in a given culture have their influence. Semihistorical reminiscences may compress an entire tribe, clan, or dynasty into a single person. And these in turn must be fitted into or stretched over a comprehensive scheme of world history—eras, dispensations, ages, or cycles that are themselves often determined by number symbolism. Finally, the desire of each religion to demonstrate its own value by testifying to its antiquity cannot be overlooked.

The primary point remains: this type of exaggeration is an affirmation of the greatness of past saints. There is no correlative need to minimize people of the present, unless originality is carelessly defined as utter novelty instead of in its basic sense of "returning to the source." Once people become conscious of a historical process they seek to comprehend it by means of orderly patterns. They call these systems discoveries, revelations, superstitions, insights, or deductions, according to their explanations of the origins of the ideas. And the value of these systems lies not in their historical veracity but in their ability to embrace and enhance present life and meaning.

Mahavira

It is tempting to examine the outward events in the life of a great person in an attempt to understand inner development, much as one hopes to find in an account of Franz Schubert's family, friends, and poverty some clue to the *Unfinished Symphony*. This can be deceptively misleading in the case of Schubert and downright impossible with Parshva and Mahavira. Even if all the biographical data were available, the single important thing about the *tirthankaras* is their victory, which transcends all accidents of time and place.

A biography points out differences, whereas the pathfinders are all the same. As if to underscore this, the Jain sculptures of the twenty-four *tirthankaras* in any temple are identical but for a small identifying emblem on the base; for example, a lion signifies Mahavira. This is merely an aid to the unlettered worshiper, just as the caption under a picture enables the reader to identify the subject. Such emblems are used in many religions; one thinks immediately of the representations of St. Mark with his identifying lion on European churches, especially in Venice, where he is the patron saint.

Recognizing the relative unimportance of the external details of Mahavira's life, we may summarize them very briefly. He was born near the center of early Indian civilization in the Ganges Valley, not far from where the Buddha gained his enlightenment. His parents, as tradition affirms of all twenty-four *tirthankaras,* were of the Kshatriya or warrior-ruler caste, not of the Brahmins. This has given rise to inconclusive speculations as to whether Jainism and Buddhism (which was also founded by a Kshatriya) were attempts to restore that caste to its former preeminent position. He was given the name Vardhamana ("the increasing one"), but nothing is known of the future *tirthankara's* childhood and youth. Apparently he married and had a daughter prior to the death of his parents when he was thirty. At that time he received permission from his older brother to become a mendicant. Plucking his hair out in five handfuls—traditional practice only required shaving the head—the young man spent the next twelve years "self-exiled from the universal farce of the force of life," in Heinrich Zimmer's apt phrase. After the first thirteen months he discarded what minimal clothing he had worn, equally avoiding shade in the torrid Indian summer and shelter in the chill of winter. At the end of the dozen years he reached his goal of *kaivalya,* described below. Mahavira taught for thirty years after that time and, again like the Buddha, he used the common vernacular of the area rather than the classical Sanskrit of the Brahmins. When he died at the age of seventy-two as a result of voluntary self-starvation, the record claims over half a million lay and monastic followers of Mahavira's doctrine. Although there is reason to regard this figure as inflated, the more interesting detail in view of later sectarian development is that women comprised more than half the total.

Kaivalya

There have already been indications in Mahavira's life story of an uncompromising severity. We may therefore expect to find a certain coldness in Jain characterizations of the ultimate state, at least as seen from the unenlightened perspective. Since these descriptions vary from those given by Hinduism we shall adopt a different term for the Jain goal, although this does not imply any necessary distinction in the experience itself. The scriptures of the two religions tend to use *moksha, kaivalya,* and several other terms interchangeably.

Kaivalya is literally solitude, isolation, the state of not being connected with anything else. In contrast to some forms of Hinduism and Buddhism, the common sense of the Jains led them to affirm the real existence of the world around them, including their own bodies. The Hindu concept of *maya,* that the world of our experience is in some sense less than real, was entirely rejected. That same Jain common sense refused to equate the world with Atman/Brahman or any other unifying principle. This universe is not only there; it is there in all its multiplicity. Jainism demanded neither denial nor deification of the world, but detachment from it. Existence is not an evil in itself, and *kaivalya* does not imply cessation of it.

The absolute self-sufficiency of the *tirthankara* is the result of an intentional withdrawal from the world, physically as well as psychologically, into a state of total imperturbability. On a lower level, most of us have had the experience at times of becoming so engrossed by our thoughts that we failed to notice noises, smells, visual distractions, and even physical discomforts. One aspect of *kaivalya* is simply this shutting off of the senses that relate us to our outer environment. But there is another level of perceptions that is completely inward, including our awareness of hunger, thirst, and other physical and mental satisfactions and longings. This level must also be shut off. What then is left? What is that which exists in utter isolation and enjoys the perfect self-sufficiency that is *kaivalya?* The Jain answer is the individual, perfected *jiva,* and we must inquire into the meaning of that term before summarizing the concept of *kaivalya.*

The Living and the Dead

Among orthodox Hindu philosophies, Jainism resembles Sankhya and Yoga in the way it divides the universe into two basic types of substances, which the Jains call *jiva* and *ajiva*. *Jiva* means "alive" and *ajiva* means "not alive." Each category contains an infinite number of atomlike parts, eternally existing and eternally separate. Every discrete object in the entire universe is inhabited by a single *jiva,* the essence of which is consciousness. *Hylozoism,* the belief that everything is alive, has been advocated by various philosophers, and the term is applicable to Jainism if the distinction between "everything is alive" and "everything is inhabited by life" is not overlooked. To clarify the Jain view, let us ask some questions that quickly arose in debates with Hindu and Buddhist philosophers. Where does the *jiva* dwell in an object? What happens to this *jiva* when, for example, a clay pot is dropped and shatters into many pieces? Is there a difference between the *jivas* inhabiting, for instance, a clay pot, an ant, and a human being? And lastly, how does the *jiva* become imprisoned in a mass of nonliving matter (*ajiva*) in the first place?

Jains respond that the *jiva* cannot be localized in any part of an object but permeates it entirely, just as the light from a lamp fills a room. Although the clay was in its entirety the abode of a single *jiva,* the moment it is broken other *jivas* immediately occupy each fragment. This argument necessitates two additional assertions about the nature of the *jiva.* First, it is capable of expansion and contraction, instantly adapting to the size of its home. Second, remembering that the number of *jivas* is infinite, it follows that there are *jivas* that are not embodied in this world. They are still a part of the cosmic process of evolution and transmigration, however, and may simply arrive here as a result of becoming disembodied in one of the numerous higher or lower worlds than ours. Indeed this ascent and descent of *jivas* is the tide of the universal life-process, continuous and everlasting. The Jain shares with the Hindu the assumption that heavenly beings—including gods—and the denizens of the several hells are all subject to the universal laws of karma and reincarnation. The gods are to be regarded as *jivas* wearing temporarily favorable masks, but they are in need of liberation or *kaivalya* no less than other beings and must eventually be reborn in human form to achieve that goal.

Jivas are classified according to the number of sense organs they possess. For example, a plant's *jiva* has only the sense of touch, while an animal's *jiva* possesses all five of the normal senses. The human animal shares with the gods and certain hellish beings an additional inner sense organ called *manas* or mind, by means of which we are able to think rationally. With the final question as to how the *jiva* becomes imprisoned in a body, we come to the unique Jain conception of karma.

Karma

As in Hinduism, karma is the law of cause and effect applied to the moral realm. But while the Hindu is content to state that karma is the abstract valency resulting from activity, and that it determines one's future birth, the Jain tendency to see reality in concrete terms leads to defining karma as a subtle form of *ajiva,* that is, a material substance having color and weight. Just as gold is found in alloyed form in mines, so *jivas* are found in varying degrees of karmic bondage. Although the *jiva* is by nature transparently lucid, karma particles flow into it through its sense organs. By the glue of desire or distaste, they attach themselves to the *jiva,* clouding, obscuring, and coloring its innate consciousness and also weighing it down.

Depending on the amount of karma attached to it, each *jiva* has a "specific gravity" and rises or falls in the universe, conceived in the form of a giant cosmic person. According to Jain belief, the world in which we now live is located at the waist level of this cosmic being. All actions create new karma, but ethical activities produce karma that is more quickly sloughed off. The process of living burns up karmic substance but also attracts fresh supplies, and this conflagration continues until we realize that abstention is necessary from action of every type. Even virtue is a fetter, and one must cultivate perfect nonactivity in thought, speech, and deed. Once the *jiva* has been relieved of every gram of karmic ballast, its natural buoyancy causes it to float to the very top of the universe, where it remains eternally diaphanous and omniscient, an "independent bubble that enjoys solitary effervescence," basking forever in its own self-effulgence.

Summary of *Kaivalya*

We have now come full circle back to the Jain concept of *kaivalya*. By comparing it with Hindu thought, we can see clearly the similarities and differences.

First, like Hindu *moksha, kaivalya* is not the product of good deeds, thoughts, or intentions, but results from the absence of all karma, good or bad. Second, while the conquest of karma for the Hindu is essentially a psychological process, for the Jain it is in the broadest sense a physiological endeavor. The Hindu Atman is a passive observer behind the scenes, unaffected by karma and eternally free if the person would only recognize it. The Jain *jiva* is actively involved and changed by the accumulation of karma that fastens it to the cycle of rebirth. Separation of the *jiva* from lifeless matter (*ajiva*) is not a change of consciousness to overcome illusions or delusions, but a gradual and difficult process of disentanglement worked out in real time and real space, in an actual historical process in a real world. Third, unlike the Hindu Atman, the freed *jiva* does not recognize any unity with some larger cosmic reality but maintains a separate existence at the summit of the universe. Having no sense organs, it is marked by an omniscience that results from direct awareness rather than sensory input. The *jiva* in the state of *kaivalya* can be pictured as a sphere with mirrored surfaces on the outside and on the inside. Impermeable but radiant from the outside and utterly self-sufficient and blissful inwardly, it is like a self-contained universe that neither influences nor is influenced by anything outside itself.

It remains to be said that the Jain is fully aware that the process of achieving *kaivalya* is a difficult one. The last person to attain it is believed to have died sixty-four years after Mahavira, and it is expressly admitted that some *jivas* will transmigrate for all eternity. There is a cause for optimism, however. Jainism rejected all ideas of fatalism and held that the sole prerequisite for *kaivalya* was birth in human form. "Pluck the fruit of human birth," says one Jain scripture, urging us not to take this life lightly. Now we see through a glass darkly—literally!—but the process of cleansing that glass is in our power and could begin immediately.

What to Do Before Doing Nothing

Up to this point we have intentionally emphasized the unequivocal demands placed on the Jain by his idea of perfection. The primarily physical world-model of Jainism, in contrast to the nonmaterial concept of reality in Hinduism, tended to deemphasize psychological factors. Although not denying the importance of thought processes, Jainism tied the concept of karma much more to the deed than to the intention motivating the deed. For example, Jains and Buddhists are both vegetarians, but the Jain automatically accumulates bad karma if he accidentally eats meat from his begging bowl; this is not true of the Buddhist. It takes only a little reflection to realize that there is a fundamental truth in the Jain position. However good my intentions may be in helping another motorist to change a flat tire, they are of little practical value if the car slips off the jack. Despite its lack of explicit psychologizing, Jainism must have had an intuitive awareness that humans are prone to rationalize their actions to themselves and to put those actions in the best possible light. It has continually shown itself unwilling to allow its followers this false comfort. Like its Indian compatriots Hinduism and Buddhism, Jainism has regarded the conquest of self-delusion as absolutely essential to religious progress.

The ultimate ethic of Jainism, as we have seen, is abstention from all activity, since actions of any type produce karma. That this abstinence extends even to eating is evident from Mahavira's self-starvation. Although that practice is still regarded with approval by the Jains (and it might be argued that the concept of human dignity dictates not only the right to live but the right to choose not to live), it is hedged by many restrictions. Obviously it is foolish to take one's own life without first being purified from all karma, since that would simply bring about another incarnation. With this in mind, however, starvation is allowed if the person is thoroughly ready for another life by reason of decrepitude, incurable illness, or a physical or mental condition making the performance of duties impossible. A healthy body is to be guarded from disease, but a hopelessly unhealthy one is to be rejected as one discards a worn-out garment that is beyond repair. The contemporary controversy over euthanasia (mercy killing) would arouse little debate in the Jain community.

Earlier we referred to ethical activities producing karma that is more easily cast off, and this implies that there are intermediate steps to the ultimate goal. These steps are the practical ethics of Jainism. Much of the territory covered by Jain ethics is familiar, whether from the Bhagavad Gita, the Ten Commandments, or the Analects of Confucius. Jain Yogic practices are not essentially different from those of Hinduism and Buddhism. The distinctiveness of Jainism is found rather in those elements of traditional morality that are singled out for special emphasis, and in particular the cornerstone of Jain ethics, *ahimsa*.

Ahimsa

Of the conditions governing earthly existence, none is more tragic to contemplate than one stated bluntly in the Bhagavata Purana, a Hindu text: "Life is the life of life." In its starkest form, this means that in order to remain alive each of us must daily impose the death penalty on other living things, or at least serve as an accomplice in premeditated murder. Putting it another way, this inevitable and unceasing slaughter proclaims an ethic of power pressed into the service of a consciously or unconsciously egotistical judgment that the life of the victim is less worthy of continuance than that of the slayer. The major portion of Mahavira's teaching, and of all Jain ethics, is concerned with this grim and sobering fact.

Ahimsa, noninjury, is the first of the five vows required of a Jain monk, and the other four are considered by Jain commentators merely as details of the first. All life is sacred to the Jain, and intentional or unintentional harm done to any living thing produces bad karma. Recalling that every object is inhabited by a *jiva,* we see that Jainism expands Albert Schweitzer's concept of reverence for life into reverence for the entire universe. *Ahimsa* also has affinities with Gandhi's nonviolent campaigns of *satyagraha* (truth-force), in which injury to others was strictly forbidden, even at the expense of one's own life. There are similarities too with the writings of St. Francis of Assisi. Yet no other religion has stressed the pivotal importance of this principle of noninjury as consistently and broadly as has Jainism. Certainly the rape of the environment, so long a part of Western civilization and only recently beginning to be recognized as a problem of tremendous magnitude, would have been unthinkable in a Jain society.

It would be entirely wrong, however, to see *ahimsa* in any sentimental light. The Jain doctrine of noninjury is based on rational consciousness, not emotional compassion, and on individual responsibility, not on a social fellow feeling. Hindu monism could regard injury to others as injury to oneself; the Jain held that there were innumerable separate *jivas* and therefore could not use the Hindu rationale. The motive in Jainism is self-centered and entirely for the purpose of individual *kaivalya*. And yet, though the emphasis is on personal liberation, the Jain ethic makes that goal attainable only through consideration for others.

Except for those who have gained *kaivalya,* the perfect practice of *ahimsa* is obviously impossible. Jainism is eminently practical in its dictates in this regard, yet unwilling to compromise further than is absolutely necessary. Hinduism was normally content to symbolize its reverence for all life by its treatment of the cow. Jains rejected this kind of symbolic allegiance to a principle as too easy a method of placating one's conscience.

Ahimsa in Practice

Three groups of distinctions governed the application of the principle of noninjury in daily life. First, the Jains distinguished between lay members of the community and the ascetics, and recognized different gradations among the latter. The lines are not rigidly drawn, however. Lay members of the Jain community have always been considered members of the ascetic order, and many engage in a periodic temporary retreat as monks or nuns. The traditional twelve vows of the Jain householder are essentially the same as the five vows of the monk, differing only in the vigor of observance that is expected. Moderation is the keynote for householders, and severity for ascetics. There is a single ethical code for all, and the ascetic life is a continuation of the householder's life, without new rules being imposed. Although the monks exert religious control over laity, the latter are given the right to excommunicate a monk who is deemed to have fallen below the standards established by the entire community. This close relationship between monk and layman is undoubtedly one of the important factors in the survival of Jainism in India. Buddhism, which tended to regard laity merely as patrons of the order of monks and established no organic connection between the two, virtually disappeared from the land of its origin.

Second, Jains distinguished between four types of injury—accidental, occupational, protective, and intentional. Protective injury is that which results, for example, when a hungry wolf is shot in a crowded chicken yard. Lay Jains are required to abstain entirely from intentional injury and, as far as possible, from accidental injury. All four types are forbidden to the monk. A widespread misconception needs to be corrected concerning occupational injury. Despite the inevitable destruction of life involved in such vocations as agriculture and soldiery, they are not forbidden to the Jain. More than half the Jains in southern India are engaged in farming, and the profession is mentioned without disapproval in Jain scriptures. Jains can also be, and some are, warriors. We may recall that all of the *tirthankaras* were of the warrior-ruler caste. It remains true nonetheless that many Jains have eschewed occupations that unavoidably entail injury, and this accounts for the disproportionate number who have entered banking, commerce, and other mercantile trades.

The third set of distinctions concerns the classification of *jivas* according to the number of senses they posses, as mentioned earlier. The karma produced is directly related to the number of senses of the injured *jiva*. Injury to plants therefore has less serious karmic consequences than injury to animals. The laity tries especially not to injure any *jivas* of two or more senses, that is, the moving ones. Vegetarianism is universal in the Jain community, but because of the danger of injury to insects, even such vegetables as potatoes, onions, garlic, carrots, and radishes are avoided.

The manifestations of this concern for life are legion among Jains. No furs, plumes, or silks are worn. Leather is kept to a minimum and must in any event be from naturally dead animals. Food is eaten during the day, since there is too much danger of injuring insects in cooking at night. The Jain will not use an open light nor leave a container of liquid uncovered, lest a stray insect be destroyed; even with this precaution, liquids are always strained before use. Monks and often some lay members will wear a cloth over their mouths to avoid accidental injury to insect life, and for the same reason a soft broom is used to sweep the path in front of one's feet. Nor will a Jain step on any plant if it can be avoided. Foot travel is severely curtailed during the rainy season, following Mahavira's example, because of the increased insect population during those four months. The preoccupation with *ahimsa* is further exemplified by a Jain hospital for stray or disabled birds in Delhi and a rest house for old or diseased animals in Bombay. In these and other sanctuaries, creatures are kept and fed until they die a natural death.

I have listed some of the ways in which Jains have sought to apply in their daily lives Mahavira's appeal not to interfere in the lives of others. It would be wrong, however, to conclude that *ahimsa* only prohibited physical violence. An early Jain text says, "With the three means of punishment—thoughts, words, deeds—you shall not injure living beings." Lying is defined by the Jain, for example, as speaking hurtful words. And noninjury must also be referred to oneself. Passions and desires cause self-injury, and proper practice of *ahimsa* includes not maiming oneself in overly extreme asceticism.

Jainism's all-encompassing ethical principle can be summarized as follows: Do your duty, and do it as humanely as you can—not just toward other Jains nor even all humankind, but toward the entire world.

Perhaps, Maybe, or Somehow

The evolution of Jain doctrines was a product in no small measure of dialogues with Hindu, Buddhist, and other thinkers. There is evidence that Mahavira himself engaged in such debates, defending and refining his insights. While the considerable contributions of the Jains in philosophy, and especially logic, are more properly the philosopher's domain, one aspect of Jain logic requires the attention of students of religion. That is the concept of multiple viewpoints, an idea surprisingly anticipatory of modern theories of relativity. To grasp the Jain view, a bit of background is necessary.

Hindu thought on the ultimate reality of the universe tended toward rather static conceptions. Insofar as Brahman and Atman were described at all, terms such as *absolute being, pure existence, unchanging,* and *eternal* were used. Buddhism's approach, in contrast, was to deny any permanency whatsoever in a world visualized as continually changing. Early Buddhist philosophy denied the existence of an Atman behind the world process that Hindus were inclined to describe as *maya,* delusion. What the Hindu regarded as delusion, the Buddhist took as reality, and vice versa. The following chart will help clarify these two distinct and exclusive ways of thinking:

Hindu reality	Buddhist reality
static	dynamic
changeless	changing
eternal	temporal
space categories	time categories
being	becoming
the "One"	the "Many"
universal	particular

The modern philosopher Alfred North Whitehead wrote, "In the inescapable flux, there is something that abides; in the overwhelming permanence, there is an element that escapes into flux."[1] The necessity for philosophical self-consistency led Hinduism to make an absolute of the "something that abides," the "overwhelming permanence"; Buddhism for its part tended to absolutize the "flux" or change. It is as if the former described a river in terms of its water and banks, while the latter focused on its flow.

To counter the proponents of these diametrically opposed positions, Jains developed a position knows as *syadvada,* the way or path of "perhaps, maybe, or somehow." *Syadvada* states simply that judgments resting on different points of view may differ without any of them being wholly wrong. In a world where human beings are limited by space and time, where the eyes that look toward the north cannot simultaneously see the south, where the person who stands in Istanbul cannot at the same time be in Montreal, where finally we know that the airplane pilot of the twentieth century cannot concurrently be driving a chariot in the early Roman Empire, all judgments must necessarily reflect a particular viewpoint. A limited and incomplete judgment is called a *naya,* and all human knowledge is a compilation of *nayas,* judgments resulting from different attitudes. The Jains were thus able to accept equally the Hindu views of "being" and the Buddhist views of "becoming," but took neither in a way that their partisan advocates desired or found comforting.

Western thought has increasingly emphasized the importance of the "standpoint of the observer" in the post-Einstein era. We now realize that since the earth, sun, and stars are all in motion, the point of stability is merely a matter of definition. We have learned that the Ptolemaic or geocentric view of the universe—that the sun revolves around the earth—and the Copernican or heliocentric view—that the earth revolves around the sun—are both human constructs. We need not decide ultimately between the wave theory of light and the particle theory, nor between a system of numbers founded on the decimal system or some other base. Each alternative can provide a frame of reference (a *naya*) for further judgments and practical use and is in that sense true. But each contains an element of falsehood in assuming that a fixed point of reference exists in reality, whereas the fixed point is purely a definition.

The Jain doctrine of *syadvada* is nonabsolutist and stands firmly against all dogmatisms, even including any assertion that Jainism is *the* right religious path. Like Bernini's pillared colonnade in front of St. Peter's Basilica in Rome, *syadvada* reaches out to embrace all viewpoints (*nayas*) as containers of truth—and error—depending on the observer. Obviously Jainism does not resort to religious conversion, for it is both noncritical and noncompetitive in relation to other religions.

Although the phrase "the Middle Way" is traditionally applied to Buddhism, it is clear that in their concept of *syadvada* the Jains also have a claim to that title. Perhaps, maybe, or somehow the truth may be discerned in the most contradictory assertions in this world of infinite complexity.

A Divided Community

After what has been said about *syadvada,* it may be surprising to find that Jainism split into two major sects and has been subject to continued divisions and subdivisions over scriptural interpretation and minor elements of religious practice. Yet this is perhaps inevitable in a religion that, though a small minority in India, is so widely distributed geographically, and that at the same time seeks to structure every detail of life.

The historical origins of the great schism are obscure. It is possible that Mahavira already had followers representing two different views that pre-dated his teaching. But one probable tradition ascribes the rift to a time of famine at the beginning of the Maurya Empire in the late fourth century B.C.E., when members of the Jain community migrated from their original home in the Ganges Valley to South India. Upon their return after the lengthy absence, they discovered that certain practices had changed among those who had remained behind. It is certain at least that the division was complete by the end of the first century C.E., and it has persisted to the present, with each group maintaining that it preserves the fundamental teachings of Jainism.

The names of the sects capture their primary difference: the Digambara or "sky-clad," and the Svetambara or "white-clothed." The former group places strong emphasis on not owning any personal property, and hence its monks and when possible its lay members are to clothe themselves only in the sky, that is, practice nudity. Other differences seem relatively minor to the outsider, and there are practically none about the basic creed of Jainism. For example, the Digambaras hold that the perfected Jain lives without food and that no woman can reach *kaivalya*. The Svetambaras disagree and in turn advance two doctrines rejected by the Digambaras. First, Svetambaras claim that Mahavira was conceived in the womb of a Brahmin woman and the embryo was then transferred divinely to the wife of a Kshatriya. Second, the Svetambaras are the source of the tradition that Mahavira was married and had a daughter. Probably because of their view on women attaining *kaivalya,* Digambara texts do not mention this. Both sects agree that the original scriptures of Jainism, called the fourteen Purvas, were gradually lost. Digam-baras assert that a secondary level of scripture, the eleven Angas, also disap-peared, but Svetambaras claim to have these books; they are the basic Svetambara scriptures. The Digambara canon is much less well defined, un-doubtedly because of the Digambara's concentration on ascetic practices and owning nothing.

The probable influence of the Islamic conquest of India is to be seen in the formation of the Sthanakavasi sect in the eighteenth century. The Muslim religion strictly forbids the use of images for worship. The Sthanakavasi reformers declared that statues of the *tirthankaras* were idolatrous and condemned the ornateness of the Jain temples and rituals. They continue today as a subdivision of the Svetambara sect, holding their religious meetings in puritanically severe buildings (*sthanakas*), from which the sect name was derived.

While all Jain sects would admit that nudity is necessary for *kaivalya,* even Digambara monks will wear clothes in public nowadays, justifying their practice as a concession to the human frailty in these degenerate times. Indeed, it is customarily required that the Digambara laity wear at least two pieces of cloth for all religious ceremonies. Among Svetambaras, the monk is no longer a homeless wanderer except in theory, and even Digambara monks remain stationary during the monsoon season in imitation of Mahavira and to avoid injury to the swarms of living things during that period.

Caste

As far as documentary evidence allows us to conclude, Parshva and Mahavira did not advocate a doctrine of caste, but they appear to have recognized four classes of people, basing the division on activities rather than birth. The development of caste in the Jain community has occurred mainly in the past thousand years and can be seen as (1) a natural extension of the hierarchical belief in *jivas* of varying numbers of senses, (2) a product of the seemingly universal human need for social status and prestige, and (3) most important, the influence of the Hindu social structure on a minority group living in its midst. Much more than among Hindus, caste is a social rather than a religious institution for Jains. But if the Jain religion as such does not acknowledge caste distinctions, neither has it obstructed their growth and practice.

Lists of the proverbial eighty-four Jain castes differ, but they show that the names were derived mainly from places of origin, not occupations. Occupational subcastes were developed within this larger scheme. The majority of Jains consider themselves Vaisyas, and there are practically no Jain Sudras. Until the fourteenth century there were no food barriers, but complex prohibitions now govern intercaste dining and marriages, though not as rigidly as in Hinduism. Exact parallels to the Hindu four castes are found among Jains in South India, and heredity plays the major role in determining caste.

The Current Scene

We may well wonder whether a religion of less than two million members, and gradually decreasing in proportion to the total Indian population, can afford the luxury of caste and sect divisions. More than half the Jain castes have fewer than five hundred members, and there are many bachelors not of choice but of necessity, due both to caste restrictions and to a general Indian tradition against widow remarriage. The latter is further aggravated by the very early marriage of young girls, increasing the probability of widowhood. Since Jain theory holds that no one will attain *kaivalya* in the present age, it may seem rather futile to quibble over whether clothing or one's sex makes a significant difference in reaching that goal.

Despite calls for unity from those who clearly perceived the problems, conferences to revitalize Jainism at the beginning of this century did not cross sectarian boundaries. Although as a result of those conferences there has been a profusion of new organizations and social services—hospitals, schools, colleges, newspapers, libraries, educational and research scholarships, and rest houses for people and other animals—these have tended to foster separatist tendencies rather than to overcome them. Human labors and financial resources continue to be spent on duplicating temples and community institutions for specific sects or castes. Liberal organizations such as the Jain Young Men's Association and the Jain Widow Remarriage Association, both of which sought to transcend secretarian divisions, have thus far had little impact on the Jain community as a whole. Especially since the beginning of this century, many Jains regard themselves and are regarded by others as Hindus, though there are recent indications that some Jains are countering this tendency with a new pride in their religion.

It is true nevertheless that the number of Jains continues to dwindle slowly to the present day. Lest this be seen in the wrong perspective, however, we need to remember that the size of their religion is not of great concern to most Jains. Their worldview has consistently held that Jainism would decline and eventually die out completely—to be reborn again in the history's next ascending cycle.

Worship Without Divinity

There are few religious shrines in the entire world that can compare in ornateness, lavishness, and astonishing splendor with the finest Jain temples, whether we speak of the white marble structures on Mount Abu or the sacred city of more than 850 temples at Shatrunjaya, both located in the state of Gujarat in western India. At these and other sacred sites, wealthy Jain families have spared no money or effort in erecting shrines worthy of their religious heritage. And yet if we inquire into the function of these temples, we find ourselves in a seeming quandary.

Let us summarize initially what Jain worship cannot be, in the light of what has already been presented about the religion. First, it should go without saying that there are no animal sacrifices, in view of the centrality of *ahimsa*. Moreover, inasmuch as the *tirthankaras* have achieved *kaivalya* and are therefore not in contact with the world, they cannot respond to worship, prayers, or sacrifices. Nor can anyone or anything else. Each of the infinite number of *jivas* in the universe is pursuing its own evolution, a path of self-help unaided by any divine being. The concept of a god or gods above this process is wholly superfluous to the Jain world, and there is, strictly speaking, no room for devotional practices (*bhakti*). Finally, there are no real congregational rituals among Jains, although there are periodic festivals and sometimes personal occasions to which others may be invited.

The function of ritual worship in Jainism has been well stated by Jagmanderlal Jaini: "Faith brings us to truth; philosophy makes us grasp it; ethics makes us practice it; and ritual makes us one with it."[2] For convenience, we will consider Jain rituals under two main headings: regular observances at the temples, and periodic observances, such as festivals, fasts, pilgrimages, and rites for special individual occasions. In both categories, the outward forms resemble Hinduism, and on the popular level it is probable that even the motives and inner meanings do not differ significantly from Hindu worship.

Temple Worship

As a general rule, the Jain layman goes to his local temple every morning, usually accompanied by his wife. Formal worship consists of anointing the statues of the *tirthankaras* with colored paints. A temple attendant follows behind with a pail of water and a cloth to cleanse the images, for it is the act of the worshiper that creates good karma or merit, not its subsequent fate. The action is performed not for the *tirthankara,* but for the worshiper. The statue, like a mirror, is not affected by the one looking at it. The alabaster figures are temporarily colored, just as the *jiva* is colored by its karma, but the cleansing reveals once again their inner luminosity as a reminder to the worshiper of his ultimate religious goal.

In contrast to Hinduism, it may be seen that the priest has no necessary role in Jain temple worship. Since the object of Jain worship is self-transformation rather than to obtain the favor of any divine being, there is no rationale for the development of complex rites of propitiation or appeasement. The growth of a professional priesthood was further hampered by an early Svetambara doctrine that no Jain should earn a living from his religion. The preservation of the religion was left to the monks, whose single duty other than seeking *kaivalya* was to preach, to instruct, and to explain the doctrines of Jainism to the laity.

About seven centuries ago, however, Jain worship began to assimilate many characteristics from Hinduism, possibly as a result of the need for survival in the face of a common religious foe, Islam. Jains whose former role had been merely to take care of the images in Digambara temples gradually came to assume a priestly function. In Svetambara temples, Hindu Brahmins were employed as priests, and we must recall that, as in Hinduism, the priest is a technician who is versed in the proper forms and rituals, not necessarily a religious person himself. With the coming of Hindu priests came the introduction of worship of Hindu gods and goddesses for minor boons, the offering of flowers and food to the *tirthankaras,* and the addition of caste and family deities. There is no scriptural support for these practices, of course, and they are ultimately inconsistent with Jain beliefs. But although they have been the targets of criticism by some reformers, these rites continue to permeate Svetambara Jainism and have reached to a lesser extent even into the conservative Digambara sect.

Periodic Observances

As Jainism came under Hindu influence, the mythology and heroes of the latter were transformed and adapted to conform to Jain principles, and Hindu festivals were reinterpreted. For example Divali, the popular Hindu festival of lights in the late autumn, was explained as a commemoration of the death of Mahavira, whose disciples lighted lamps when "the light" had departed from the world. Various ceremonies to mark significant moments in life, from conception to becoming a *tirthankara,* are largely modeled after comparable Hindu rituals. It appears that early Jainism was wholly unconcerned with such "rites of passage," but Digambara Jains today list fifty-three different occasions for such observances. Pilgrimages confer great merit as in Hinduism, and more than one hundred places are considered worthy of visitation by Digambara Jains. Few of these pilgrim goals are for both main sects, and the Svetambaras have their own list, comparable in size. A pilgrimage to certain holy places entitles the Jain to adopt a special pilgrimage surname as in Islam, where the pilgrim to Mecca may from that time on add the title "Hajji" (pilgrim) to his name.

Insofar as Jainism differs today from Hinduism in its periodic observances, these distinctions center around voluntary fasting, the practice of total *ahimsa.* Theoretically the layman should enter a monastery and abstain from all food on each full moon and new moon day. While few now observe the full rite, it is still customary in our time for the layman to fast as a monk at least once a year, and many Jains of all sects undertake ten to twelve days of fasting in their homes every month. The most auspicious dates for fasting differ between sects, being determined by the priests in their role as astrologers.

The Jain New Year, falling in late July or August, is the occasion for a widely observed fast of monks and laity together, lasting eight days for Svetambaras and fifteen for Digambaras. It is preeminently a time for penance, confession, and renewal, and in that sense resembles the ten-day period in

Judaism leading from the Jewish New Year's Day to Yom Kippur, the day of atonement. Among Jains, the New Year fast is marked by repaying debts and asking forgiveness of others—Jains, non-Jains, and even animals—for short-comings during the preceding year.

A recent sociological survey of the Jain community suggests that the practice of fasting may be decreasing among the laity, although the limited sample used in the study does not justify a firm conclusion.[3] It still remains true that the feasting and revelry associated with holy days in other religions are conspicuously absent from Jainism.

Conclusion

Like Buddhism, Jainism is a religion of purely human origin. Its teachings revolve around a fundamental injunction to avoid harm to all living things, traced strangely enough to a group of founders who came from the warrior caste. Throughout its long history Jainism has shown itself capable of adaptation when absolutely essential but has tenaciously held to its core doctrines. In fact its very refusal to change or compromise has in no small way contributed to its survival in a land where the waxing and waning of religious movements has been a recurrent phenomenon. Jain religious, commercial, and intellectual contributions to India are far out of proportion to this religion's small and still diminishing numbers.

If one main purpose of religion is to keep the "is" and the "ought to be" in a tight tension, Jainism has been very successful. That tension is basically the responsibility of each individual Jain, but neither monk nor layperson has been afforded any comfort by the religion if the balance is tipped too far from the ideal toward the practical. Perfection for the Jain is not an abstract concept, but a state of being toward which every moment of every life should be a single step.

Albert Schweitzer, Jainism, and Reverence for Life

Ara Paul Barsam

Ara Paul Barsam is a Schweitzer scholar from Oxford University who has been en-
gaged as an ethicist in peacemaking in Armenia. Here Barsam addresses a theme that
is not often discussed but is of great importance for our understanding of reverence for
life: the Jain concept of ahimsa *and its probable impact upon Schweitzer. In this care-*
fully argued essay Barsam observes that Schweitzer was influenced by a variety of
ideas and individuals, but "his rapport with Jainism and ahimsa *helped him to artic-*
ulate and discern the meaning of 'reverence.' "

Although several scholars have attempted to analyze the content of Albert Schweitzer's work, few have commented on the sources of his
ethical innovation. In 1952, a doctoral student at Harvard University wrote
to Schweitzer in Lambaréné and asked him to comment on the major influences on his work. Schweitzer's initial response is vague: "I have never taken
into account just what philosophy has had special influence upon me."[1]
Later in the letter, however, he responds, "I felt, even at the age of eighteen,
that Schopenhauer's [work] under the influence of Indian thought . . . was
an event for me."[2] Schweitzer concludes, "Forgive me for not complying
with your wishes. . . . You will have to find the answer to your question in
the works I have written."[3]

A close examination of Schweitzer's thought on Indian religions provides many clues that help to answer the question to which the doctoral student directed his letter. This paper argues that Schweitzer's thought, and

207

specifically his development of reverence for life, was possibly influenced by Indian religious thought and, in particular, the Jain principle of *ahimsa* (non-violence, noninjury).[4]

This essay is divided into seven sections. Part 1 presents an overview of Schweitzer's formative childhood experiences with animals. Part 2 offers an account of his early exposure to and interest in Indian ethical thought. Analysis of his "ethical mysticism" is presented in part 3, as well as a discussion of how his study of Jainism possibly fortified the foundation of reverence for life. Part 4 provides an overview of Jainism and the historical development of *ahimsa*. Part 5 explores Schweitzer's analysis of Jainism and *ahimsa* and some of the connections between Schweitzerian and Jain ethics. Part 6 examines his notion of the "will-to-live" and the Jain concept of the *jiva* (soul). Part 7 comments on Schweitzer's comparative method.

1. Indications of Reverence for Life in Schweitzer's Childhood and Youth

Schweitzer's sensitivity to suffering is evident from an early age. In *Memoirs of Childhood and Youth,* an autobiographical essay of his first nineteen years in Upper Alsace, he gives numerous indications of the sympathy he felt for other forms of life, especially for the animal world. He relates how he "never really knew light-hearted youthful enjoyment of life."[5] He was invariably disturbed by the pain he found present in the life around him:

> As far back as I can remember, I have suffered because of the misery I saw in the world. . . . What especially saddened me was that the poor animals had to suffer so much pain and misery. The sight of a limping old horse being dragged to the slaughterhouse in Colmar by one man while another beat it with a stick haunted me for weeks.[6]

Puzzled by the lack of consideration given to animals in his traditional nightly prayers, Schweitzer did not forget to pray for nonhuman creatures:

> Already before I started school it seemed quite incomprehensible to me that my evening prayers were supposed to be limited to human beings.

Therefore, when my mother had prayed with me and kissed me good-night, I secretly added another prayer which I had made up myself for all living beings. It went like this: "Dear God, protect and bless all beings that breathe, keep all evil from them, and let them sleep in peace."[7]

Shortly after he began his schooling, one event apparently made a deep impression:

Heinrich Bräsch and I had made ourselves rubber band slingshots with which we could shoot small pebbles. One spring Sunday during Lent he said to me, "Come on, let's go up to Rebberg and shoot birds." I hated this idea, but I did not contradict him for fear he might laugh at me. We approached a leafless tree in which birds, apparently unafraid of us, were singing sweetly in the morning air. Crouching like an Indian hunter, my friend put a pebble in his slingshot and took aim. Obeying his look of command, I did the same with terrible pangs of conscience and vowing to myself to miss. At that very moment the church bells began to ring out into the sunshine, mingling their chimes with the songs of the birds. It was the warning bell, half an hour before the main bell ringing. For me, it was a voice from heaven. I put the slingshot aside, shooed the birds away so that they were safe from my friend, and ran home. Ever since then, when the bells of Passiontide ring out into the sunshine and the naked trees, I remember, deeply moved and grateful, how on that day they rang into my heart the command "Thou shalt not kill."[8]

Schweitzer summarized the moral lesson of his experience as follows: "The way in which the commandment not to kill and torture worked on me is the great experience of my childhood and youth. Next to it, all others pale."[9]

Memoirs of Childhood and Youth offers several other accounts of Schweitzer's interaction with animals in his early years. On at least one occasion, he writes of his "being deeply stirred by the suffering in the world around us" as "the great experience of [his] life."[10] These events led to one of his strongest convictions:

> From such experiences, which moved my heart and often put me to shame, there slowly arose in me the unshakable conviction that we may inflict death and suffering on another living being only when there is an inescapable necessity for it and that we must all feel the horror of thoughtlessly killing and causing pain. This conviction has driven me ever more powerfully. I have become more and more certain that in the depths of our hearts we all feel this.[11]

This conviction, writes biographer George Seaver, led "him to give up shooting and fishing while in his teens; the captivity of wild animals in a menagerie was a horror to him second only to the training of domestic animals for an exhibition, and the sight of thirsty frightened cattle cramped together in a jolting railway truck was a nightmare."[12]

In these accounts of his childhood, the reader is presented with Schweitzer's own selected history. It is chronologically noteworthy that in the spring of 1923 he had completed the first two volumes of *The Philosophy of Civilization*. While traveling across Switzerland that same summer, he used a two-hour train stopover to visit his friend, the prominent Zurich psychologist and pastor Dr. Oscar Pfister. Pfister "urged me to tell him some incidents of my childhood just as they would come into my mind," as the psychologist wanted to publish them in a young people's magazine.[13] Later, Pfister sent him the shorthand notes he had taken during those two hours. But Schweitzer requested that they not be published as is; he wished for the notes to be left with him to edit and complete. Shortly before his departure for his second stay in Africa in 1924, he finished editing the reflections of his childhood and youth.

Inasmuch as Schweitzer was cognizant of Pfister's plans to publish the memoirs, it is possible that he (intentionally or unintentionally) recounted those memories that were most in accord with his mature self. At the very least, it is evident that he edited the text such that many of his reflections take on a heavy didactic form. This sermonic undertone was most likely employed in order to evince an emotional response in the youthful readers whom he anticipated to be his audience. Written almost immediately after *The Philosophy of Civilization,* his childhood memoirs supplement his ethical reflections directed to a younger audience often in the form of moral parables. It is hard to judge, then, whether these are Schweitzer's genuine reflections or whether they possibly reflect a later understanding of reverence for life.

It is important to emphasize that these experiences were not "plain narrative" but rather were remembered stories. However, the unfolding of reverence for life may be reasonably viewed as linked to what may be seen as some formative mystical-ethical experiences in his early life. His childhood experiences with animal suffering may have provided him with a basis from which to search other religions and philosophies for an ethic that supported these intuitions. Indeed, after his introduction to Indian thought, it is evident that Schweitzer extends his understanding of the moral to include concern not just for animals but for all living beings.

2. Previous Research

Previous efforts to trace the intellectual origins of Schweitzer's thought focus strictly on the possible influences from Western thought. Eastern religious thought and ethics, despite his substantial writing on the subjects, have been largely ignored.

Numerous scholars have rightly suggested that the ideas and terminology of both Immanuel Kant and Arthur Schopenhauer are present in his philosophical works. More boldly, in an attempt to discover the roots of Schweitzer's notion of reverence, Charles Joy, in his introduction to Schweitzer's essays on Goethe, claims that the term "reverence for life" stems from Goethe's *Wilhelm Meister*:[14] "Somehow what Goethe had written and taught must have become so integral a part of Schweitzer's subliminal self that he failed to recognize in the words that came to him [reverence for life] on the mount the accents of Goethe's voice."[15]

At one point in *Wilhelm Meister*, three older men remark to young Wilhelm, "One thing there is which no child brings into the world with him; and yet it is on this one thing that all depends for making man in every point a man. If you can discover it yourself, speak it out." After much reflection, Wilhelm shakes his head and asks what it is. The three men then exclaim, "Reverence!" Wilhelm pauses. "Reverence!" the three men declare again: "All want it, perhaps you yourself."[16] The men continue to explicate this threefold reverence: reverence for that which is above us, around us, and below us. The last type of reverence is not isolated, but rather calls one to stand forth and revere that which is beneath the earth and nourishes us.

Schweitzer, however, calls one to revere not only that which sustains us from below, but also all beings in the universe. The fundamental feature of his reverence is its boundlessness; it includes all life. Whereas Goethe thinks of reverence for the earth that nourishes us, Schweitzer understands it to include "the mosquito that stings us, the snake that bites us, and the bacterium that kills us."[17] He understands the problems that such a boundless ethic presents but still maintains a limitless reverence.

Joy concludes that to "say that Schweitzer's idea of reverence for life came originally from *Wilhelm Meister,* although Schweitzer himself has forgotten the spring from which he drank, is not, however, to depreciate his originality."[18] Though Schweitzer and Goethe shared philosophical views, Schweitzer's vision is broader. He develops the notion of reverence into an ethic, for which there is no evidence in Goethe's work. Although Joy may be correct in highlighting the connections between Goethe's term "reverence" in *Wilhelm Meister* and in Schweitzer's reverence for life, influences upon the content of his ethical system can be shown to stem from his early knowledge of Indian thought and his enduring study of *ahimsa*.

Background and Timing

In 1900, at the age of twenty-five, Schweitzer set himself the grandiose task of analyzing many of the major religions and great philosophies of the world as well as the writings of various mystics. The vast majority of this work was published in 1923 in *The Decay and Restoration of Civilization* and *Civilization and Ethics,* parts 1 and 2 of *The Philosophy of Civilization.* In these two volumes, he rejects many past efforts in Western philosophy to posit ethical foundations in civilization and advances his own ethic of reverence for life. This ethic, he believes, is the means to realizing mystical union with "infinite Being"[19] while simultaneously engaging actively and ethically in the world; it is an "ethical mysticism."

Schweitzer intended to follow the two parts of *The Philosophy of Civilization* with two other volumes, *The World-View of Reverence for Life* and *Civ-*

ilized State.[20] In the third volume, he initially wanted to devote a chapter to his studies of Eastern religions, philosophies, and mystics. However, his exploration of these three forms of thought continued for more than three decades, and the resulting manuscripts exceeded the confines of a single chapter. Although Schweitzer does not explain how existing mystical or ethical doctrines directly influenced the development of reverence for life, several neglected manuscripts from his third volume show that he undertook major studies of Indian ethics and mysticism at least two decades before (and still while) he was writing *The Philosophy of Civilization.* These manuscripts, published as *Indian Thought and Its Development,* reveal his praise and rejection of various aspects of Indian religions and provide a key to understanding one possible influence on reverence for life.

"What I like about Indian ethics," writes Schweitzer, "is that it is concerned with the behavior of a human being to all living beings and not merely with his attitude to his fellow humans and to human society."[21] Inasmuch as reverence for life appears to be the closest Western analogue to the Jain principle of *ahimsa,* it is of little surprise that he heralds the development of "the commandment not to kill and not to injure as one of the greatest events in the spiritual history of mankind."[22] However, reverence for life not only resembles the principle of *ahimsa,* but it also partly developed out of and in reaction to Schweitzer's study of the Jain principle of nonviolence now present in various forms in several Eastern religions. His adulation here is not to be taken as offhand praise or an isolated remark, but rather as a signaling of an intellectual influence.

Early Influence of Indian Thought on Schweitzer

How did Schweitzer's awareness of Indian religions first develop? In the preface to *Indian Thought and Its Development,* he writes, "Indian thought has greatly attracted me since in my youth I first became acquainted with it through reading the works of Arthur Schopenhauer."[23] At the Mulhouse Gymnasium his favorite teacher was Wilhelm Deecke, "an enthusiastic follower" and a former student of Schopenhauer. Three months before Schweitzer died, he wrote to the Asiatic Society in Calcutta, India:

I studied Indian philosophy early on, when I was attending the University of Strasbourg, Alsace, even though no course was being given on that subject. But then, around 1900, Europe started getting acquainted with Indian thought. Rabindranath Tagore[24] became known as the great living Indian thinker. When I grew conversant with his teachings, they made a deep impact on me. In Germany it was the philosopher Arthur Schopenhauer who first recognized the significance of Indian thinking. A pupil of Schopenhauer's was director of the Mulhouse Secondary School in Alsace, which prepared students for the university. His name was Deecke. In this way I got to know Indian thinking at an early date. And by the time I completed my doctoral examination in philosophy, I was familiar with Indian thought. By then I was teaching at the University of Strasbourg. Focusing as I did on the problem of ethics, I reached the conclusion that Indian ethics is correct in demanding kindness and mercy not only toward human beings but [also] toward all living creatures. Now the world is gradually realizing that compassion for living creatures is part of true ethics.[25]

This correspondence is significant for at least three reasons. First, written just a few months before Schweitzer's death at the age of ninety, the timing of the letter offers a mature account of the influence of Indian thought from his youth onward. He did not come to Indian ethics only as support for his earlier childhood "ethical mysticism," but rather was introduced to new ethical principles and extended his moral considerations.

Second, Schweitzer realizes that his own ethical conclusions follow the same path as "Indian ethics" in its incorporation of all living beings within the realm of moral consideration. In a later correspondence with Prime Minister Lal Bahadur Shastri, he acknowledges again that "my ideas are known in India and are consistent with Indian ideas."[26] He recognizes that he is reaching many of the same conclusions that had been reached previously by some Indian religions. Long before he articulated reverence for life, Schweitzer was convinced of the import of a "boundless" ethic and was cognizant of its origins outside his own thought. Concern for "all living beings," he acknowledges, has "existed for Indian thought for more than two thousand years"[27] and is "first clearly expressed by Jainism"[28] in the ethic of *ahimsa*.

Third, as similarly evidenced in other writings on the topic, this letter highlights how his approach to Indian religions and ethical thinking merits criticism for its frequent undifferentiated use of the terms "Indian thought," "Indian ethics," "Indian religions," and the "philosophy of the Indians." Like many other Western scholars of that time, he often used these terms to refer to Jainism, Buddhism, Hinduism, and other Indian religions without adequately distinguishing their varied beliefs and practices. His application of such terminology suggests in some sense a monolithic conception of the diverse religious and ethical beliefs and practices. Despite the fact that his text on Indian religions underscores the differences and developments of thought between various Indian religions, his utilization of such general terms causes confusion in determining to which Indian religion he is referring.

At first reading, Schweitzer's use of such general terms appears to allow for little in-depth analysis on the influence of a specific Indian religion. However, close examination of his text in conjunction with an inquiry of Indian religious thought is more illuminating. For instance, when Schweitzer states "I reached the conclusion that Indian ethics is correct in demanding kindness and mercy not only toward human beings but toward all living creatures," he is not referring to "Indian ethics" in general but more specifically to the ethic of *ahimsa*. He is not concerned with the Brahman ethic of ritual sacrifice, which he rejects as "unethical," but instead is referring to the Jain principle of *ahimsa,* which promotes nonviolence to all living beings. It is possible that in his letter to the Asiatic Society and in many other writings, he wanted to display the widest possible affinity between reverence for life and the ethics of other Indian religions and, therefore, grouped them together as one entity.

In another passage on his appreciation of *ahimsa* (already cited), Schweitzer again refers to it under the heading of "Indian ethics":"What he likes about "Indian ethics" is its concern with "the behavior of a human being to all living beings and not merely with his attitude to his fellow humans and to human society."[29] This quotation reemphasizes both his interest in "Indian thought" because of its ethical concern with all living beings and his misleading use of the terms "Indian thought" and "Indian ethics." Though the ethic of *ahimsa* is present in various forms in several Indian religions, it is clear from Schweitzer's own examination of Indian religions that he understood concern for "all living beings" to be most closely associated with the Jain principle of *ahimsa*. His lack of attention to detail appears intentional, and not to stem entirely from lack of knowledge:

The deliberate brevity of my treatise may give occasion to all kinds of misunderstanding. I had no intention of describing Indian philosophy in detail, but only wanted to show how it regards the great problems of life and how it undertakes to solve them. To bring this as clearly as possible into the light of day I drew my sketch with broad, firm lines. This is why anybody who is at home in Indian thought will miss so many details which in his eyes belong to the ideas and thoughts concerned and specially characterize and color them.[30]

Despite Schweitzer's acknowledgment that his intentional exclusion of detail may result in "all kinds of misunderstanding," he nonetheless proceeds in this fashion.

3. Schweitzer's "Ethical Mysticism"

Schweitzer's term "ethical mysticism" encapsulates his belief that the moral and the spiritual are inextricably linked. "Mysticism," he states, "must never be thought to exist for its own sake. It is not a flower, but only the calyx of a flower. Ethics is the flower."[31] Mysticism puts one "on the road of inwardness, but not on that of a viable ethic."[32] Schweitzer reduces the purpose of mysticism to its capacity to engender higher ethical awareness in realizing its own end of spiritual union with the Divine.

He understands mysticism usually to refer to an experience of inwardness without correlation to the external world and the concerns of other life. By contrast, the goal of *"ethical* mysticism" is to enable humans to be engaged actively in the world around them and thereby attain spiritual union with "infinite Being." Ethical mysticism implies an active relationship between the human person and other life; through interaction with other life, union with the Divine is afforded. Schweitzer believes that an ethical mysticism eliminates the problems of passivity traditionally associated with mystics. Schweitzer's description of mysticism and its connection to ethical activity has been the source of confusion. Although some of his writings have a mystical style, they do not primarily provide descriptive reports of individual experiences, as do most other mystical writings. His writings include reflections on the role of mysticism in society and ethics that transcend the concerns of the personal mystical experience.

Schweitzer introduces an important distinction between different forms of mysticism, which was maintained throughout his life. He rejects pantheistic or monistic identification between humans and God. Ethical mysticism endorses union with the Divine but not direct identification. There is still an "I-thou" relationship, however close those two may be; mystical union means both unification and differentiation. Monism implies the loss of consciousness and involves a fusion of the individual, without distinction or qualification, with the Divine. The "great danger," he states, is that of making such identification "an end in itself." [33] This passivity does not satisfy Schweitzer inasmuch as "ethical existence," not passive harmony with the Divine, is seen as "the highest manifestation of spirituality." [34] For him, mysticism "is valuable only in proportion as it is ethical." [35] It is "valuable" insofar as it involves ethical activity. He rejects quietism, that is, all forms of spirituality that do not result in action. It is through participation in the community of life, not strictly in contemplation, that one connects to the Divine:

> It is only through the manifestations of Being, and only through those with which I enter into relations, that my being has any intercourse with infinite Being. The devotion of my being to infinite Being means devotion of my being to all the manifestations of Being which need my devotion, and to which I am able to devote myself.
>
> Only an infinitely small part of infinite Being comes within my range. . . . But by devoting myself to that which comes within my sphere of influence and needs me, I make spiritual, inward devotion to infinite Being a reality. [36]

The manifestations of Being, or infinite Will-to-live, are the various wills-to-live (lives) in the natural world. This passage highlights Schweitzer's dogmatic view that union with the infinite Will-to-live occurs only by assisting other wills-to-live. His is a mysticism of action, or what he calls "practical mysticism." He does not give mysticism a theory of intellectual realization, but of praxis. By virtue of its active concern for other life, ethical mysticism leads one to its Creator. This threefold, interdependent relationship among humans, life, and Creator introduces a distinction in Schweitzer's understanding of mysticism. He departs from mysticism as traditionally understood; it is mysticism not only to a heightened spiritual end but also to a higher ethical purpose.

The Will-to-Live

Schweitzer's ethical mysticism emerges out of reflection upon the "will-to-live" (*Willen zum Leben*).[37] He states, "The essential thing to realize about ethics is that it is the very manifestation of our will-to-live."[38] The notion of the "will-to-live" is central to reverence for life, as his mysticism is one of the "will."

His specific use of the "will" is derived from Schopenhauer, the principal advocate of the German voluntarist philosophical school, who first articulated the phrase in *The World as Will and Idea* (1819).[39] For Schopenhauer, ethical activity should be founded upon an intuition, "the will," "whose most immediate manifestation is the whole organic life."[40] Schopenhauer, who adapted Kant's noumenal/phenomenal distinction,[41] claimed that we are aware of ourselves in two distinct ways: in the cognitive fashion through which we come to know external things, as well as "from within," which may be described as the "will," or more accurately as "will-to-live."[42]

Schweitzer lauds Schopenhauer as the first person to acknowledge "the essence of things in themselves, which is to be accepted as underlying all phenomena," as will-to-live.[43] Whereas Kant denied that the "thing-in-itself" was knowable, Schweitzer believed that the thing-in-itself was the "will-to-live" and readily ascertainable through the physiological makeup of animate phenomena.[44] Since the basis of one's own self is experienced as will-to-live, Schweitzer believes the basis of all animate phenomena in the world, by analogy with himself, similarly to be will-to-live.[45]

Schweitzer's metaphysics begins with the supposition that despite the diversity of individual things in the natural world, they all manifest the same inner essence. From a comprehension of oneself (the microcosm), one is able to acquire knowledge of the world (the macrocosm); the key to understanding the world is self-understanding. His argument largely rests on whether knowledge that originates from inner experience of the will-to-live is more reliable than knowledge derived from empirical examination of the outer, physical world. The nonempirical quality of the will-to-live as the core self is a presupposition of his work.

Life-View and Worldview

Lee Ellerbrock wrote that the word *Lebensanschauung,* commonly translated as "life-view" or "view of life," implies the subjective perspective of an individual as to "what his life means to him and what purpose he wishes to give his life." [46]

Weltanschauung, usually translated as "worldview," or even more broadly as "theory of the universe," is used by Schweitzer to refer to the universe and all that it comprises. More specifically, *Weltanschauung* is the aggregate of thoughts that an individual holds about the nature and purpose of the universe as well as the role of humankind within it.

Worldview normally encompasses life-view, as one's understanding of the cosmos largely determines a conception of human life and personal existence. Schweitzer maintains that "so long as it was possible to cherish the illusion that the two [worldview and life-view] were harmonious and each completed the other, there was nothing to be said against the combination." [47] He believes that Western moral philosophy has made a crucial error in its attempt to arrive at a life-view through its understanding of the world:

> To understand the meaning of the whole—and that is what a worldview demands!—is for us an impossibility.
>
> I believe I am the first among Western thinkers who has ventured to recognize this crushing result of knowledge. . . . Resignation as to knowledge of the world is for me not an irretrievable plunge into a skepticism which leaves us to drift about in life like a derelict vessel. . . . A worldview which fails to start from resignation in regard to knowledge is artificial and a mere fabrication, for it rests upon an inadmissible interpretation of the universe. [48]

Instead, he claims that one's worldview should stem from a prior life-view:

> The last fact which knowledge can discover is that the world is a manifes-
> tation . . . of the universal will-to-live.[49]
>
> Our relation to the world as it is given in the positive certainty of our
> will-to-live, when this seeks to comprehend itself in thought: that is our
> world-view. Worldview is a product of life-view, not vice-versa.[50]

Our conception of life and the world, Schweitzer holds, should be composed of those convictions given in our will-to-live. He maintains a pessimism about matters of knowledge that prevents him from locating a
comprehension of the universe alongside a wholly affirmative attitude to
life. He wants to found a *Weltanschauung* on optimism, that is, on an affirmative attitude toward life.

Schweitzer maintains that Western thought has failed to develop a
strong foundation for ethics because of its assumption that world- and life-
affirmation must be logically deduced from knowledge about the world.
From this assumption it followed that "an intelligent purposive meaning
must be attributed to the universe as a whole before the meaningfulness of
human life can be established."[51] The predator-prey relations in the natural
world prevent him from locating a basis for ethics in the workings of the
world; he is resolute that there is little or no discernible moral purpose in
nature:

> Nature knows no reverence for life. It produces life in thousands of the
> most meaningful ways and destroys it in thousands of the most senseless
> ways. . . . Creatures live at the cost of the lives of other creatures. Nature
> allows them to commit the most terrible cruelties. Nature is beautiful and
> sublime, viewed from the outside. But to read in its book is horrible. And
> its cruelty is so senseless![52]

And:

> The world is a ghastly drama of the will-to-live divided against itself. One
> existence makes its way at the cost of another. . . . The solution is not to
> try to get rid of dualism from the world, but to realize that it can no longer
> do us harm. This is possible, if we leave behind us all the artifices and un-
> veracities of thought and bow to the fact that, as we cannot harmonize our

life-view and our worldview, we must make up our minds to put the former above the latter. *The volition which is given in our will-to-live reaches beyond our knowledge of the world. What is decisive for our life-view is not our knowledge of the world but the certainty of the volition which is given in our will-to-live.*[53]

Schweitzer views the world as parasitic, full of death and apparent cruelty. For him, creation is at best "ambiguous": in the words of Andrew Linzey, "it seems to affirm and deny God at the same time."[54] Outside us, the will-to-live manifests itself as a creative-destructive force, leaving the physical world absent of a morally affirmative telos. For this reason, Schweitzer maintains that in order to develop a system of thought upon which to found ethics, our worldview must not be based on the workings of the natural world. Since an ethical principle cannot be discerned in the world processes, one cannot base a *Lebensanschauung* (a life-view and ethical reflection) on a *Weltanschauung* (a worldview and theory of the universe). It follows that ethics should stem from our life-view, which is born out of the affirmation of the will-to-live. For Schweitzer, one's experience inwardly as will-to-live transcends that which one sees outwardly in the world.

He rejects the possibility of total knowledge of the workings of the world. Rather, one has to acquire a "knowing ignorance" (*docta ignorantia*), an "enlightened ignorance," which "admits how absolutely mysterious and unfathomable the world and life are."[55] The enlightened mind's first move should be an act of resignation: it abandons its desire for complete understanding about the universe or God from what the world reveals to us. Skepticism about absolute knowledge of the world need not produce cynicism, as an optimistic-ethical attitude to "life" (life-affirmation) is not dependent on an optimistic-ethical interpretation of the world.

The certainty with which Schweitzer speaks of the individual finding a "noble and valuable" life-view through the will-to-live leads one to believe that he does not recognize the boldness of his conviction. However, as he finds the will-to-live to be the most immediate and highest knowledge available to the individual, it is to him the soundest foundation for an ethical system. His theory of ethical optimism is not verifiable but is a postulate or demand of the will-to-live that claims for itself knowledge independent of empirical sources.

Affirmation and Negation Philosophy

Schweitzer distinguishes Indian and European thought largely on the basis of world- and life-affirmation and world- and life-negation philosophies. For Schweitzer, world- and life-affirmation consists of this:"that a person regards existence as he experiences it in himself and as it has developed in the world as something of value *per se.*"[56] World- and life-negation, conversely, consists of "a person regarding existence as he experiences it in himself and as it is developed in the world as something meaningless and sorrowful, and he resolves accordingly (*a*) to bring life to a standstill in himself by mortifying his will-to-live, and (*b*) to renounce all activity which aims at improvement of the conditions of this world."[57] Neither of these two world- and life-views is established by circumstances in the outer, physical world. Rather, each is founded upon an understanding of the inner determination of the will.

Affirming the will-to-live, "life-affirmation," is "natural" because it corresponds with the instinctive will-to-live in each of us that "urges" to maintain life. For Schweitzer, the human body and all living beings instinctively affirm life by virtue of the fact that they *will* to stay alive. With every beat of the heart, there is a (subconscious) affirmation of life within us, what he considered to be an "instinctive will-to-live" or an "instinctive reverence" for one's own life. The will-to-live, by virtue of the fact that it strives to maintain life, is an affirmation of life. By consciously affirming life, humans act in accord with the inner will-to-live and "confirm an instinct" by repeating it in their "conscious thought."

From Schweitzer's perspective, world- and life-negation philosophies largely developed through the rise of Jainism and Buddhism. From the onset, both religions emphasized the doctrine of reincarnation and karma. "It was only when the idea of reincarnation began to interest the masses," he explains, "and when fear of constantly returning to existence began to rule people's minds, that there arose the great movement towards renunciation of the world which then continued for centuries."[58] Liberation from the cycle of rebirths (*samsara*), that is, the attainment of *moksha* or *nirvana*, can be accomplished through freedom from the physical world and from the will-to-live.

World- and life-negation is problematic to Schweitzer for many reasons. Most specifically, our inner will, the will-to-*live*, affords us the highest knowledge of both ourselves and, by analogy, the world. When we ask what sort of knowledge we acquire from our will, only the optimistic, "life-affirming" attitude emerges as a logical response for him. He stands in opposition to Schopenhauer's conviction that "everything which helps to deaden the will-to-live is good" and maintains that life is intrinsically good and is to be promoted. To turn the will-to-live into will-*not-to-live* would involve a self-contradiction; unless one decides on a self-chosen death,[59] he or she would be forced to make constant concessions to the will-to-live in order to stay alive:

> To remain alive, even in the most miserable fashion, presupposes some activity conducive to the maintenance of life. Even the hermit, who is most strict of all people in his world- and life-negation, cannot escape from that. He picks berries, goes to the spring, fills his drinking-cup, perhaps even washes himself now and then.
>
> Passing from concessions to concessions, which have to be made if those who live the worldview of world- and life-negation are to remain alive, the decision is reached that what really matters is not so much actual abstention from action as that people should act in a spirit of non-activity and in inner freedom from the world so that action may lose all significance. In order not to be obliged to confess to themselves how much of world- and life-negation is abandoned, they have recourse to a method of regarding things which savors of relativity.[60]

World- and life-negation is deemed untenable. In order to maintain basic physical existence, one is forced to make "concessions" to the body's will-to-live and, therefore, to life-affirmation.[61] Schweitzer holds any "concession" to remain alive (that is, eating or drinking) is inconsistent with life-negation. The notion that individuals follow life-negation in a spirit of nonattachment, and not in a literal manner of total nonmovement, is also dismissed as relativistic.

Schweitzer's understanding of affirmation and negation philosophy is to some extent based on an oversimplified polarization between Western and Indian religious worldviews. Such notions represent ideal types. In his scheme, world- and life-affirmation promotes social service and meaning-fulness of life, while world- and life-negation takes little interest in the world and exalts immobility. As Radhakrishnan comments in *Eastern Religions and Western Thought,* "to divide peoples into those who will not accept the world at all and those who will accept nothing else is hardly fair."[62] Schweitzer presents a caricature of an Indian mystic lost in contemplation and with lit-tle interest in the world, while his or her Western counterpart is actively en-gaged in the world and in fruitful union with the Divine.

Interreligious dialogue was in its early stages at the time when Schweitzer lived. His study of Indian religions poses many methodological questions that highlight the shortcomings of his research. As far as we know, Schweitzer never saw Indian religious life in practice. He never ac-quired a personal knowledge of Indian religions and did not study them from within each tradition through their own adherents.[63] He did not read Sanskrit, and, at the time of his writing, there were few Indian texts trans-lated into German and little critical research available on such subjects. Often those works that were accessible reflected many of the same preju-dices about Indian thought that Schweitzer held. Also, since his text on In-dian thought lacks footnotes, it is difficult to trace his sources beyond a few authors mentioned in passing.[64] These issues raise the question as to what historical, philosophical, or theological knowledge of Indian religions he held when comparing them to his beliefs. His criticisms are those of an outsider and are not always factual.

Schweitzer's approach to other religions is less factually descriptive than it is typological and evaluative, in particular with regard to his ethical in-quiry. The primary interest of his text on Indian thought is an examination of the extent to which various Indian ethical doctrines are in accord with his own ethic of reverence for life. Schweitzer inappropriately uses his *own* ethic and his *own* world- and life-view as the basis from which to evaluate other religious and ethical thought. He is partial to those notions that are in accord with his own views and often dismissive of alternative ideas.

Ethics and Worldview

Schweitzer's notion of "life-affirmation" concerns the intrinsic value of life. His "ethical" world- and life-affirmation has an added component that elevates it beyond an endorsement of mere existence. This entails active participation to help all life-forms in the world to thrive.[65] He writes, "Ethics demands of someone that he should interest himself in the world and in what goes on in it; and, what is more, simply compels him to action."[66] Since the "world" encompasses all life-forms, ethical world-affirmation refers to an individual's self-devotion to both human and nonhuman life alike.

In Indian thought, which at various times has displayed elements of world- and life-affirmation, the spirit of world- and life-negation "occupies a predominant position."[67] Schweitzer is adamant that Indian thought is not entirely pessimistic; his text focuses on the discovery of life-affirmation interwoven with negation philosophy. Conversely, in European thought, though periods of world- and life-negation can be found, such as in Neoplatonism, Gnosticism, and Stoicism, affirmation philosophy is dominant.

The greatest problem for world- and life-negation arises from ethics, which for Schweitzer includes the principle of "active love." If world- and life-negation is concerned with ethics, then he believes that it is forced to make such serious concessions that "it ceases to exist." Since ethics "compels" one to action in the world, life-negation (withdrawal from worldly affairs) and ethics become incongruous: "The ethical premises the taking of interest in the welfare of beings that belong to this world, and this regard for terrestrial affairs points to world- and life-affirmation, however slight the tendency towards it may be."[68]

For "negation" ethics to transcend the "inner" ethic of self-perfection by becoming interested "in the world and what goes on in it," it must be operative in the world. In order to "escape this fate" of inconsistency, Indian thought attempts to stay within the boundaries of world- and life-negation by limiting itself to a *non*-active ethic. Such an ethic, claims Schweitzer, can only demand two things from a person. First, "that in a spirit of kindliness completely free from hatred he should seek true inner perfection, and [second] that he should show forth this by *refraining* from destroying or damaging any living thing. . . . *Active love it cannot demand of him.*"[69] As "negation" philosophy becomes more ethical (that is, takes an interest in the welfare of other beings), it "renounces" itself. Nonetheless, Indian ethical thought is credited for having "pushed forward to a stage of knowledge which is quite outside the purview of European thinking";[70] it places all life in the realm of ethical consideration.

According to Schweitzer, European ethical world- and life-affirmation needs to extend its moral consideration to all living beings, while India's universal ethics needs to align itself with world- and life-affirmation. Examination of his understanding of the major components of Indian and European thought reveals an affinity between his reverence for life and what seems to be the integration of the Jain ethic of *ahimsa* with life-affirmation. Reverence for life synthesizes these twin concerns, and Schweitzer appears indebted to Indian thought for a confirmation of his ethical ideas. In working through these conflicts between world- and life-views and the "boundless" ethical considerations in Jainism, it seems that he was simultaneously finding a base upon which to establish his own ethic.

4. Jainism and the Development of *Ahimsa*

In order to understand better the relevance of Jainism for Schweitzer's thought, some closer examination of its precepts and practices is needed. This section focuses primarily on the development and framework of *ahimsa* within Jainism.

From the sixth to fifth century B.C.E., India is marked among political, social, economic, and artistic achievements by the propagation of Jainism, Buddhism, and other heterodox religious sects. In opposition to the Brahmans, many ascetics and spiritual aspirants (*sramanas*) rejected the Vedic tradition. In their origin, both Jainism and Buddhism were *sramana* movements; whereas the Vedic tradition was believed to be founded on inequality, Jainism and Buddhism were established on ideas of greater equality (karma). Brahman inequality was held to be manifested in three ways: (1)

through social class, that is, the caste system; (2) through things such as prosperity here and heaven thereafter; and (3) through ethical consideration of living beings and the Vedic ritual sacrifices. These three views, and particularly the last one, were addressed by the development of the ethic of *ahimsa,* loosely translated as nonviolence or noninjury. The principle and practice of *ahimsa* is most closely identified with the Jain tradition.

The Relation of *Ahimsa* to Karma and Rebirth

The name Jainism is derived from the word *jina,* meaning conqueror. Jains are followers of the path established by the Jinas who were said to have "conquered" the suffering (*dukkha*) in this world. (See the essay by Ronald M. Huntington, "Jainism and Ethics," above.) *Ahimsa,* a practice of noninjury that respects all living forms, constitutes the primary religious and moral precept for all Jains. In the presence of a holy person, a Jain aspirant repeats the ancient formula: "I will desist from the knowing or intentional destruction of all great lives. As long as I live, I will neither kill nor cause others to kill. I shall strive to refrain from all such activities, whether of body, speech, or mind." [71]

The first written documents in Jainism offer a doctrine of rebirth that advances strict adherence to the ethical principle of *ahimsa.* [72] Lord Mahavira's message was that birth and caste were of no importance, and that one's karma was of the utmost significance. [73] One's future happiness depended on the elimination of karma that was directly related to avoiding the injury or destruction of any *jiva* (soul or life-monad). However, since *jivas* or souls are held to be ubiquitous in the natural world, it is evident that to perform almost any physical action without harming them is extremely difficult. This belief in the "vitality" or "livingness" of natural objects resulted in the application of *ahimsa* to minimize violence to other *jivas.*

Harmful action (*himsa*) is held to result in karmic bondage, where "the soul is invaded and weighed down by subtle matter." [74] This bondage ensures that upon death, the *jiva* will be reborn either in this world or another world (*samsara*), as opposed to achieving a state of liberation and bliss at the top of the universe. The more harm one commits, the greater the karmic bondage and the worse the state of rebirth that one can expect. As such, an active life in the world inevitably holds too much *himsa,* and hence bondage, for one easily to attain a better rebirth, let alone total liberation.

W. J. Johnson maintains that the practices of Jains are conditioned by three separate but interrelated beliefs. First, nearly all matter in the natural world is alive; that is, matter contains souls (*jivas*). Second, violence or injury to any living being is unethical. Third, actions inevitably have results that will affect future states and future rebirths of the agent. This third belief, the doctrine of karma, entails a strict observance of ethical tenets based on *ahimsa.*

For Jains, *ahimsa* "is not simply the first among virtues but *the* virtue; all other restraints are simply elaborations."[75] Of the five *Anuvratas,* the fundamental tenets of Jainism that afford the follower the means whereby karmic influx can be contained, *ahimsa* is the first. Though *himsa* is often understood as harm done to others, for Jains it refers additionally to injury to oneself—to that behavior which hinders the soul's capacity to attain liberation. P. S. Jaini writes, "The killing of animals, for example, is reprehensible not only for the suffering produced in the victims, but even more so because it involves intense passions on the part of the killer, passions which bind him more firmly in the grip of *samsara.*"[76] The abandonment of harmful action represents the soteriological goal.

The more harm one performs, the heavier the karmic bondage and the worse the rebirth. To avoid bondage, it is necessary to observe a vow of nonviolence toward all creatures. In order to liberate oneself from the negative influences of karma, Jains take a series of vows (*vratas*) that are believed to aid them in a purging of karmic residue previously accumulated through bad activity. The Jains' path to liberation consists of fourteen stages of purification centered around the ethic of *ahimsa.* In the early doctrines of Jainism there is little mention of the possibility of meritorious activity (*puñña*); only by restraint from action can one decrease the amount of bad karma "stuck" on the *jiva* and attain a better rebirth. The central concern of Jain practice is, therefore, to act in a manner that (ideally) entails no *himsa* and hence no further bondage.

Action Versus Intention

It is evident that at least in early Jainism, physical activity of any sort is harmful to other *jivas* and thus binding; what matters most is the effect on the injured, not the subjective state of the agent responsible for the injury. The intention behind one's actions is important in the early texts only insofar as it could lead to or away from *himsa*. In regard to the mechanism of karmic bondage, it is specifically action, or the restraint thereof, that matters when the soteriological consequences of an action are determined. The *Dasaveyaliya Sutra,* an early text on ascetic practice, elucidates these points:

> One who walks, (stands, sits, lies down, eats, and speaks) carelessly, will hurt living beings. He binds evil karman, that is his bitter reward.
>
> One should walk, stand, sit, and lie down carefully; if he eats and speaks carefully, he does not bind evil karman.[77]

Early monastic rules underscore that what is significant for salvation is the actual physical harm done, its cause being secondary. Jain thought later shifted away from strictly an emphasis on one's actions to a focus on the intentions of the individual committing *himsa*. The impact of this doctrine of internalization on Jain doctrine is apparent in the writing of Umasvati.

Umasvati's *Tattvartha Sutra*

The first textual synthesis of Jain doctrine is Umasvati's *Tattvartha Sutra* (Manual for Understanding the Reals), written between 150 and 350 C.E. The *Tattvartha* was an attempt to systematize various components (epistemological, metaphysical, cosmological, ethical, and practical) of the Jain path to purification. The text developed a doctrine of the mechanism of bondage (*bandha*). The new synthesis advanced a *kasaya* doctrine, positing greater or lesser degrees of bondage as the result of the degree of intention that motivated the act.

The *Sarvarthasiddhi,* commenting on *Tattvartha Sutra* 6.4, states that there are two kinds of karma: (1) *"samparayika,* leading to *samsara,"* and (2) *"iryapatha,* caused by vibrations."[78] This distinction marks an important shift in Jain thought inasmuch as the emphasis is not only on activity, but also on the mental state that accompanies it. The *Sarvarthasiddhi* thus differentiates between actions brought about through passion, which result in *himsa,* and passion-free actions that do not. Significantly, nearly the whole emphasis, at least doctrinally, is changed to the internal state of the agent. Umasvati's definition of *himsa* ("Injury is the destruction of life out of passion"[79]) highlights the development of a more inclusive and lay-compatible ethic.

Ahimsa and Active Compassion

Observed by almost all members of the Jain community, the basic restraints are dietary in nature. Jains do not partake of meat, alcohol, honey, or any of five kinds of figs. These products are prohibited because they hold many forms of life, specifically numerous *nigodas* (microorganisms). The strict adherence to vegetarianism is the hallmark of the Jains, as their refusal to consume meat constitutes the most fundamental expression of *ahimsa.* Such restrictions are far stricter for monks and nuns.[80]

Though renunciation plays a significant role in Jainism, it is important to note that *ahimsa* represents not only noninjury as a negative duty, but also implies "the presence of cultivated and noble sentiments such as kindness and compassion for all living creatures."[81] In spite of the negative particle "non," it is not a negative ideal. *Ahimsa* has another role, that of *karuna* (compassion), and calls forth positive action to alleviate the suffering of all.[82] As Shah notes, *ahimsa* is a positive virtue and "resolves itself as *jiva-daya,*[83] compassion for living creatures."[84] For instance, recently Jains have established animal and bird sanctuaries (*panjara polas*) in India and elsewhere, tree-planting schemes, and other initiatives to help preserve the environment. This "positive" or "life-affirmation" aspect of *ahimsa* is absent in Schweitzer's critique of Jainism.[85]

It is apparent that from Schweitzer's understanding, reverence for life makes a departure from Jain ascetics' application of *ahimsa;* it prescribes not only noninjury to other life, but also enjoins "active love" or practical care. However, when understood less narrowly than Schweitzer apprehended it, *ahimsa* shares more in common with reverence for life than he may have initially realized.

5. Schweitzer's Esteem for Jain Ethics

In Jainism, emphasis rests largely on the purificatory aspect of the liberation process. Schweitzer grasps this notion when he states the "idea of being exalted above the world is replaced by that of keeping pure from the world—an event full of significance for the thought of India!"[86] Jain ethics recognizes that from ethical or nonethical conduct there ensues a higher or lower form of rebirth, and that by the practice of *ahimsa* one can attain liberation from the cycle of rebirths (*samsara*). Life-negation does not "claim to be above all ethics," he states, "but desires to be the supreme ethic. What is new, then, in Jainism is the importance attained by ethics."[87]

Although Jainism upholds life-negation, it is importantly the first religion to seek "to give ethical significance to world- and life-negation."[88] Schweitzer supports the Jains' departure from the traditional ethics and ceremonial sacrifices of the Brahmins. This "endeavor explains how in Jainism not to kill and not to harm living creatures (*ahimsa*) first becomes a great commandment."[89] In Jainism, "world and life-negation first assumes an ethical character";[90] the high importance in Jainism ascribed to the principle not to kill and not to injure makes the development of *ahimsa,* from Schweitzer's standpoint, *"one of the greatest events in the spiritual history of mankind."*[91] Through *ahimsa,* humans reach "the tremendous discovery that ethics knows no bounds!" "So far as we know," he claims, "this is for the first time clearly expressed by Jainism."[92] Starting from its principle of abstention from action (life-negation), Jainism realizes that the demands of ethics are, in principle, "boundless" and encompass every life-form.

The Limitations of *Ahimsa*

Whereas Schweitzer understands the ethic of *ahimsa* to advance strictly *non-violence* and to refer to the avoidance of actions that constrain the soul's potential to attain *moksha,* reverence for life additionally posits an active compassion for all life. It is because Jesus' "ethic of love" promotes the principle of activity that he believes it to correspond to world-affirmation and reverence for life. As Jesus' emphasis on love (*agape*) suggests, the ethical implications of reverence for life are greater than a promotion of nonviolence to other wills-to-live. They involve active concern for all life.

Schweitzer states that the "characteristic attitude of Indian thought is less a positive reverence for life, than a negative duty to refrain from destroying."[93] This "ideal of inactivity obstructs the way to the real ethics of active love."[94] It is not enough to refrain from violence toward other wills-to-live; one must also seek to promote and help all the wills-to-live with which one comes in contact. Only "by taking heed of all creation would [ethics] put us in a spiritual relationship with the entire universe."[95] It is evident that Schweitzer's analysis of Jainism largely neglects Umasvati's emphasis on intention (*kasaya*) or the "positive virtues," such as compassion (*karuna*), inherent in *ahimsa* as emphasized by Jain thinker Srimad Rajachandra.

Schweitzer is critical of the Jain concept of *ahimsa* because it did not grow from "a feeling of compassion" but stemmed from a desire to remain "undefiled" by the world. He states, "It was for his own sake, not from a fellow-feeling for other beings, that the pious Indian of those ancient days endeavored very strictly to carry out the principle of non-activity in his relations to living creatures."[96] That many early Jains interfered with Brahman sacrifices to save animals suggests that *ahimsa* encouraged action as part of its practice. Indeed, despite this opening criticism, Schweitzer maintains, "When once the *ahimsa* commandment has become generally accepted, it operates with educative effect. It arouses compassionate feeling and keeps it awake. . . . It remains the great merit of [Jain] thought that it held fast to knowledge imparted to it by a marvelous dispensation of providence and recognized its importance."[97]

Once established, *ahimsa* awakens compassion in its adherents. Schweitzer concludes, "Whatever opinion one may form as to the historical origin of this great ethical principle, it cannot detract from its importance."[98] Schweitzer and Jainism converge in accepting responsibility for the welfare of all wills-to-live and *jivas*.

The Division of the Will-to-Live

Following Schweitzer's critique, Jainism does not address how the "law of necessity" makes total abstention from harm to other life impossible. Although he finds the elaboration of *ahimsa* significant, Jainism, according to Schweitzer, neglects to examine the ethic from "every side and to concern itself with the problem contained in it."[99] Ethics "without limits" cannot be fully realized, but he wrongly suggests Jainism does not acknowledge the problems intrinsic to a boundless ethic of nonviolence: "However seriously someone undertakes to abstain from killing and damaging, he cannot entirely avoid it. He is under the law of necessity, which compels him to kill and to damage both with and without his knowledge. . . . Again and again we see ourselves placed under the necessity of saving one living creature by destroying or damaging another."[100]

This passage helps to illumine two ideas central to Schweitzer's study of Indian thought and discussion of reverence for life. First, he articulates the same charge against Jainism often directed against him: application of *ahimsa* (or reverence for life) without qualification is impossible. One cannot maintain life without harming or killing some other life and, therefore, absolute adherence to an ethic of nonviolence to other life (*jivas*) cannot be sustained. This notion leads to Schweitzer's emphasis on "resignation" as an integral aspect of ethics, as explored in the following section.

This first point is related to the second idea, what Schweitzer calls the problem of the "law of necessity." The world, from his view, "is a ghastly drama of the will-to-live divided against itself";[101] one existence is necessarily predicated upon the life of another. Gandhi similarly emphasizes, "All life in the flesh exists by some violence. . . . The world is bound in a chain of destruction. In other words, violence is an inherent necessity for life in the body. . . . None, while in the flesh, can thus be entirely free from violence, because one never completely renounces the 'will to live.' "[102]

The "necessity" of some violence, at least at first appearance, seems to work against *ahimsa* and reverence for life. The "law" eliminates the possibility of complete adherence to each ethic's principles. However, both Jainism and Schweitzer deal with this problem. In Jainism, Umasvati's *kasaya* doctrine distinguishes intentional and unintentional violence. Also, it is recognized that at least some harm must be committed to one-sense beings to nourish one's body, as will be examined in part 6.

Unaware of such distinctions in Jainism, Schweitzer charges that it "incomprehensibly clung fast to [this] illusion, as if not-killing and not-harming were completely possible of fulfillment by anyone who takes the matter seriously." [103] More broadly, he remarks that the "history of the world teachings on the subject may be summarized in the motto, 'Avoid absolute ethics, and thus keep within the realm of the possible.' " [104] Although Schweitzer is cognizant that absolute ethics "cannot be completely achieved" in practice, he believes "that fact does not really matter." [105] The import of an ethic should not be judged on the basis of whether it is *"practicable"* as opposed to *"absolute."* [106] Reverence for life propounds responsibility for all life and does not appoint a maximum limit as to how one should act. It is an absolute ethic in the sense that it does not outline specific rules for each given situation and cannot, as an ethical *mysticism,* "be fitted into tabulated rules and regulations." [107] The mystical component of reverence for life is valid insofar as one takes all life into consideration.

Though reverence for life can neither make a claim to full application nor to complete realization (one cannot exist without harming other life), it does not prevent Schweitzer from enjoining others to practice it to the greatest extent possible. The "law of necessity" may make the application of reverence for life impossible, but for him it is still morally imperative to strive to that end. How does one determine the extent of violence to commit? For Schweitzer there can be no definitive answer, and his position is well summarized by Gandhi: "Life is governed by a multitude of forces. It would be smooth sailing if we could determine the course of action only by one general principle, whose application at a given time was too obvious to need even a moment's reflection. But I cannot recall a single act which could be so easily determined." [108]

Every individual is to decide how best to reduce the circle of violence and to offer assistance to other life. [109] Schweitzer's discussion of the "law of necessity" reveals his distress over the fact that life necessarily involves violence and affords a clearer picture of the mystical value that he attaches to reverence for life. At the same time, it illumines how far he is from equating "reverence" with the inviolability of life.

Resignation

Schweitzer maintains that one needs to acquire an intellectual "resignation" to the "law of necessity." "Resignation" does not mean pessimism about the world: "Resignation is the vestibule through which we enter ethics. Only one who in deepened devotion to his own will-to-live experiences inward freedom from outward occurrences, is capable of devoting himself in profound and steady fashion to the life of others." [110]

This understanding of intellectual resignation is analogous to the Stoic ideal of *apatheia,* implying a certain inner liberty or dispassion from the external happenings in the world over which one does not have control. "When we speak of resignation," Schweitzer writes, "it is not sadness to which we refer." [111] Such a state may imply detachment, but not indifference; it consists not in ceasing to feel external happenings, but in no longer yielding to them. "Resignation" is the inward detachment from the world that helps enable one "to work in the world." [112] In this sense, resignation is to be understood as positive, not negative: "True resignation is not a becoming weary of the world, but the quiet triumph which the will-to-live celebrates at the hour of its greatest need over the circumstances of life. It flourishes only in the soil of deep world- and life-affirmation." [113]

Resignation is the means by which Schweitzer guards against pessimism. It is important for him that one does not expect to understand the world completely, inasmuch as the "creative" is bound to the "destructive." One needs to be "determined solely by what is given within," [114] that is, the affirmation of life given in the will-to-live.

Reverence for Life: Principle and Practice

Reverence for life is not a principle or a strict set of obligations. Shorn of its mystical aspect, Schweitzer's ethic looks absolutist and impractical. However, that is precisely how he wished not to be read. He never explicitly propounds a scale of values. Reverence for life is an experience of the inherent value of all life that, in turn, helps to guide one's actions.

Schweitzer's refusal to systematize ethics as reverence for life is not meant to impede one's behavior by establishing an inflexible rule. The very word "reverence" (*Ehrfurcht*) indicates to us that Schweitzer is not depicting obedience to moral law but the promotion of the good, which in turn "requires a holistic response of the individual including attitude, disposition, motive as well as action." [115] This notion is evidenced by Schweitzer's statement that "in the traditional language of religion," he speaks of "love" instead of "reverence for life." [116] Ethics cannot be systematized because "reverence for life, including love and compassion, must attend to the situation in which it finds itself." [117] He describes the distress such decisions caused him:

> I have just killed a mosquito that was buzzing around me in the lamplight. In Europe I wouldn't kill it even if it were bothering me, but here, where mosquitoes spread the most dangerous form of malaria, I take the liberty of killing them, although I don't like doing it. The important thing is for all of us properly to mull over the question of when damaging and killing are permissible.
>
> Much will be achieved once people become reflective and wisely realize that they should damage and kill only when necessary. That is the essence. The rationalization of individual cases is a different matter. Someone brought me four pelicans whose wings had been so badly slashed by unfeeling people that they cannot fly. It will take two or three months before their wings heal and they can fly freely. I have hired a fisherman to catch the necessary fish to feed them. I always pity the poor fish to the depths of my soul, but I have to choose between killing the fish or the four pelicans who would surely starve to death. I do not know whether I am doing the right thing in deciding one way instead of the other. [118]

Philosophically, Schweitzer is resolute that moral hierarchies between species are in theory groundless:

> To undertake to establish universally valid distinctions of value between different kinds of life will end in judging them by the greater or lesser distance at which they stand from us human beings. Our own judgment is, however, a purely subjective criterion. [119]

In contrast to his philosophical position, Schweitzer's examples often reveal a consistent preference of human life to other life, and mammals to more elementary life-forms. Though (consciously or unconsciously) his examples reveal a practical, species-informed hierarchy, he was *not* offering the reader universally valid rules as to which specific life to preference in a given scenario. He believed each individual must decide in each situation how to act most compassionately.[120] "We must perceive every act of destruction always as something terrible," and, guided by this awareness, he counsels that we "ask ourselves, in every single case, whether we can bear the responsibility as to whether it is necessary or not."[121]

"Active Compassion" and *Ahimsa*

Schweitzer suggests that there are other values of greater import than the strict preservation of life. For example, he maintains that prolonged and intense suffering is "a more terrible lord of mankind than even death":[122]

> In many ways it may happen that by slavish adherence to the commandment not to kill compassion is less served than by breaking it. When the suffering of a living creature cannot be alleviated, it is more ethical to end its life by killing it mercifully than it is to stand aloof. It is more cruel to let domestic animals which one can no longer feed die a painful death by starvation than to give them a quick and painless end by violence. Again and again we see ourselves placed under the necessity of saving one living creature by destroying or damaging another.
>
> The principle of not-killing and not-harming must not aim at being independent, but must be the servant of, and subordinate itself to, compassion. It must therefore enter into a practical discussion with reality.[123]

Active compassion supersedes a strict observance of the principle of nonviolence. Schweitzer feels that Indian ethics has not addressed the problem of the relationship between humans and other life inasmuch as "it commands only compassionate non-killing and non-harming and not compassionate helping."[124] Such active compassion may, for him, include killing an animal in pain rather than standing "aloof" and watching it suffer. The words "necessity" and "ethical" in the above quotation provide an important clue for the reconciliation "of the apparent conflict between

Schweitzer's concern for civilization and his insistence that reverence for life is absolute and universal." [125]

The conflict between the "necessary" and the "ethical" is, in large measure, caused by his understanding of the ethical as disassociated from the relative, instrumental, utilitarian, or even necessary. In *The Philosophy of Civilization,* Schweitzer claims that "all destruction of and injury to life, under whatever circumstances they take place, [ethics] condemns as evil." [126] Ethical conflicts are not abolished, but rather, the individual is forced to decide "how far he can remain ethical and how far he must submit himself to the necessity for destruction of and injury to life, and therewith incur guilt." [127]

In *Indian Thought and Its Development* as well as in his autobiography, Schweitzer speaks of a feeling different from "evil" or "guilt" over the necessity of taking other forms of life: the individual "bears *responsibility* for the life that is sacrificed." [128] In these two texts, published ten and twelve years after *The Philosophy of Civilization* respectively, he acknowledges that reverence for life allows for "ethical activity," which entails killing of some nonhuman life. It is possible that Schweitzer altered his position slightly in the interim period and offers a more considered statement in his later works.

Throughout his writing, Schweitzer repeatedly highlights this tension between the "universality" of reverence for life and the "necessity" of sacrificing some wills-to-live to help others. [129] He underscores the importance of the choice between the necessary and the ethical as well as the sense of responsibility one should feel when forced to sacrifice life. In other words, killing may sometimes be "necessary," but it can never be "ethical" as such. To create a hierarchy of values among different life-forms or to keep "adjustments between ethics and necessity all ready for use in order to ease one's conscience" would be unethical. "The good conscience," he never ceases to remind us, "is an invention of the devil." [130]

The principal practice by which one can alleviate the "guilt" or "responsibility" incurred for injuring other life is to increase service to other wills-to-live. "Some atonement for that guilt," Schweitzer states, "can be found by the man who pledges himself to neglect no opportunity to succor creatures in distress." [131] The necessity of harm does not damage the absolute claims of reverence for life; it only strengthens the call for a renewed determination to its practice.

6. The Value Inherent in All Life

As noted, Schweitzer and Jainism affirm the inherent or intrinsic value in all life. Both believe that all life-forms have value in themselves, independent of human estimations; all living things are to be protected and reverenced as far as possible. For Schweitzer, it is the presence of the will-to-live that confers each being's intrinsic value: "life" is "something possessing value *in itself.*"[132] Similarly, Jainism respects the *jiva* located within all animate beings. Part 6 studies the importance of the will-to-live and the *jiva* in each ethical system.

The Centrality of the Will-to-Live in Reverence for Life

For Schweitzer, the will-to-live establishes the value of life but not distinctions within the value of life. Neither a creature's species nor its sentiency qualifies this universality: "A person is truly ethical only when he or she obeys the compulsion to help all life which he is able to assist, and shrinks from injuring anything that lives. Such a person does not ask how far this or that life deserves one's sympathy as being valuable, nor beyond that, whether and to what degree it is capable of feeling. Life as such is sacred to him."[133]

Unlike Jainism, which holds a hierarchy of being from one-sense to five-sense creatures, our relation to the nonhuman world, Schweitzer posits, should not be one of moral hierarchies or instrumentality. The self, as will-to-live, finds its source of value not entirely in itself, but rather as a result of its relationship to other life and to the infinite Will-to-live. He dismisses the idea of a hierarchy of beings in nature, with humans at the top, reflecting varying degrees of intrinsic value in creation: "The ethics of reverence for life makes no distinction between higher and lower, more precious and less precious lives. . . . How can we know the importance other living organisms have in themselves and in terms of the universe?"[134]

He restates this view more forcefully in a correspondence: "and I'll be damned if I recognize any *objectively valid* distinctions in life. Every life is sacred! Value judgments are made out of subjective necessity, but they have no validity beyond that. The proposition that every life is sacred is absolute. In this respect I will always remain a heretic. It is a question of principle, one that reaches deep into the foundation of my outlook on life." [135]

Though in practical matters humans must make decisions about the relative priority of diverse life-forms, our judgment on this matter is subjective and anthropocentrically informed. Such decisions should not be taken as an objective measure of the intrinsic value of other life. To establish "universally valid distinctions of value," from Schweitzer's point of view, invites mistreatment by dismissing some life-forms as less important than others and expendable. He stands against the Protagorean maxim in which humans are the measure of all things. Distinctions cannot be defended by establishing the importance different life-forms hold in the universe, as humans cannot know what cosmic importance they play. Human wants, needs, and benefits, Schweitzer tells us, cannot be the sole basis by which we judge the value of other creatures.

The Centrality of the *Jiva* in Jain Thought

Jainism posits that the *jiva* is permanent and suffers or benefits from the fruits of its karmic deeds. It is the *jiva* that, as a result of the karma it acquires, passes through the series of rebirths and finally obtains liberation through the elimination of its karma. The *jiva* is held to be conscious, regardless of how undeveloped it may be, and is present even in the least-developed form of life, the *nigoda*.

Within the Jain universe a *jiva* may be characterized in five ways according to the number of senses it possesses. The *Ekendriya jivas* are one-sense beings, just above the *nigoda,* which possess a sense of touch. The *Ekendriya jivas* are subdivided into *Prithvikaya, Apakaya, Teukaya, Vayukaya,* and *Vanaspatikaya.*[136] All the *Ekendriya jivas* have the capacity to suffer, hence the quest for total renunciation and nonactivity.

The *Be-indriya jiva* possesses two senses: touch and taste. These include animalcules, worms, mollusks, leeches, and earthworms. Though Jain mendicants seek to refrain from injuring or killing anything in the *Ekendriya* class, the vow of *ahimsa* for the layperson begins at the *Be-indriya* group. In the next class, *Tri-indriya,* are those beings which, in addition to touch and taste, have a sense of smell. In this group are ants, fleas, moths, and centipedes. *Corendriya* possess the fourth sense of sight. Wasps, mosquitoes, gnats, flies, and locusts are included under this heading. The fifth sense added to the *jiva* is that of hearing, and this refers to fish, birds, animals, humans, infernals, and gods.

Regardless of how many senses a being may possess, Jains regard the existence of a karma-bound and alterable soul as self-evident. Such a soul "is the reality without which [their] entire world-view and quest for salvation would be meaningless." [137] The significance of upholding the inviolability of such subtle creatures is underscored in the opening portions of the *Acaranga Sutra:* "Take note—there are innumerable tiny beings individually embodied in earth. Take note—there are some people who truly control themselves, safeguarding even these beings, while others fail to do so and thus are only pretending to be renunciants." [138]

The *Acaranga Sutra* later claims that the element bodies suffer, as do all other living beings; their suffering is likened to that of a blind and mute person "who can neither see who it is that hurts him nor express his pain." [139] It has been suggested that the Jains are inappropriately focused on "lower" beings to the detriment of their interest in "higher" animals and humans. However, this criticism fails to appreciate that the ascetic has already, as part of his or her lay vows, established a pattern of nonharmful behavior toward "higher" creatures. The ascetic's concern for the welfare of the *Ekendriya* and element bodies does not exclude this prior vow but rather expands it.

Parallels

Whereas for Schweitzer the will-to-live is the physical and spiritual dynamic of life, in Jainism the *jiva* is the life-force and soul of each being. Both arrive at a focus on the will-to-live and the *jiva* through meditation on life and existence itself.

According to Schweitzer, "if we ask, 'What is the immediate fact of my consciousness? What do I self-consciously know of myself, making abstractions of all else, from childhood to old age? To what do I always return?' we find the simple fact of consciousness is this, *I will to live.*" [140] He criticizes

Descartes's dictum "I think, therefore I am" (*cogito ergo sum*) and establishes apprehension of the will-to-live as the starting point of philosophy:

> He [Descartes] built an artificial structure by presuming that a person knows nothing, and doubts all, whether outside himself or within. And in order to end doubt, he fell back on the fact of consciousness: *I think.* . . . Who can establish this fact that he thinks, except in relation to thinking *something?* And what that something is, is the important matter.[141]
>
> True philosophy must start from the most immediate and comprehensive fact of consciousness, which says, "I am life which wills to live in, in the midst of life which wills to live."[142]

For Schweitzer, this proposition is not "an ingenious dogmatic formula,"[143] nor does it need to make "any pretensions to high titles or noble-sounding theories to explain its existence."[144] Rather, it comes about through physiological makeup and the unity of all life: "This, then, is the nature and origin of ethics. We have dared to say that it is born of physical life, out of the linking of life with life."[145]

Similarly, in *Sacred Books of the East,* Hermann Jacobi states that Jainism arrived at the concept of the soul "not through the search after the Self, the self-existing unchangeable principle in the ever-changing world of phenomena, but through the perception of life. For the most general Jain term for soul is life (*jiva*), which is identical with self (*aya, atman*)."[146] Jainism views the existence of a bound and alterable self as readily evident. External proofs for this reality "are considered redundant and superfluous; the simple experience of self-awareness (*ahampratyaya*) is proof enough."[147] Jaini explains: "Even doubt—for example, 'is there really a self here?'—supports this view when one asks the further question, 'Who is it that has the doubt?' The answer given, of course, is *jiva,* the basic 'I' that stands behind all human actions."[148]

Both analyses are centered upon the interactions of the will-to-live, or *jiva,* with other life. It is the presence of the will-to-live, or *jiva,* that establishes the intrinsic value of the being, and not necessarily the stage of development or number of senses it possesses that entitles it to moral regard. Ethical consideration does not depend on what human beings possess alone, but rather on that which they share in common with all other beings. Inasmuch as the will-to-live and the *jiva* are held to be omnipresent in the universe, there is a call to treat all beings nonviolently.

Most significant, reverence for life and *ahimsa* are principally concerned with the individual's ethical and spiritual development. For Schweitzer, the highest form of development is to attain mystical union with the Divine through ethical action with other life. In Jainism, the reduction of violence toward other life through *ahimsa* and the elimination of one's karma represent the telos of ethical action. Each ethic occupies the center of these religious convictions.

7. "Valuable treasures of thought"

Schweitzer believed that Indian and Western forms of thought could benefit from one another: "Both are the guardians of valuable treasures of thought. Both must be moving along the path towards a way of thinking which shall . . . eventually be shared in common by all humankind." [149] The significance of a comparative study of Indian and Western thought is that each can become cognizant of its own "inadequacies" and be "stimulated to turn in the direction of what is more complete." [150] "For there must indeed arise a philosophy profounder and more living than our own and endowed with greater spiritual and ethical force. . . . From the East and from the West we must all keep look-out for this [ethic]." [151]

Although it is likely that Schweitzer considered reverence for life to be this global ethic, he saw signs of ethical rapprochement in contemporary Indian thinkers' application of *ahimsa,* such as Gandhi and Tagore. Though at times Schweitzer asserts the superiority of his own thought over Jainism, more often he sought to infuse each with the ethical and spiritual qualities of the other so that a "more perfect and powerful form of thought" would arise.

Schweitzer's comparative ethical study (and his resultant ethical innovation) bears similarity to Keith Ward's notion of "convergent spirituality." The adherent of a "convergent spirituality" model "must move, not to a neutral vantage-point free of all traditions, but towards building bridges to traditions other than our own. In this way, the tradition we start from may receive an access of new life and understanding, without having to set aside its own distinctive perspective and contribution."[152]

Schweitzer did not work from an unbiased or "neutral vantage-point"; rather than abdicating his judgments, he mirrored some of the prejudices and misunderstandings of Indian thinking that many Western scholars held at that time. Nonetheless, he tried to "build bridges" with other traditions through his academic texts and, more personally, by devoting numerous correspondences to Indian and Asian individuals in an attempt to highlight the mutuality of thought between reverence for life and the ethics of their religions. Schweitzer can be seen to enhance what he believes to be the essential ideas of Christianity—Jesus' "ethic of love"—with the "boundless" ethical considerations established in Jainism and manifested in the ethic of *ahimsa*. Reverence for life unites his twin concerns of "active love" with regard for all living beings. In this way, he may have received access to a new understanding of extended moral consideration without renouncing his understanding of Jesus' ethic.

In Schweitzer's comparative ethical study, development occurs through a process akin to what Paul Tillich referred to as "a dialectical union of acceptance and rejection."[153] Ward similarly terms such a method one of "dialectical interaction," where opposing views are not abandoned but "are seen in dynamic and complementary interaction."[154] To this end, Schweitzer states, "When Western and Indian philosophy engage in discussion, they must not contend in the spirit that aims at the one proving itself right in opposition to the other."[155] However (inaccurately) critical at certain points his commentary may be toward Jain ethics, his interaction with *ahimsa* displays signs of fruitful engagement. He does not emphasize one religion to the necessary exclusion or detriment of the other, but rather attempts in his own ethical consideration to imbue each with the most critical and complementing ideas. As Ward notes:

> By a creative conversation of traditions, one can gain new insights into the relation of the human and the divine, the finite and the infinite. . . . One tradition does not have to be rejected, to accept another. Nor need one just artificially graft parts of one tradition onto another in a way which is

untrue to both. There can be genuine interchange, as each stresses aspects the other has under-emphasized. That is why I find it particularly helpful to encourage conversation between Indian and Semitic traditions. Their characteristic emphases are so initially different that they each have the capacity to extend the other in fruitful ways.[156]

Although Schweitzer stressed the import of Jesus' ethic, he also emphasized the need for a transformation of Christianity. He writes that "what has been presented as Christianity during these nineteen centuries is merely a beginning, full of mistakes,"[157] and he is particularly concerned that it "hardly acts on its spiritual or ethical principles."[158] Such a transformation possibly included the incorporation of ethical insights from other religions—though the details of his innovation do not appear to have been worked out in a systematic fashion. Perhaps it was because the characteristic emphases of Christianity and Jainism were initially so different that these distinctions extended Schweitzer's ethical thinking in a way that helped him articulate reverence for life.

Through his research, Schweitzer admittedly developed a "strong rapport with" and "profound understanding of the grandeur of Indian thought,"[159] as well as an "inner relationship to its great representatives both in antiquity and in the present day."[160] In turn, many Jain scholars have met his esteem with appreciation for reverence for life.[161] As such, reverence for life can be seen as an important catalyst between Western and Indian ethical thought.

Schweitzer reacts to a great range of intellectual stimuli, assimilating, modifying, picking and choosing, and then gradually constructing his own ethic. Although he claims reverence for life "flashed" into his mind while on a voyage on the Ogowe River in Gabon, it is evident that the ethical ideas present in this phrase were cultivated long beforehand. Among the significant influence of Jesus, St. Paul, and others, Schweitzer's rapport with Jainism and *ahimsa* helped him to articulate and discern the meaning of "reverence."

CHAPTER 15

The Legacy of Albert Schweitzer's
Quest of the Historical Jesus

James M. Robinson

James M. Robinson, professor of New Testament at Claremont Graduate University, is a leading scholar of the New Testament and early Christian literature and the author of the insightful introduction to the 1968 English edition of Schweitzer's Quest of the Historical Jesus. *Here Robinson offers new perspectives on how Schweitzer built his own life and ethic on his understanding of the life of Jesus.*

Albert Schweitzer's *Quest of the Historical Jesus* made a sensation in theological circles when it first appeared in 1906, and it continues to be remarkably well known by the public at large.

This is not because anyone today has actually read it. But the never-ending quests of the historical Jesus all begin by referring to Schweitzer as the point of departure.

Actually, what is most familiar in the book itself, even to the extent of having been set to music, is the concluding paragraph, with which I therefore begin:[1]

> He comes to us as one unknown, without a name, as of old, by the lakeside, he came to those people who knew him not. He speaks to us the same word: "Follow me!" and sets us to the tasks which he has to fulfill for our time. He commands. And to those who obey him, whether they be wise

or simple, he will reveal himself in the toils, the conflicts, the sufferings which they shall pass through in his fellowship, and, as an ineffable mystery, they shall learn in their own experience who he is. (403)

This sublime, eloquently poetic prose seems to say it all, and yet in a sense says it all too well for it to have much down-to-earth concreteness for us. So I want to back up to "the toils, the conflicts, the sufferings" of Jesus, as Schweitzer saw them, and only then think of Schweitzer himself, as one of "those who obey him." For it is "the toils, the conflicts, the sufferings which they pass through in his fellowship" that is the "legacy" of *The Quest of the Historical Jesus* in Schweitzer's own experience, and, one might hope, in our own.

Thus I invite you to stir up your courage and risk taking with me a guided tour of Schweitzer's own "life of Christ," with which he concludes *The Quest of the Historical Jesus.*

Schweitzer begins with Jesus' parables about sowing, followed by the reaping of grain at harvest time:

> In these parables it is not the idea of development, but of the apparent absence of causation which occupies the foremost place. The description aims at suggesting the question, how, and by what power, incomparably great and glorious results can be infallibly produced by an insignificant fact without human aid. . . .
>
> What the parables emphasize is, therefore, so to speak, the in itself negative, inadequate character of the initial fact, upon which, as by a miracle, there follows in the appointed time, through the power of God, some great thing. They lay stress not upon the natural, but upon the miraculous character of such occurrences.
>
> But what is the initial fact of the parables? It is the sowing. . . .
>
> And the initial fact which is symbolized? Jesus can only mean a fact which was actually in existence—the movement of repentance evoked by the Baptist and now intensified by his own preaching. . . .
>
> If we look into the thought more closely we see that the coming of the kingdom of God is not only symbolically or analogically but also really and temporally connected with the harvest. The harvest ripening upon

earth is the last! With it comes also the kingdom of God which brings in the new age. When the reapers are sent into the fields, the Lord in heaven will cause his harvest to be reaped by the holy angels. . . .

The analogical and temporal parallelism becomes complete if we assume that the movement initiated by the Baptist began in the spring, and notice that Jesus, according to Matt. ix. 37 and 38, before sending out the disciples to make a speedy proclamation of the nearness of the kingdom of God, uttered the remarkable saying about the rich harvest. ["The harvest is plentiful, but the laborers are few; pray therefore the Lord of the harvest to send out laborers into his harvest."]

. . . The initial fact to which Jesus points, under the figure of the sowing, is somehow or other connected with the eschatological preaching of repentance, which had been begun by the Baptist.

. . . In the movement to which the Baptist gave the first impulse, and which still continued, there was an initial fact which was drawing after it the coming of the kingdom, in a fashion which was miraculous, unintelligible, but unfailingly certain, since the sufficient cause for it lay in the power and purpose of God. . . .

Jesus must have expected the coming of the kingdom at harvest time. And that is just what he did expect. It is for that reason that he sends out his disciples to make known in Israel, as speedily as may be, what is about to happen. (356–58)

Schweitzer's view of Jesus' mood is as follows:

We must always make a fresh effort to realize to ourselves that Jesus and his immediate followers were, at that time, in an enthusiastic state of intense eschatological expectation. We must picture them among the people, who were filled with penitence for their sins, and with faith in the kingdom, hourly expecting the coming of the kingdom, and the revelation of Jesus as the Son of Man, seeing in the eager multitude itself a sign that their reckoning of the time was correct. (386)

Hence the mission of the Twelve, reported practically verbatim in Matthew 10, according to Schweitzer, was intended by Jesus as his final act before the end:

He tells them in plain words (Matt. x. 23) that he does not expect to see them back in the present age. The Parousia [the appearance at the end of time] of the Son of Man, which is logically and temporally identical with the dawn of the kingdom, will take place before they shall have completed a hasty journey through the cities of Israel to announce it. [Matt. 10.23: "When they persecute you in one town, flee to the next; for truly I say to you, you will not have gone through all the towns of Israel, before the Son of Man comes."] (358–59)

Schweitzer described "the significance of the sending forth of the disciples and the discourse which Jesus uttered upon that occasion" as follows:

Jesus' purpose is to set in motion the eschatological development of history, to let loose the final woes, the confusion and strife, from which shall issue the Parousia, and so to introduce the supra-mundane phase of the eschatological drama. (371)

Schweitzer was convinced that "at the time of their mission," Jesus "did not expect them to return before the Parousia" (386). But that is in fact what did happen:

There followed neither the sufferings, nor the outpouring of the Spirit, nor the Parousia of the Son of Man. The disciples returned safe and sound and full of a proud satisfaction; for one promise had been realized—the power which had been given them over the demons. (364)

Schweitzer drew the inevitable consequence:

It is equally clear, and here the dogmatic considerations which guided the resolutions of Jesus become still more prominent, that this prediction was not fulfilled. The disciples returned to him; and the appearing of the Son of Man had not taken place. The actual history disavowed the dogmatic history on which the action of Jesus had been based. An event of supernatural history which must take place, and must take place at that particular point of time, failed to come about. That was for Jesus, who lived wholly in the dogmatic history, the first "historical" occurrence, the central event which closed the former period of his activity and gave the coming period a new character. . . .

The thoroughgoing eschatological school [of Schweitzer himself] . . . recognize[d] in the non-occurrence of the Parousia promised in Matt. x. 23 the "historic fact," in the estimation of Jesus, which in some way determined the alteration in his plans, and his attitude toward the multitude.

The whole history of "Christianity" down to the present day, that is to say, the real inner history of it, is based on the delay of the Parousia, the non-occurrence of the Parousia, the abandonment of eschatology, the progress and completion of the "de-eschatologizing" of religion which has been connected therewith. It should be noted that the non-fulfillment of Matt. x. 23 is the first postponement of the Parousia. We have therefore here the first significant date in the "history of Christianity"; it gives to the work of Jesus a new direction, otherwise inexplicable. (359–60)

Thus Jesus' first encounter with actual history, as distinct from the dogmatic history he tried to superimpose on reality, was when he sent the Twelve out on a hurried effort to convert Israel into a mass repentance that would pressure God into initiating the end of time even before the Twelve could return. Hence Jesus did not expect to see them again until after the end, in the kingdom of heaven itself. But what came was not the end, but the disciples returning a bit sheepishly from their mission. The mass repentance that Jesus thought would be triggered by their mission to Jewish villages and which would in turn trigger the end of the world did not take place. For Jesus, this was a terrible letdown. He felt compelled to change his strategy:

This change was due to the non-fulfillment of the promises made in the discourse at the sending forth of the Twelve. He had thought then to let loose the final tribulation and so compel the coming of the kingdom. And the cataclysm had not occurred. . . .

In leaving Galilee he abandoned the hope that the final tribulation would begin of itself. If it delays, that means that there is still something to be done, and yet another of the violent must lay violent hands upon the kingdom of God. The movement of repentance had not been sufficient.

When, in accordance with his commission, by sending forth the disciples with their message, he hurled the fire-brand which should kindle the fiery trials of the Last Time, the flame went out. (389)

So Jesus determined to march on Jerusalem, there to provoke his own martyrdom as an alternate way to cause God to bring in the end:

His death must at last compel the coming of the kingdom. . . .

The new thought of his own passion has its basis therefore in the authority with which Jesus was armed to bring about the beginning of the final tribulation. . . . For now he identifies his condemnation and execution, which are to take place on natural lines, with the predicted pre-Messianic tribulations. This imperious forcing of eschatology into history is also its destruction; its assertion and abandonment at the same time. (390–91)

For this heroic resolve ended in a second, even more painful encounter with actual history, leading to his last anguished cry, "My God, my God, why have you abandoned me?":

What is really remarkable about this wave of apocalyptic enthusiasm is the fact that it was called forth not by external events, but solely by the appearance of two great personalities [John the Baptist and Jesus]. . . .

The Baptist and Jesus are not, therefore, borne upon the current of a general eschatological movement. The period offers no events calculated to give an impulse to eschatological enthusiasm. They themselves set the times in motion by acting, by creating eschatological facts. It is this mighty creative force which constitutes the difficulty in grasping historically the eschatology of Jesus and the Baptist. Instead of literary artifice speaking out of a distant imaginary past, there now enter into the field of eschatology men, living, acting men. It was the only time when that ever happened in Jewish eschatology.

There is silence all around. The Baptist appears, and cries, "Repent, for the kingdom of heaven is at hand." Soon after that comes Jesus, and in the knowledge that he is the coming Son of Man lays hold of the wheel of the world to set it moving on that last revolution which is to bring all ordinary history to a close. It refuses to turn, and he throws himself upon it. Then it does turn, and crushes him. Instead of bringing in the eschatological conditions, he has destroyed them. The wheel rolls onward, and the mangled body of the one immeasurably great man, who was strong enough to think of himself as the spiritual ruler of humankind and to bend history to his purpose, is hanging upon it still. That is his victory and his reign. (370–71)

Schweitzer drew the inevitable consequences for his own time:

Whatever the ultimate solution may be, the historical Jesus of whom the criticism of the future . . . will draw the portrait, can never render modern theology the services which it claimed from its own half-historical, half-modern Jesus. . . .

In either case, he will not be a Jesus Christ to whom the religion of the present can ascribe, according to its long-cherished custom, its own thoughts and ideas, as it did with the Jesus of its own making. Nor will he be a figure which can be made by a popular historical treatment so sympathetic and universally intelligible to the multitude. The historical Jesus will be to our time a stranger and an enigma.

The study of the Life of Jesus has had a curious history. It set out in quest of the historical Jesus, believing that when it had found him it could bring him straight into our time as a teacher and savior. It loosed the bands by which he had been riveted for centuries to the stony rocks of ecclesiastical doctrine, and rejoiced to see life and movement coming into the figure once more, and the historical Jesus advancing, as it seemed, to meet it. But he does not stay; he passes by our time and returns to his own. (398–99)

Where did this leave Schweitzer himself?

But the truth is, it is not Jesus as historically known, but Jesus as spiritually arisen within people, who is significant for our time and can help it. Not the historical Jesus, but the spirit which goes forth from him and in the spirits of people strives for new influence and rule, is that which overcomes the world. . . .

The abiding and eternal in Jesus is absolutely independent of historical knowledge and can only be understood by contact with his spirit
which is still at work in the world. In proportion as we have the Spirit of
Jesus we have the true knowledge of Jesus.

Jesus as a concrete historical personality remains a stranger to our
time, but his spirit, which lies hidden in his words, is known in simplicity,
and its influence is direct. Every saying contains in its own way the whole
Jesus. The very strangeness and unconditionedness in which he stands before us makes it easier for individuals to find their own personal standpoint
in regard to him. (401)

This heroic figure, who called God's hand by laying hold of the wheel of
history and giving it a drastic turn, is in a sense less the historical Jesus, as he
is understood today, than Albert Schweitzer himself. What did Schweitzer
find "hidden in his words"?

Schweitzer's own theological movement was called "thoroughgoing eschatology" or, more literally, "consistent eschatology." By that he meant that
one should carry to its ultimate consequences Jesus' terribly painful discovery that his dogmatic obsession with eschatology was untenable and should
be given up, once and for all, in a thoroughgoing, consistent way. But the
language to bring to expression its "ineffable mystery," "hidden in his words,"
came to Schweitzer first in a riverboat heading for Lambaréné: reverence for
life, respect for everything that is alive.

In a sense, this was culturally conditioned: German culture at the time
he was young was tired of an endless series of rehashes, such as neo-
Gothicism and neoclassicism, which gave America most of its repetitious
church steeples and courthouses of the last century. So the young people of
Schweitzer's time turned to nature, hiking in the woods and coming home
laden with garlands of greenery that they draped in their homes and, in ar-
chitecture, on the facades of their buildings. It is not the dead hand of re-
hashed tradition, but rather the freshness of the life of nature that is what
speaks to us.

But this does not inevitably lead to Lambaréné. Rather he sensed "his
spirit, which lies hidden in his words." One only has to read the text that had
impressed Schweitzer most in his reconstruction of Jesus, the mission of the

Twelve in Matthew 10, to hear the voice that led him to change careers, to study medicine, and to head for Lambaréné:

> Then Jesus summoned his twelve disciples and gave them authority over unclean spirits, to cast them out, and to cure every disease and every sickness. . . . These twelve Jesus sent out with the following instructions: "Go nowhere among the Gentiles, and enter no town of the Samaritans, but go rather to the lost sheep of the house of Israel. As you go, proclaim the good news, 'The kingdom of heaven has come near.' Cure the sick, raise the dead, cleanse the lepers, cast out demons. You received without payment; give without payment. Take no gold, or silver, or copper in your belts, no bag for your journey, or two tunics, or sandals, or a staff; for laborers deserve their food. Whatever town or village you enter, find out who in it is worthy, and stay there until you leave. As you enter the house, greet it. If the house is worthy, let your peace come upon it; but if it is not worthy, let your peace return to you. If anyone will not welcome you or listen to your words, shake off the dust from your feet as you leave that house or town. . . . See, I am sending you out like sheep into the midst of wolves; so be wise as serpents and innocent as doves. . . . When they persecute you in one town, flee to the next; for truly I tell you, you will not have gone through all the towns of Israel before the Son of Man comes. A disciple is not above the teacher, nor a slave above the master; it is enough for the disciple to be like the teacher, and the slave like the master."

It is this text that Schweitzer took so literally as spoken by Jesus to the Twelve that he built his life of Christ upon it—but then built upon it his own life. This is what he meant by the hauntingly sublime language with which *The Quest of the Historical Jesus* closes:

> He comes to us as one unknown, without a name, as of old, by the lakeside, he came to those men who knew him not. He speaks to us the same word: "Follow me!" and sets us to the tasks which he has to fulfill for our

time. He commands. And to those who obey him, whether they be wise or simple, he will reveal himself in the toils, the conflicts, the sufferings which they shall pass through in his fellowship, and, as an ineffable mystery, they shall learn in their own experience who he is.

CHAPTER 16

The Sermon on the Mount

Compiled by Early Followers of Jesus

The New Testament Sermon on the Mount is a radical statement of ethical piety, and as such it has profoundly affected the life and thought of Albert Schweitzer, as the essays in the present volume attest. The Sermon on the Mount has also had a profound impact upon Tolstoy, Bonhoeffer, Gandhi, and other thinkers and activists to the present day. This text is found in the Gospel of Matthew, and it presents Jesus, after the manner of Moses, discussing the law and ethical issues up on a mountain or hill. Occupying chapters 5–7 of Matthew, the Sermon on the Mount may be compared to Luke's Sermon on the Plain, found in chapter 6 of Luke's Gospel. Today scholars commonly consider the sayings of Jesus within the Sermon on the Mount as having derived from Q, the traditional synoptic sayings source that most likely was compiled during the first century and probably was a source used by Matthew and Luke in the composition of their gospels. Thus these sayings of Jesus may be among the very oldest materials we have relating to the historical Jesus. The significance of the Sermon on the Mount for Schweitzer's ethic of reverence for life may be noticed throughout the sermon, but perhaps particularly in the command to love neighbors and enemies and in the statement of ethical reciprocity: "So in everything, act toward others the way you want others to act toward you." The present translation is by Marvin Meyer. For an excellent commentary on this sermon, see Hans Dieter Betz, The Sermon on the Mount *(Minneapolis: Fortress Press, 1995).*

When Jesus saw the crowds, he went up the mountain, and after he sat down, his followers came to him. And he opened his mouth and began to teach them, and he said,

Blessings on the poor in spirit,
for theirs is heaven's kingdom.
Blessings on those who grieve,
for they will be comforted.
Blessings on the gentle,
for they will inherit the earth.
Blessings on those who hunger and thirst
for justice,
for they will be fed.
Blessings on the merciful,
for they will be treated mercifully.
Blessings on those with clean hearts,
for they will see God.
Blessings on those who work for peace,
for they will be called God's children.
Blessings on those who are oppressed
for the sake of justice,
for theirs is heaven's kingdom.
Blessings on you when people insult you
and oppress you
and tell all kinds of evil lies about you
on account of me.
Rejoice and be glad,
for your reward is great in the heavens.
That is how they oppressed the prophets
who came before you.

You are the salt of the earth.
But if salt becomes tasteless,
how can it become salty again?
Then it is good for nothing
except to be thrown out
and trampled by people.

You are the light of the world.
A city set on a hilltop cannot be hidden.
Nor do people light a lamp
and put it under a basket,
but on a lamp stand,
and it gives light to everyone in the house.
That is how your light should shine before people,
that they may see your good deeds
and praise your Father in the heavens.

Do not think I have come to undo
the Torah or the prophets.
I have come not to undo
but to complete.
For in truth I tell you,
Until heaven and earth fade away,
not one yodh,
not one serif will fade away from the Torah,
until everything is done.
So whoever breaks one of the smallest of these rules
and teaches people to do the same
will be called the smallest in heaven's kingdom.
But whoever does them and teaches them
will be called great in heaven's kingdom.
For I tell you,
Unless your justice is greater
than that of the scholars and Pharisees,
you will never enter heaven's kingdom.

You have heard our ancestors were told,
You must not murder,
and whoever murders
deserves judgment.
But I tell you,
Everyone who is angry with a friend

deserves judgment,

and everyone who says to a friend,

You fool,

deserves the sentence of the court,

and everyone who says,

You moron,

deserves the fire of Gehenna.

So if you are offering your gift at the altar

and you recall that your friend has something

against you,

leave your gift there at the altar.

First go and make peace with your friend,

and then return and offer your gift.

Come to terms quickly with your accuser

while the two of you are on the way,

or else your accuser may hand you over to the judge,

and the judge to the officer,

and you will be thrown into prison.

In truth I tell you,

You will never get out of there

until you have paid the last coin.

You have heard people were told,

You must not commit adultery.

But I tell you,

Everyone who eyes a woman and desires her

has already committed adultery with her in the heart.

If your right eye causes you problems,

gouge it out and throw it away.

For you are better off losing one body part

than having your whole body thrown into Gehenna.

And if your right hand causes you problems,

cut it off and throw it away.

For you are better off losing one body part

than having your whole body go into Gehenna.

People were told,
Everyone who divorces his wife
must give her divorce papers.
But I tell you,
Everyone who divorces his wife,
except for reasons of unfaithfulness,
makes her go through adultery,
and everyone who marries a divorced woman
commits adultery.

Again, you have heard our ancestors were told,
You must not break an oath,
but you must keep your oaths
made to the Lord.
But I tell you,
Do not swear any oath,
not by heaven,
because it is God's throne,
nor by the earth,
because it is the stool for God's feet,
nor by Jerusalem,
because it is the city of the great king.
And do not swear an oath by your head,
because you cannot make one hair white or black.
Your word should be Yes yes, or No no.
Anything beyond that is from the evil one.

You have heard people were told,
An eye for an eye
and a tooth for a tooth.
But I tell you,
Do not fight back against someone evil.
If someone slaps you on the right cheek,
turn to the person the other also.
If someone wants to sue you and take your shirt,

let the person have your coat also.
And if someone compels you to go one mile,
go with the person a second mile.
Give to one who begs from you,
and do not refuse one who wants to borrow from you.

You have heard people were told,
You must love your neighbor,
and you must hate your enemy.
But I tell you,
Love your enemies,
and pray for those who oppress you,
that you may be children
of your Father in the heavens.
Your Father makes the sun rise
on the evil and the good,
and makes it rain
on the just and the unjust.
For if you love those who love you,
what reward should you get?
Even tax collectors do as much, don't they?
And if you greet only your friends,
what is so special about that?
Even gentiles do as much, don't they?
So be complete,
as your heavenly Father is complete.

Be careful not to parade your life of justice
before people,
to be noticed by them.
If you do, you will get no reward
from your Father in the heavens.
So when you give to charity,
do not blow your own horn,
as phonies do in synagogues and on the streets,

that they may be praised by people.
In truth I tell you,
They have their reward.
But when you give to charity,
do not let your left hand know
what your right hand is doing,
that your charity may be done in secret.
And your Father, who sees in secret,
will reward you.

And when you pray,
do not be like phonies.
For they love to stand and pray
in synagogues and on street corners,
that they may show off to people.
In truth I tell you,
They have their reward.
When you pray,
go into your room and close the door
and pray to your Father who is in secret.
And your Father, who sees in secret,
will reward you.

And when you pray,
do not ramble on and on like the gentiles,
for they think they will be heard
because they talk so much.
Do not be like them.
For your Father knows what you need
before you ask.

So pray like this:
Our Father in the heavens,
your name be honored,
your kingdom come,

your will be done
on earth as in heaven.
Give us today
our bread for the day,
and free us from our debt
as we also have freed those in debt to us.
And do not bring us to trial,
but rescue us from the evil one.

For if you free people from their faults,
your heavenly Father will also free you.
But if you do not free people,
neither will your Father free you from your faults.

When you fast,
do not look downcast, like phonies.
For they put on long faces,
that they may show off their fasting to people.
In truth I tell you,
They have their reward.
When you fast,
arrange your hair and wash your face,
that you may show your fasting not to people,
but to your Father who is in secret.
And your Father, who sees in secret,
will reward you.

Do not store away for yourselves treasures on earth,
where moths and bugs devour
and where robbers break in and steal.
But store away for yourselves treasures in heaven,
where neither moths nor bugs devour
and where robbers do not break in or steal.
For where your treasure is
your heart will also be found.

The eye is the body's lamp.
So if your eye is healthy,
your whole body will be enlightened,
but if your eye is sick,
your whole body will be darkened.
And if the light within you is darkness,
how dark it is!

No one can serve two masters.
For a person will either hate one and love the other,
or be loyal to one and despise the other.
You cannot serve God and wealth.

That is why I tell you,
Do not worry about your life,
what you will eat or what you will drink,
or about your body,
what you will wear.
Isn't life more than food,
and the body more than clothing?
Look at the birds of heaven.
They do not plant or harvest or store in barns,
and your heavenly Father feeds them.
You are worth more than they, aren't you?
Can any of you add an hour to your life
by worrying?
And why worry about clothing?
Observe the wild lilies,
how they do not prepare or work or spin.
But I tell you,
Not even Solomon at the peak of his glory
was decked out like one of them.
If that is how God clothes the wild grass,
which is here today

and tomorrow is tossed into an oven,
how much more will God clothe you,
you who have so little trust?
So do not worry and say,
What shall we eat,
or what shall we drink,
or what shall we wear?
All this is what the gentiles seek.
For your heavenly Father knows you need all this.
Seek God's kingdom and God's justice first,
and all this will be yours as well.
So do not worry about tomorrow,
for tomorrow can worry about itself.
Each day's trouble is enough for the day.

Do not judge, that you may not be judged.
For the judgment you give
will be the judgment you get,
and the standard you use
will be the standard used on you.
Why do you see a splinter in your friend's eye,
but miss a log in your own eye?
Or how can you say to your friend,
Let me take the splinter out of your eye,
when, look, there is a log in your own eye?
You phony,
first take the log out of your own eye,
and then you will be able to see well enough
to take the splinter out of your friend's eye.

Do not give what is holy to dogs,
and do not throw your pearls to pigs,
or else they may trample them underfoot
and turn and attack you.

Ask and it will be given to you,
seek and you will find,
knock and the door will be opened for you.
For everyone who asks receives,
and everyone who seeks finds,
and for one who knocks
the door will be opened.
Or is there a person among you
who will serve a stone
if your child asks for bread?
Or will serve a snake
if your child asks for fish?
So if you, flawed as you are,
know how to give good gifts to your children,
how much more will your Father in the heavens
give what is good to those who ask!

So in everything,
act toward others
the way you want others to act toward you.
This is the Torah and the prophets.

Enter through the narrow gate.
Wide is the gate and open is the way
leading to destruction,
and there are many who enter through it.
Narrow is the gate and difficult is the way
leading to life,
and there are few who find it.

Be careful of false prophets,
who come to you in the guise of sheep
but underneath are ravenous wolves.
By what they produce

you will know what they are.
Grapes are not harvested from thorns, are they,
or figs from thistles?
Every good tree produces fine fruit,
but a rotten tree produces bad fruit.
A good tree cannot produce bad fruit,
nor can a rotten tree produce fine fruit.
Every tree that does not produce fine fruit
is chopped down and tossed into a fire.
By what they produce, then,
you will know what they are.

Not everyone who says to me,
Master, master,
will enter heaven's kingdom,
but only one who does
the will of my Father in the heavens.
On that day many will say to me,
Master, master,
didn't we prophesy in your name
and exorcise demons in your name
and perform many miracles in your name?
Then I shall announce to them,
I never knew you.
Get away from me,
you wrongdoers.

For everyone who listens to these sayings of mine
and acts on them
will be like a smart person
who built a house on bedrock.
The rain fell, the flood came,
and the wind blew and battered that house,
but it did not collapse,

for its foundation was on bedrock.
And everyone who listens to these sayings of mine
and does not act on them
will be like a foolish person
who built a house on sand.
The rain fell, the flood came,
and the wind blew and beat against that house,
and it collapsed,
and its collapse was great.

And so, when Jesus had finished these sayings, the crowds were amazed at his teaching. For he was teaching them as a person of authority, not like their scholars.

PART FOUR

Reverence for Life and Education

CHAPTER 17

Teaching Reverence for Life

Nikki Lindberg

From 1995 to 1999 Nikki Lindberg was an administrator for the Albert Schweitzer Institute in Connecticut, with a special interest in developing strategies and programs for teaching reverence for life. In this essay she introduces programs and activities that incorporate ethical thinking and service concerns into the education of children and young people. As she describes the programs, "I think we are giving young people the opportunity to ask questions and to discover reverence for life through Albert Schweitzer, what he did, what he thought, what he wrote, and what he stood for. Their world will certainly be the better for it."

The Albert Schweitzer Memorial Foundation was founded in 1984, with the support of Rhena Schweitzer Miller, to perpetuate the philosophy of Albert Schweitzer. It was a volunteer organization that in 1990 put together a major conference at the United Nations to honor Dr. Albert Schweitzer on the twenty-fifth anniversary of his death. The conference addressed subject areas of particular interest to Dr. Schweitzer: health, the environment, animal and human rights, theology, music, and world peace. Speakers included such well-known figures as writer Norman Cousins, zoologist Jane Goodall, President Benjamin Hooks of the NAACP, and President Oscar Arias of Costa Rica. It was the largest conference of its kind held by a nonprofit organization at the UN.

As a natural outgrowth of this successful conference, the foundation became the Albert Schweitzer Institute for the Humanities (now called the Albert Schweitzer Institute). It adopted the following mission statement: "To perpetuate Albert Schweitzer's philosophy of reverence for life through programs of education and action." Some of these programs focus upon the education of young people and the incorporation of ethical reflection and service into curricula.

According to the AASA (the American Association of School Administrators), the juvenile violent crime arrest rate increased by 60 percent between 1985 and 1995. We only have to go to the movies or scan a few video games to see the violence with which young people are surrounded. During 1996, 19 percent of the people arrested for violent crimes were under eighteen years old.

AASA also references a survey conducted by Northeastern University which indicates that the vast majority of law enforcement officials agreed that "educational and preventive services are more likely to be a deterrent to youth crime than is construction of more prisons. America could sharply reduce crime if government invested more in programs to help children and youth get a good start."

◆　　◆　　◆

To help children and youth get a good start, Dr. Albert Schweitzer gave us major, invaluable, and—I will even venture to say—incomparable teaching tools:

The first teaching tool Albert Schweitzer gives us is his example as a role model.

In a letter to Norman Cousins, Dr. Schweitzer wrote, "I decided I would make my life my argument. I would advocate the things I believed in, in terms of the life I lived and what I did." As Cousins later commented, "Dr. Schweitzer's greatness does not lie primarily in what he accomplished during his lifetime. Rather, it lies in what others have done because of his example."

Young people respond well to Albert Schweitzer's life story. He is a source of great interest and his example is an exceptional one.

The second teaching tool he gives us is his philosophy of reverence for life.

Dr. Schweitzer devoted many years to the study of theology and philosophy and earned his Ph.D.s in both fields. He then earned his medical degree, having decided to devote the remainder of his life to serving people in need. He went on to build his hospital in Africa, where he continued his intellectual pursuits, searching for a concise expression of his philosophy. In the following passage, Dr. Schweitzer recounts how his philosophy of reverence for life first occurred to him:

> I resolved to devote the entire trip to the problem of how a culture could be brought into being, that possessed a greater *moral depth* and *energy* than the one we lived in. I filled page after page with disconnected sentences, primarily to center my every thought on the problem. At sunset on the third day, near the village of Igendja, we moved along an island set in the middle of the wide river. On a sandbank to our left, four hippopotamuses and their young plodded along in our direction. Just then, in my great tiredness and discouragement, there flashed upon my mind, unforeseen and unsought, the phrase, 'reverence for life.' The iron door had yielded: the path in the thicket had become visible. Now I had found my way to the idea in which affirmation of the world and ethics are contained side by side! . . . Only by means of reverence for life can we establish a spiritual and humane relationship with both people and all living creatures within our reach.

There is film footage showing Dr. Schweitzer talking about this moment. His eyes are twinkling, his excitement is clearly visible, and it is hard to help but feel it, too.

The third teaching tool Dr. Schweitzer gives us is his writing—a voluminous record of his thoughts from childhood onward. It provides resources for even very young children to tap into, to begin honing their own character values.

Reading, for example, with young students about Albert Schweitzer's experience of going bird-shooting with his friend in Günsbach, where he spent his childhood, prompts the following questions: Why did he not wish to shoot a bird? Was he concerned about losing the friendly relationship with the boy he was with if he did not shoot it? Have you ever done anything you felt was wrong but had reasons for doing it anyway? Why did you make the decision you made? In retrospect, would you make the same decision today?

Or, reading about the time when Albert refused to wear his winter coat to school because the boys in the village were too poor to have one: Was this about friendly relationships, too? What was Albert thinking? What would you have done? Why?

There are many stories Dr. Schweitzer tells that young children respond to because they are real. They relate the stories to their own circumstances and think about life in a new way. There are examples in his writing that present ethical questions appropriate for all ages to discuss. That is one of the beauties of Dr. Schweitzer's writing: the range is so broad.

◆　　◆　　◆

In 1995, the Albert Schweitzer Institute moved onto the campus of Choate Rosemary Hall, a private secondary school in Wallingford, Connecticut. This move provided the institute with a laboratory and a partner for developing its youth programs.

Not long after we had settled in, the headmaster of Choate Rosemary Hall, Edward Shanahan, and the Wallingford superintendent of schools, Dr. Joseph Cirasuolo, came to us with a proposition for student collaboration. They were seeking an opportunity for their students to relate in ways other than the competitive environment of sports. Interschool student relationships were not friendly. Would the Albert Schweitzer Institute spearhead the development of a program that would bring students together? Shanahan and Cirasuolo said that they would work with the institute closely.

◆　　◆　　◆

This resulted in a very successful program conducted during the 1996–1997 academic year with a group of fifteen students, five from each of the two public high schools and five from a private high school. The program had three phases:

• A six-week extracurricular course on Albert Schweitzer. Each session was guided by faculty but led by students who prepared the discussion questions.

• A local community service project, selected and planned by the students.

• A two-week community service project in a developing country.

The text provided to students in the course segment of the program covered Dr. Schweitzer writing about human rights, animal rights, peace issues, music—the array of subjects we associate with him. The kinds of discussion questions prompted by the students after thinking about these issues were:

- True or false: Man is superior to the other fifteen to seventeen million identified species on earth.
- Do humans rank the worth of certain species? How?
- You are a poor farmer in a tropical rainforest. You own several acres of land, but the crops are not doing well. Would you sell this land to a logging company to support your family? What other choices are there?
- What do you think about when you hear Bach's *Toccata and Fugue in D minor?* Try to identify colors, emotions, shapes, or natural happenings.

For local community service projects, the group members chose to paint the bleachers at the community playground and to work at the food bank. They also collected clothing, toys, and supplies for the people in Suriname, South America, where they would be doing their international community service work. In addition, the institute welcomed volunteers for its own humanitarian aid program. The volunteers sorted and packed medical supplies for shipment to developing countries.

The two-week community service program in Suriname was an adventure for the students as well as a dramatic learning experience about different cultures, ethnic structures, and economic levels. The students spent time in the rainforest, where they met those who depend upon it for their livelihoods. The students were also houseguests of community leaders and the diplomatic corps, and they worked in an orphanage and in a junior detention center, painted a clinic, and planted pineapples. They had opportunities to enter the life of the community, including participating in Pagua, a communitywide festival with similarities to Carnaval in Brazil. Part of this festival's ritual includes "painting" everyone in sight with brightly colored powders.

In communicating with the first interschool group a year later, we learned that all but one of the students continued to be interested and involved in community service work in their schools, colleges, or communities, and 50 percent of them had advocated or were leading a community service project. Several of them made the same statement on their evaluations of the project: "This experience changed my life."

The experience affected how they viewed other people, their classmates, people in the town where they lived, and those from different cultures. It affected how they viewed natural resources and the world around them. It affected how they viewed themselves and, most important, their role and potential contribution to society.

Months later, a teacher whom I had not met before came to my office and spoke about one of the participants in the program who came from a very poor family. This student was tough and streetwise, and she had never been outside Connecticut. The teacher wanted me to know that the girl had changed—she had become thoughtful and considerate. Those qualities were always there, of course, but they had not been given an opportunity to surface above what were perceived as survival traits for her teen years.

Bringing the Schweitzer philosophy to young people can serve to develop leadership qualities in them. It can serve to build a strong and wise citizenry. It can also serve to guide those who might otherwise have taken a wrong turn in life.

A Schweitzer text that was developed for this project, and the workbook that resulted, became the first of our series of Schweitzer Action Packs. We called them Action Packs because they involve learning, discussion, and service.

The desired result is that young people using the Action Packs will "make their lives their argument," the way Albert Schweitzer did. We hope that doing community service becomes part of the fabric of their lives.

With the institute's Action Pack for high school students in hand, work began on the development of three additional Action Packs: one for kindergarten through grade 2; one for grades 3, 4, and 5; and one for grades 6, 7, and 8. A diverse group of teachers from public, private, and parochial schools have volunteered their time to work on the packs relating to the grades they teach. Each pack includes:

- An age-appropriate text about or by Albert Schweitzer
- A teacher's guide and discussion questions
- Ideas for community service.

◆ ◆ ◆

The K-2 Action Pack has been tested by a number of teachers.

Sue Mattingly, who used the pack in her second-grade class at the Israel Putnam Elementary School in Meriden, Connecticut, submitted the following report:

Background: The students were an enthusiastic, multicultural group. The class included children from different family structures (both parents, one parent, foster parents, etc.) and different income levels. The group of twenty came from apartments, individual homes, low-income housing, and the shelter.

The poster of Albert Schweitzer generated a lot of curious comments and questions: "Who is that guy?" "Why are there children near him?" "What a strange chair he is sitting in!"

After about a week, I introduced Albert Schweitzer by reading the picture book we had put together and by telling the children a few little stories I had recalled from my own reading.

Interest was building and there were lots of questions, covering everything from "Was his wife pretty?" to "What happened to his hospital and the animals?"

I continued using the packet by next playing the tape (Albert Schweitzer playing Bach on one side and African music on the other) and rereading the children's book. Then each child wrote and illustrated what they thought was their favorite part of the book. Those papers were full of interesting, innocent insights. Again, there were many questioning comments: "He is like me, I love animals." "I have trouble sometimes in school, maybe I'll get smart and do something important like him some day." "I wish he was still alive so he could remind people to be kind."

◆   ◆   ◆

What I had planned was a few weeks in length, but I soon realized that the children were completely engaged with Albert Schweitzer and his philosophy, so I needed to do much more.

◆   ◆   ◆

The themes of friendship, caring, service, and courage came alive as we worked through the packet. Students made puppets and maps of Africa, created posters to advertise Schweitzer's ideas to our school, and had many lively discussions.

Student learning was unbelievable! Parents and siblings commented to me on what a worthwhile project it was. One parent, in an end-of-the-year letter to me, wrote a positive comment mentioning the important Schweitzer unit:"I feel that my child was part of such a memorable learning experience."

Our culminating activity was a visit from Rhena Schweitzer Miller. We prepared questions, and the children were very excited. It was an experience I will never forget.

While Mrs. Miller was observing, I wanted her to see some of the children's thinking as they completed a simple activity, What They Could Do to Make the World a Better Place. The children's learning can be seen from the following comments they made on their drawings:"I will always be kind and think about other people and creatures."" I will remind people to treat animals with respect because they are special too.""I will always work hard and do my best because every little person can make our world a better place." "If kids keep telling adults to use the Golden Rule, maybe they'll start using it too."

◆　　◆　　◆

Later . . .

◆　　◆　　◆

Schweitzer became part of our classroom as we continually practiced caring, respect, friendship, and courage in all we did. These themes followed the ideas of the Responsive Classroom, which was a part of my teaching philosophy. Students become responsible for their classroom and their own learning. I often heard children saying things such as "Dr. Schweitzer wouldn't have liked that," in relation to a news story about an animal that was hurt. "Come on, don't say that. Remember what Dr. Schweitzer said. Use the Golden Rule." To a student who acted shy and was afraid to answer a question:"Come on, have courage like Dr. Schweitzer. He wasn't afraid to try something new."

Even at the end of the year the students related things back to our unit on Dr. Schweitzer. (I used the packet in late February through mid-March.) It was a very worthwhile project that carried over into much of what we did for the rest of the year.

◆　　◆　　◆

Now . . .

◆　　◆　　◆

Former students have asked me if the new class has met Parsifal (Albert Schweitzer's pet pelican) yet, and when class members are going to learn about Dr. Schweitzer, because "he's a really important guy" (the words of a very tough little nine year old).

The packs for grades 3, 4, 5 and 6, 7, 8 are in the process of being tested. When final adjustments have been made, they will be put into production. Our hope is that teachers in schools throughout the country will choose to incorporate them into their school programs. The exposure to the values espoused by Albert Schweitzer must start when children are very young and must be reinforced until ethical thinking and generosity of spirit are part of their natures.

Another route the institute is taking toward helping students discover reverence for life for themselves is through a series of interschool workshops. These are organized in partnership with the School for Ethical Education in Bridgeport, Connecticut, and offered for middle or high school students.

They are structured as follows: several schools, selected for their diversity—inner-city, country, private, public, and parochial—are invited to send a team of five or six students and one teacher. The teams come to Choate Rosemary Hall, where the institute is located, for one full day. During most of the day, the teams are split up and become part of new teams made up of representatives from all the schools. At this point students work with others they have not met before. The agenda includes guided explorations of common character values, case studies involving ethical choices, and discussions of what characteristics make up an ideal community.

The workshop exercises vary depending on visiting faculty. One of the workshop exercises included a segment on tolerance and acting out students' worst fears. The mixed group of students put a number of widely held prejudices out on the table for open discussion.

At the end of the day, the school teams reconnect with their own schoolmates to think about how they can contribute to the betterment of their communities. They plan service projects they will begin back in their own schools or communities.

The institute and the School for Ethical Education follow up with the teachers that participated. The following describes some of the projects the students have undertaken.

One group of middle school students developed welcome kits for new students at school. Another provided tutoring services for elementary students after school and set up visits to a nearby senior citizens home.

Within the high school groups, one team expanded to include additional students interested in programs with intergenerational connections. Approximately ten students visited local senior homes twice a week. Another high school group developed a needs assessment, conducting community interviews to evaluate what service projects would be most useful in the community. Possible projects included volunteering with the soup kitchen and organizing a recycling project.

A teacher and group of students in one school we worked with chose to stay together and form a Schweitzer club dedicated to continuing their learning and involvement in matters related to reverence for life—human rights, peace, and health issues.

A second club was formed by a theater group in Yugoslavia, whose members bring their dramatic performances into orphanages and senior centers as a result of their workshop experience.

Part of our future thinking includes ways to expand and support the Schweitzer clubs, including chat rooms over the Internet and youth leadership conferences. Another way the institute promotes Albert Schweitzer's legacy is by recognizing young people who are role models themselves. The Albert Schweitzer Environmental Youth Award has been presented annually to individuals or groups of students between the ages of twelve and eighteen who have initiated a project to effect positive environmental change.

The 1998 award recipient, Michael Anderson, was a high school student from Oklahoma who founded an organization called Environmental CPR to expand community recycling operations, organize awareness campaigns, and offer educational programs involving numerous volunteers, county officials, and club members.

Brandon Kingsbury, a middle school student from Florida, received the second-place award in 1998 for his three-year project, which researched whether a local power plant was contributing to acid rain. The award reflects Dr. Schweitzer's ethic of reverence for life, which emphasizes each person's responsibility to all forms of life on our planet.

The 1999 recipient, Melissa Poe, founded one of the world's largest environmental action groups for kids: Kids F.A.C.E.—Kids For a Clean Environment. She started at the age of nine, strongly affected by a TV show she saw which indicated that the world might not be a healthy place when she grew up. "Help me stop pollution," she wrote President Bush in 1989. She became an organizer of the first order. Kids F.A.C.E. is now an organization with three hundred thousand members worldwide.

Are we teaching reverence for life? I think we are giving young people the opportunity to ask questions and to discover reverence for life through Albert Schweitzer, what he did, what he thought, what he wrote, and what he stood for. Their world will certainly be the better for it.

CHAPTER 18

Student Essays on Albert Schweitzer and Reverence for Life

The student essays presented here derive from the Chapman University course "Albert Schweitzer: His Life and Thought," taught annually as a course in peace studies, philosophy, and religious studies. They confront issues that may be addressed in the context of Schweitzer's ethic of reverence for life: finding meaning in life through twelve-step programs, making everyday decisions, setting standards for eating, deciding on abortion, considering the rights of animals, and living a life of responsibility in action. The essays are published here with the permission of the students.

Finding Meaning in Life   Joie Karnes

How is a person to find meaning in life? According to Albert Schweitzer, in his book *Out of My Life and Thought,* the only way of giving meaning to one's existence is to "raise his physical relationship to the world to a spiritual one." This first involves passive inward experience, then active experience with the world. Schweitzer claims this will lead to an ethical affirmation for all life, which he refers to as reverence for life. In this essay I will look at these two stages of passive and active relationship to the world and how I think Schweitzer went through these steps in his own life to reach his ethic of reverence for life. I will also include some of the ways I think he lived this ethic. I will conclude with questions about what Schweitzer calls elemental thinking and how Schweitzer and others seem to arrive at the starting point of this journey.

The passive inward experience that leads to a spiritual relationship with the world begins with resignation. It occurs when, feeling subordinate to world events, one moves toward "inward freedom from the fate that shapes his external existence." This inner freedom affords one the strength needed to succeed in everyday difficulties and to become a "deeper and more inward person, calm and peaceful." Schweitzer considered resignation as the "spiritual and ethical affirmation of one's own existence," and to be capable of accepting the world, one must go through the "trial of resignation" (233).

The active role is different from the passive in that the spiritual relationship one has with the world is not seen in isolation. Schweitzer writes, "On the contrary, one is united with the lives that surround him; he experiences the destinies of others as his own. He helps as much as he can and realizes that there is no greater happiness than to participate in the development and protection of life" (233). Schweitzer continues this line of thought to the conclusion that once a person begins considering the mystery of one's individual life and then connects that to all that lives in the world, the ethic of reverence for life will naturally be reached . One will then live this ethic. As a result, life will be more difficult than a self-centered life would have been, but life will be "richer, more beautiful, and happier" because of it. For Schweitzer it will become, "instead of mere living, a genuine experience of life" (234).

Schweitzer seemed to be a contemplative person even in childhood. However, I wonder if some of the influences that led him to such deep inner reflection included being able to excel in so many areas. Some of us might be deluded into thinking that if only we were at the top of our game, whether it be basketball, business, or art, we would find the meaning of life. If we do not find meaning, it could be because we never made it to the top. We could die trying the wrong path and never know it. Schweitzer did not have the luxury of that delusion. He was not only at the top in one area, he was accomplished in many. The thought of success in any endeavor as the solution to the question of meaning in life could be experientially proven false by Schweitzer. (This is my speculation, of course, not Schweitzer's.)

After receiving much acclaim in diverse fields (music, organ building and playing, theology, and philosophy), he decided to serve others by becoming a doctor of medicine and practicing in Africa. His extraordinary efforts to accomplish this goal were interrupted in the early years by World

War I. At first he was denied, as a German citizen, the opportunity to practice medicine in a French colony. Next, he and his wife were taken to an internment camp as prisoners of war. Then he returned home to Alsace to find the horrors of war all around him, including the news that his mother had been trampled to death by soldiers on horses. How could someone who did so much good in the world experience so much bad? It seems that—by itself—life led in the service of others, as the solution to the question of meaning in life, could also be proven false (experientially) by Schweitzer.

Schweitzer went into a depression after the war. Could it be the combination of all of these factors (broad exceptional success, service of others, and death and destruction) that led him to experience the feeling of subordination to world events on a profound level? Perhaps this is when he combined his religious background and training with his introspective nature to reach experientially the passive inward experience he later articulates as part of the journey toward living the ethic of reverence for life.

From caring for Africans in his hospital to sharing his food with ants under his house, Schweitzer clearly exemplifies one who has a relationally active role with the universe. While he seemed to have always been sensitive, he learned over time the importance of not hurting animals and the importance of helping them. He also seemed to have learned about relationships with people. As a child, he was said to have had a mean temper and once actually hit his sister in the face. In school, he had not participated in a study group until he was in his thirties at medical school, and he was resistant to join even then, in spite of the obligation he felt to serve others and the joy he received in so doing.

Schweitzer had a fantastic ability to remember specific details in his life that related to his ethical development. For example, when a Jewish man walked through town with his cart and was made fun of by the Christian children, Schweitzer learned from the humble dignity and compassion the man showed the ignorant children (including Schweitzer). During the war, when Schweitzer and his wife were laden with more baggage than they were strong enough to carry, a stranger offered to help them. From that point on, Schweitzer made a point of helping those with more bags than they were able to carry. Schweitzer's role continually expanded; this is evident in his political involvement (late in life) when he was speaking out against nuclear weapons.

Schweitzer could very well have developed this active part of his theory over a lifetime of experiences in which the internal rewards for acting in the service of others were preferable to the feelings produced from harming others.

I spell out experientially some of the events that I believe could have contributed to Schweitzer's development of the ethic of reverence for life, because I subscribe to the suggestion of Bill Wilson, cofounder of Alcoholics Anonymous, that the spiritual life is not a theory; it has to be lived. What Schweitzer calls elemental thinking "starts from fundamental questions about the relationship of human beings to the universe, about the meaning of life, and about the nature of what is good" (228). I do not think people ask these questions unless they are already in the process of resignation to the world, trying to reconcile the contradictions that make acceptance of the world as it is seem impossible. When the spiritual bankruptcy of the age reaches each individual, then he or she has the ability to start on the path of resignation that leads to living the ethic of reverence for life. No matter how profound a text is, I do not think anyone will achieve true understanding from simply reading it. The service I think Schweitzer is now providing us is an example of what to do when we do look for meaning in life.

Alcoholics and addicts of all sorts are finding meaning in life in just the way Schweitzer prescribes. Through twelve-step programs people must accept their subordination to world events and develop inner freedom and serenity, and to keep life they are told they have to give it away in the service of others. The basic premise is that of reverence for life. Some people are better at incorporating reverence for *all* life (not just human life) than others, but I think there is hope. Personal responsibility for all of a person's actions (which Schweitzer also emphasized) is crucial to twelve-step programs and is also an essential component of reverence for life. Perhaps programs like these will help usher in what Schweitzer believed we needed: "a new spiritual force strong enough to evoke a new spirit in humankind" (243).

Reverence For Life: Making Decisions   Maria Tafoya

We tend to look at "the big picture." For most people, reverence for life refers to human life, not the "lower" life forms. Even those who are actively involved in caring for the ecosystem might work to preserve another species, but not necessarily care about individuals within a species. They might express concern for the species of earthworm, even avoid stepping on one, yet not go to the length of moving it out of the street so it may survive longer. Albert Schweitzer saw life a bit differently.

He believed, like the Jains, in "unconditional respect for all forms of life" (see the video entitled *Ahimsa,* a production of KRMA-TV, Denver, 1987). The stories about Schweitzer feeding the ants in his study reflect statements by Jains that "all life is equal . . . therefore, I look on even an ant as equal to me." How, then, was Schweitzer able to make life and death decisions between living organisms? As a physician he knew that the choices were necessary, and seemingly he had no difficulty in making these decisions when the question was the survival of a bacterium over the survival of a human. He said, "The necessity to destroy and to injure life is imposed upon me. . . . In order to preserve my own existence, I must defend myself against the existence which injures it" (Schweitzer, *The Philosophy of Civilization,* 316).

A while ago I was told that I had cervical cancer, and that a number of organs would need to be removed in order to kill the existing cancer and to prevent its spread. I certainly had no crisis of conscience when I was faced with the destruction of cancer cells versus my continued life. I was extremely grateful when I learned that much of the tissue that was removed, and thus killed, was healthy, since it meant the cancer had not yet begun to spread. Nor did I object to killing bacteria when I was told to use antibacterial soap to keep my incision from developing an infection. I certainly agree with Schweitzer that any organism which threatens my existence should be destroyed. Killing cancer cells or a flu virus is a fairly easy decision, of course. There are certainly much more difficult decisions to be made about which organism should live, even in life-threatening situations.

In the video *Ahimsa* it was noted that many Jains are physicians, and thus are faced with these kinds of issues every day. After mentioning the tuberculosis and cancer clinics established and maintained by Jains, a monk who had been a physician was introduced. He spoke of one of the most controversial of all health issues, abortion, saying, "Killing is wrong, but in cases where termination of the pregnancy is desirable because of the health of the mother . . . this is accepted medical practice, and is accepted among ethical people as well." If the pregnancy threatens the life of the mother, then the choice may be made to terminate the pregnancy, thus losing one life instead of two. It was not stated but can be inferred that if no life is endangered by the pregnancy, then an abortion would not be accepted among ethical people. Obviously, these decisions are made on a case-by-case basis. Schweitzer also saw the need to approach each situation individually, making the decision regarding the necessity of killing over and over again.

Schweitzer's lifestyle, if it had been based in *ahimsa,* would seem paradoxical. He fed ants, yet killed fish for Parsifal the pelican. For most of his life he was not a vegetarian and enjoyed the various meats that appeared at his daily meals. However, reverence for life is not entirely based in *ahimsa.* It should be remembered that, although Schweitzer admired some of the tenets of Jains, saying "their ethics is correct in demanding kindness and mercy not only to human beings but to all living creatures," he rejected Jainism as a complete ethical system (Ara Paul Barsam, "The Influence of Jainism on the Thought of Albert Schweitzer," paper presented at the conference "Albert Schweitzer at the Turn of the Millennium"; compare Barsam's essay, Chapter 14). Schweitzer felt that Jainism did not go far enough, that *ahimsa* was merely a practice of nonviolence and avoidance of hurt, whereas he felt that "it is not enough to avoid the bad, one must do good. . . . Reverence for life requires deliberately working toward healing" (Barsam). He believed that "reverence for life is not to paralyze, but to open opportunities" (Barsam). These beliefs led Schweitzer to become a doctor, thus "a mass murderer of the bacteria" (Schweitzer, *The Philosophy of Civilization,* 317). Reverence for life led him to choose between lives and between goods, choosing always what he believed to be the greater good. Therefore, he could do good for Parsifal by feeding him, even though this meant he had to kill fish to do so. It should also be remembered that Parsifal would have killed the fish himself if he were not a pet, but all the pelicans I have ever met would much rather be hand fed than go fishing. Either way, however, the fish were going to become dinner.

Many Native American people see all life as interconnected. For the Navajo, as long as each piece of creation is kept in balance with all other pieces, the nation and the land will be healthy. Because every part of the world depends on every other part, it is wrong for humans simply to use that which is around them without thought. Humans depend on meat for food, but it is necessary to recognize the essence of the creature that is killed for food, and the fact that the hunter and the hunted are related. Each animal that is killed for food is thanked for giving its life and is treated with respect. Even the corn and other vegetables are thanked and celebrated. Nothing is wasted, because this would damage the balance, causing illness in the people and the land. The lack of balance and concern for the interconnectedness of all of nature by the "civilized" nations has led to environmental disaster worldwide.

If we take the time to think about them, our daily decisions about life and death are usually not as dramatic or as easy as the one I made about my cancer cells. We have to decide what to eat, whether to swat the mosquito, if we should walk around the snail on the sidewalk or place it in the grass, and so on. For many people the decision as to whether to eat meat can be a difficult one, particularly if they have not really understood where those neat plastic packages in the supermarket started out. I was raised on a farm and grew up understanding that certain animals were destined to become my dinner. We had the responsibility of caring for them to the best of our ability, not merely because we wanted healthy food, but because they were alive and deserved good treatment. The sheep and chickens we raised were given names, played with, and eventually killed, butchered, and eaten. It was part of life, according to our respective places on the food chain.

Because of these experiences I know that my hamburger used to be a cow. I know where those plastic packages started out and do not have a problem consuming what I know to have been a living creature, raised for the specific purpose of being eaten. I know that an egg I buy in the store was never fertilized, so it could never become a chicken; thus no life is endangered through my eating it. I know that buying dairy products in the store will not deprive a calf of its food, for the calf was weaned before the cow's milk was made available for sale.

I was also taught that some wild creatures were dangerous to our farm animals and to humans. At an early age I was taught to shoot, and what I was allowed to shoot at. The deadly cottonmouth moccasin was fair game, but the corn-stealing crow was not. Moccasins are not afraid of anything and will actually attack, but a crow can be frightened out of the fields. Those early teachings continue to affect my life and death decisions. Mosquitoes are annoying, but they are the main food source for fruit bats and other creatures, so I wear mosquito repellent and try to avoid swatting them. I am allergic to bees, yet I prefer to have my husband catch them and put them outdoors rather than to kill them. However, if it comes down to the bee or me, I will choose my own life every time.

It seems clear that reverence for life is an ethic that can be applied in everyday life. The important, and perhaps most difficult, point is that the decision must be made repeatedly by each person, in every situation. The big, one-time decisions such as killing cancer cells seem simple compared to the need to be constantly aware of all the life decisions that come up in a day. It should not even be thought that "this is the decision I made last time, so I will make the same one this time," since no two situations are ever exactly identical. I may have made a lifestyle decision that includes eating meat, but each time I plan a meal I make that decision again. Each time I see a bee I must decide whether to avoid it, catch it, or kill it. Reverence for life requires constant awareness that the decision should be one that is in favor of the preservation of existence and the greater good.

Reverence for Life and Eating   Timothy Johnson

I eat, therefore I am. Eating involves the taking of life to prolong one's own life, and of course those who do not eat waste away and die. If reverence for life is simply the revering of life, there would be no problem. I could just be mindful and grateful for each morsel of food I consume, either thanking the Lord or Great Spirit, the animal itself, or both.

Albert Schweitzer noted that "I am life which wills to live, in the midst of life which wills to live" (*The Philosophy of Civilization,* 309). This statement is true. There is nothing hidden or esoteric in it; it simply states the fundamental element of life and its nature. In the Sermon on the Mount Jesus said, "So in everything, act toward others the way you want others to act toward you" (Matthew 7.12). Since the ethic of Jesus and Schweitzer are the same (at least Schweitzer thought so)—that is, reverence for life—the command would be "show the same reverence for life to others that you would have them show unto you."

Schweitzer did not even soften his ethic and write it in the Mahayana Buddhist vein of "take no unnecessary life." His ethic is strictly "take no life," plain and simple: "Ethics is responsibility without limits towards all that lives" (Schweitzer, *Philosophy of Civilization,* 311). This makes his ethic an absolute, yet no "thou shalts" and "thou shalt nots" are involved.

If we are to live, we must break this simple and straightforward commandment and not show reverence for life to some unfortunate sentient being. Everyday about three meals and maybe a snack or two are eaten by the average American or European person. Everything on the plate before a person is a leg, an arm, or some other portion of sentient life. The meals usually have unnecessarily large portions, and the snacks generally are the result of boredom or indulgence.

The dilemma is between being a truly ethical person who reveres all life and is dying from starvation and sickness, or being someone who eats animals and kills bacteria to live. The former person's bacteria tell their friends to come on over, since their host will not take life. So, we may call this person a saint, but most people would not be able to subscribe to this extremely ascetic way of life. Even Albert Schweitzer himself did not do so; evidently this is not the correct solution to the great ethical dilemma of eating.

Vegetarians abstain from the eating of animal meat, and certain adherents further abstain from all animal products, including milk, honey, and eggs. At first this appears to be an answer, a solution that does not involve taking the lives of animals. However, this approach only partially solves the problem. Although vegetarians do not eat meat, they do eat vegetables, fruits, grains, and nuts. Life is still being taken, albeit green life. Their refusal to support and fund the inhumane treatment and slaughter of animals makes vegetarians seem nobler than their carnivorous counterparts.

Since Albert Schweitzer does not set up a hierarchy—for example, humans-apes-lions-cows-chickens-fish-clams-spiders-insects-celery-potatoes-bacteria and so on—being a vegetarian will not resolve the dilemma. Since all life is life, to be revered and regarded as equal, good is not done by choosing to devour one form of life over another. For example, I could eat my younger brother, or I could drink a glass of gutter water, and both cases would involve taking life.

Vegetarianism really does not solve the problem, and eternal fasting is not an option. As I attempt to think clearly, I have concluded that "take no unnecessary life" should be my guide. This means that at buffets I must eat only what I need to satisfy my hunger, instead of trying to get my money's worth. In America a restaurant meal is not considered good unless one can get another meal out of it. That plastic box sits in the refrigerator wasting away, hosting new forms of life, until it is forgotten about and later thrown away. At home, I must take only what will sustain my own being, showing an indebtedness to the Christ figures in miso soup, shrimp tempura, rice, seaweed, and green tea that died so that I may live. Truly, the only solution is to eat simply and not to excess.

Albert Schweitzer did not want to make this universal ethic a dogmatic, legalistic doctrine. Rather, he wanted each human being to find the right balance, to find the way for himself or herself. If I am indeed life that wills to live, my life must be sustained by disregarding another's will to live. This is where the dilemma begins and ends.

Although Schweitzer's reverence for life is an absolute, it is an impossible absolute. Finding the way in this ethic only comes through clear thinking, and through clear thinking comes rational judgment. Schweitzer's universal ethic does not provide ways around it, for it is simply "take no life." People must reflect upon this ethical system with their own clear thinking, which usually results in a hierarchy and a system of "thou shalts" and "thou shalt nots." As long as this legalistic doctrine of ethical action is the result of a love affair with clear thinking, Schweitzer would have no complaints. So we must, as Gandhi said, "Live simply that others may simply live," or even "Eat simply that others may simply live."

Applying the Ethic of Reverence for Life to the Issue of Abortion in America   Joie Karnes

In his book *Out of My Life and Thought*, Albert Schweitzer argues that humanity is in a period of spiritual decline. Having discovered the principle of reverence for life, which contains the ethical affirmation of life, Schweitzer wanted to effect change in the world by helping people "to think more deeply and more independently" (223). This is an interesting avenue through which to look at the abortion issue in America, whose two sides fight for the right to life and the right to choose. Each side contains an ethical principle about which Schweitzer felt very deeply. Schweitzer has reverence for life, but he also argues that independent thought is necessary for an individual to be capable of living this ethic. Therefore, I will first discuss Schweitzer's views on independent thought and how they pertain to the right to choose, and then I will discuss his views on reverence for life, relating it to the right to life. I will conclude with the consideration of how, with Schweitzerian ethics, these two can be used together.

First, a brief review of the opposing sides. The pro-life faction, which is against abortion, posits that an unborn fetus is a human life and therefore has all the rights of a human being, including the right to life. Pro-lifers argue that it is the responsibility of government to protect all human life by making abortion illegal. Some pro-lifers support abortion in the cases of rape, incest, or endangerment of the mother's life, while others do not support abortion under any circumstance. Many pro-lifers are also against sex education and birth control.

The people who support the right to have an abortion call themselves pro-choice and advocate both sex education and birth control. Some agree and some disagree with the pro-lifers that an unborn fetus is a human life. Regardless of each pro-choice person's view on the status of the fetus, the argument they defend together is that our government is not the appropriate body to make this difficult decision: the body of the mother is.

◆　　◆　　◆

William R. LaFleur wrote in his book *Liquid Life: Abortion and Buddhism in Japan* of our desire to define "life." Many think that if we could accomplish that, things would fall into place and our ethical dilemmas would begin to dissolve. He observes that our society seems to believe that with sufficient definitions, salvation from our problems can be achieved. It is "as if matters of substantive difference do not exist and the only problem we have is the relatively easy one of clarifying a few key terms." LaFleur also suggests that our desire for agreement on definitions is connected with another societal belief:"if only we could pass the 'right' laws or repeal certain other laws, our society would be on the road to solving its deepest social problems" (14).

In the case of abortion, Americans are looking to the courts for the solution to this ethical dilemma. We hope that someone else will tell us what makes a person "dead" and at what "point" in time life begins. By accomplishing this, we think we will be able to distinguish "acts that are innocuous and even charitable from ones that are murderous and cruel. Thus we try to pull off moral miracles with words and definitions" (15). In so doing, we delude ourselves into thinking that we can pass the responsibility of our ethical choices and actions from ourselves to someone or something else.

This exemplifies the reason Schweitzer described the spirit of our age as being "filled with contempt for thought" (Schweitzer, *Out of My Life and Thought,* 223). People doubt the efficacy of using thought to answer the question in life that brings meaning and substance to it, namely, what is our relationship to the universe? The problem is compounded because people not only neglect thought but also mistrust it. This is because the "organized political, social, and religious associations of our time are at work convincing the individual not to develop convictions through his own thinking but to assimilate the ideas they present to him" (224). This makes a thinking person at least inconvenient and perhaps even dangerous to organized institutions because they cannot trust him or her to comply uniformly with their agendas. It is within this uniformity that corporate bodies believe they have their power. The spirit of the age ignores the fact that human progress is a result of thought, and that there could be future achievements because of it. Instead it sets its course to discredit individual thought every way it can.

People today are constantly being exposed to influences that tend to rob them of confidence in their own thinking. The atmosphere is of intellectual dependence, and it pervades every aspect of what people hear and read, from the people they meet to the political parties and associations that claim them as their own. Corporate bodies and other organized institutions repeatedly force convictions upon the individual and refuse to let a person find herself or himself.

◆　　◆　　◆

"By the spirit of the age, then, the person of today is forced into skepticism about his own thinking, so that he may become receptive to what he receives from authority. He cannot resist this influence because he is overworked, distracted, and incapable of concentrating. Moreover, the material dependence that is his lot has an effect on his mind, so he finally believes that he is not qualified to come to his own conclusions" (Schweitzer, *Out of My Life and Thought,* 225).

Schweitzer points out that individuals are also intimidated by the "prodigious development in knowledge" (225). New discoveries are beyond their comprehension, so people are forced to accept what they do not understand. Scientific truth becomes yet another factor contributing to the doubt one has about one's own ability to judge . As a result, the modern individual no longer possesses self-confidence: "Behind a self-assured exterior he conceals an inner lack of confidence. In spite of his great technological achievements and material possessions, he is an altogether stunted being, because he makes no use of his capacity for thinking" (226).

Schweitzer warns that blindly accepting something as true without personal reflection retards the individual's advance in reason: "Our very attempt to manipulate truth itself brings us to the brink of disaster" (227). Clearly, we understand this in other areas. Take the subject of math, for example. We would never develop a math program that consisted in giving students the answers without the questions. Teaching students how to work through problems is the point of teaching a math class. If we give students the tools to solve the problems, they will have the opportunity to advance even further than we have. If we do not, we will not be passing on to future generations the ability to compute mathematically. Personal reflection on the abortion issue is not possible without sex education and the option of birth control. As students of life, we know that the stakes are high. Through fear and laziness, we run the risk of cheating ourselves out of spiritual, intellectual, emotional, and physical independence. Until we take personal responsibility for our thinking, we will be in danger of remaining like children, dependent upon others to meet all of our needs. As Schweitzer reminds us, "Only when we gain the confidence that we can find the truth through our own individual thought will we be able to arrive at living truth" (227).

◆   ◆   ◆

For Schweitzer, reverence for life answers the question of how human beings and the universe are related to one another. He asserts that all we know is this: everything that exists in the universe is the will-to-live manifesting itself. Human beings have both an active and a passive role. At the same time they are subject to world events, they are also capable of preserving or destroying the life that surrounds them (*Out of My Life and Thought*, 233). Schweitzer observes, "Once someone begins to think about the mystery of his life and the links connecting him with the life that fills the world, he cannot but accept, for his own life and all other life that surrounds him, the principle of reverence for life. He will act according to this principle of the ethical affirmation of life in everything he does. His life will become in every respect more difficult than if he lived for himself, but at the same time it will be richer, more beautiful, and happier. It will become, instead of mere living, a genuine experience of life" (234).

Schweitzer notes that some people object that the ethic of reverence for life places too high a value on natural life. He responds by pointing out that the mistake all previous ethical systems have made includes the failure to deal with this mysterious value that life possesses: "Reverence for life, therefore, is applied to natural life and the life of the mind alike" (235). In the case of abortion, this ethic places importance on both the value of the mind to decide for itself and the choice to revere life.

One of the most baffling aspects of the ethic of reverence for life is its lack of division between higher or lower and more or less valuable life. However, "it has its reasons for this omission. . . . To undertake to establish universally valid distinctions of value between different kinds of life will end in judging them by the greater or lesser distance at which they stand from us human beings. Our own judgment is, however, a purely subjective criterion. Who among us knows what significance any other kind of life has in itself, as a part of the universe?" (235).

In the abortion issue, this makes the question of whether the fetus is a human being irrelevant. It is an organism manifested in the universe with the will to live, and we are duty-bound as thoughtful beings to respect its right to life. If we choose to take that life, we must take responsibility for our actions. Ethical people will no longer be able to deem arbitrarily some life worthless and willfully destroy it: "If one has been touched by the ethic of reverence for life, he injures and destroys life only under a necessity he cannot avoid, and never from thoughtlessness" (236).

The pro-choice argument offers a perfect example of the type of situation in which an individual's right to think and to make choices can be defended, but we must always remember that with freedom comes responsibility. I believe that the pro-lifers have the right ethic at heart. Unfortunately, the means by which they are striving to obtain this ethic will inevitably preclude a person's ability to reach it. We must not only allow but also encourage all people to be thinking individuals so that we can develop into human beings who live the ethic of reverence for life. Schweitzer gives us hope and direction to achieve these ethical goals: "If people can be found who revolt against the spirit of thoughtlessness and are sincere and profound enough to spread the ideals of ethical progress, we will witness the emergence of a new spiritual force strong enough to evoke a new spirit in humankind" (243).

Reverence for Life and Animal Rights   Marianne Tardaguila

As I examine Schweitzer's ethic of reverence for life and apply it to different issues, I find there are many difficulties and problems to sift through. The more I delve into this ethic, the more I find myself in a state of mental unrest. Schweitzer often wrote about rational thinking, but there are many questions appearing in my mind, and I have not found simple answers. In reviewing chapter 26 of *The Philosophy of Civilization,* I notice Schweitzer opens by stating, "Complicated and laborious are the roads along which ethical thought, which has mistaken its way and taken too high a flight, must be brought back" (307). Then he states, "To become ethical means to begin to think sincerely" (308). So with this I will attempt to keep ethical thought to "its right direction" (307), as much as I am able.

First, I have chosen to narrow the focus of this essay to examine

Schweitzer's concept of reverence for life and how it can apply to animal rights. While studying a well-known animal rights organization, People for the Ethical Treatment of Animals (PETA), I found many different issues to be interesting or controversial in relation to some of the ethical ideas I have been pondering, such as animal experimentation and the place animals hold in our lives. Generally, animals have been in the service of humans without receiving much appreciation for how they make our lives more comfortable. For instance, we consume animals and animal products, we use them for clothing, and we enjoy them as companions and protectors. Some individuals even view certain animals and specific breeds as symbols of status. Animals are often seen as objects to be used by sports, entertainment, and business industries, as in competitive racing, hunting, riding, and breeding. Within this reality there are vast differences of opinion as to what constitutes respect for animals. PETA is one of the first groups to raise awareness of the concept of animal rights and to define what it means.

Founded in 1980, PETA is an international nonprofit organization, based in Norfolk, Virginia, that educates policymakers and the public about animal abuse and promotes an understanding of the rights of animals. With over six hundred thousand members, it is the largest animal rights organization in the world. Efforts made by this organization have resulted in closure of a horse slaughterhouse, closure of a military laboratory in which animals were shot, and discontinuance of the use of cats and dogs in all wound laboratories. In addition to this, PETA is a group that places a strong emphasis on activism, which has been effective in pressuring lawmakers to enact policy changes regarding animal rights.

As I began researching the issue of animal rights, the first question I found myself asking is whether animals should have rights. This is the most obvious question and, in my opinion, the easiest to answer. When one upholds reverence for life, it seems that respect for all of life is necessary, and this includes animals. According to Schweitzer, this is the basic principle of the ethic of reverence for life. Simply stated, it is good to encourage life; it is bad to destroy life. Moreover, a person is most ethical only when he or she honors the principle to support all life and to avoid injuring life. Following this, with the reverence for life ethic, one does not ask oneself "how valuable" is this life or that life. Instead, one should consider all of life sacred. In this regard, I believe that animal rights groups, such as PETA, are carrying out the "compulsion" (Schweitzer, 309) of ethical decision making in reverence for life.

In *The Philosophy of Civilization,* Schweitzer said if one sees an earthworm on the road after a rain, one should pick it up and place it on the grass so it can live (310). If reverence for life applies to any living thing, it encompasses our whole environment. It means unlimited responsibility. In the area of animal rights, Schweitzer maintained that one must ask whether an animal may be injured in order to create a greater good. In reference to scientific experimentation, Schweitzer wrote, "How much wrong is committed in scientific institutions through neglect of anesthetics, which to save time or trouble are not administered?" Then he continued, "How much [pain is inflicted] through animals being subjected to torture merely to demonstrate to students generally known phenomena?" (318). Clearly, animal experimentation was an issue about which Schweitzer held some very strong and definite opinions. In situations that concern animals, Schweitzer stated that the question of necessity is the pivotal point in the relations between human beings and animals, and that this question of necessity must be applied case by case.

On the web page for PETA, there is a plea stating, "Please join us and help us continue to speak out for those who cannot speak for themselves." This appeal suggests the ethical responsibility humans should hold regarding animals. It seems that Schweitzer would agree. In *The Philosophy of Civilization,* Schweitzer said that if we are aware of animal suffering, we should not act "idly," as though it were not our concern (319). But Schweitzer does not say that we should go and picket in front of a laboratory to stop animal rights abuses. Instead, he says we should recognize our indebtedness to animals. Schweitzer maintains that we need to recognize that a special relationship exists between animals and humans because of the sacrifices of animals that are made for human benefit.

On the other hand, some active members of PETA might consider it right and proper to go "underground" in order to investigate the practices of a particular laboratory in order to expose cruelty to animals. PETA operates under the belief that "animals are not ours to eat, wear, experiment on, or use for entertainment." According to its mission statement, PETA focuses its attention on four areas in which "the largest numbers of animals suffer the most intensely for the longest periods of time: on factory farms, in laboratories, in the fur trade, and in the entertainment industry." Then, PETA follows by stating that it also "work[s] on a variety of other issues, including the cruel killing of beavers, birds and other 'pests,' and the abuse of backyard dogs." This organization primarily works through public education, "cruelty investigations" and research, animal rescue, legislation, special events, celebrity involvement, and direct action.

Some of the current stories listed in *PETA News,* the organization's publication, include updates on legal policies regarding animal testing. One of the updates discusses the ongoing debate regarding the Environmental Protection Agency (EPA) ruling on a high production volume (HPV) chemical-testing program (*PETA News,* May 1999), which was introduced by Vice President Gore in February 1999. Another update states that the United States EPA has "conceded to PETA that some of the planned animal tests were not necessary. PETA has relentlessly protested the HPV program through meetings with the EPA and Congress and through grassroots efforts" (April 1999). So, it is apparent that this group has a philosophy that upholds appreciation or reverence for life. In seeing to it that some of the unnecessary testing is stopped, PETA is echoing some of Schweitzer's thoughts on the importance of questioning necessity. However, there are ethical challenges in the application of reverence for life, and there is a great deal of room for agreement and dissension.

For example, in *The Philosophy of Civilization* Schweitzer stated, "while animals have to endure intolerable treatment from heartless people, or are left to the cruel play of children, we all share the guilt" (319). Schweitzer did not tell us what to do to change any of it. He does not state that no one should eat meat, that no one should own pets, that farmers should plow their own land without the use of animals, or anything like this. Again, Schweitzer leaves it up to us to decide but emphasizes the importance of viewing each situation independently. While PETA says we should not use animals for experimentation, it neglects to mention that many people have benefited from animal testing, and some of it was considered very necessary practice. Many scientists claim that much of the progress medicine has made to date would have been severely impeded if not for the existence of medical testing. In fact, one interesting point to mention is that Linda McCartney, who was a well-known spokesperson for PETA, campaigned for years against the use of animals in medical experiments. She stated that animal experiments do not lead to reliable treatments for human diseases. However, when McCartney was diagnosed with breast cancer, she received chemotherapy—a medical treatment that was tested extensively on animals before ever being used on human beings.

According to the article "Animal Rights Not Such a Good Idea," writer Brian Carnell quoted PETA president Ingrid Newkirk as saying "we'd be against it," regarding using animal experimentation to find a cure for AIDS. The hard fact remaining is that without animal research, life-saving treatments and vaccines for many illnesses would not exist, including treatments for diabetes and polio. Many of us have benefited from animal research without even realizing it. Most medical treatments in the United States are not used for human beings until they are first tested extensively on animals, and all drugs must be tested on animals first. How many of us have even thought of this when receiving medical treatments?

Clearly, animal rights issues are just as complicated in application to reverence for life as all other issues, and, upon examination, they only become more complex. In the March 1999 issue of *Vaccine Weekly* an article, entitled "Protestors up in Arms over Experiments That Give Chimps HIV," begins with a question, "Does the prospect of developing an effective HIV vaccine justify condemning chimpanzees to death? That's the stark question dividing biomedical researchers in the U.S., now that virologists know that some strains of HIV cause the same fatal illness in chimps as they do in people." At least in this situation it appears that someone is addressing ethical concerns. In the publication *Science,* September 1998, an article titled "Strict Rules for Indian Scientists" discusses proposed rules to create a government-run system to regulate research using animals, triggering a debate in India. These new proposals, which were set to go into effect starting in October 1998, were drafted by the chair of a committee, Maneka Gandhi, who is an animal rights activist and a social justice minister. However, research groups are trying to stop the rules from going into effect by "arguing that they are extreme and threaten valuable research."

In all of this, a point can be made for and against animal experimentation. If using animal experimentation means that our family members can be cured of their illnesses, or at least achieve improvements in their quality of life, then an argument in favor of animal experimentation can be made. On the other hand, there is incredible waste in the field of animal experimentation, and I believe it comes from a basic desensitization that occurs when action precedes thought. It should not be made easy for someone to take a life. Yet, I am a person who wants the benefits of medicine without the guilt of what animals have had to sacrifice for us. Still, I acknowledge feelings of guilt. I would not want a job as a lab researcher. I prefer to take simple steps in my everyday life to begin upholding reverence for life, which I have just recently begun to put into effect.

For instance, a couple of weeks ago, after seeing the video *Ahimsa*, I became a vegetarian. I do not know if I will be able to remain a vegetarian for long unless I remain attached to what I felt and learned from watching the video. For many years I have consumed animal products and often thought of where they came from. This bothered me, but I would just put these ugly thoughts out of my mind. In the past, I have tried to make changes in my eating habits, but the changes were only temporary. Today, however, I have a newfound sense of purpose. While I may not be able to effect change in laboratory laws right now, I am able to effect change in my immediate actions, which now uphold values reflective of reverence for life. I do not remember many readings in which Schweitzer, earlier in life, comments on vegetarianism, but his ideas have offered me some direction in which I can take responsibility for my own action toward reverence for life. For my life, vegetarianism seems like a logical way to start with this ethic. After all, before I can picket in front of a lab for its exceedingly cruel practices, I must remove cruelty from my own actions, and this means not using cosmetics that include products made from animals and not consuming animals themselves.

Last, organizations such as PETA are evidence of society reflecting on itself and wanting to make changes. Though some of the organizations' practices may be considered radical, I see these practices to be extremely committed. It is also true that sometimes their position in relation to the politics of animal rights seems to be unclear, but this is true of all kinds of organizations made up of people with differing opinions. I am relieved that there are organizations such as PETA that make it their business to keep tabs on hidden agencies and what they are doing. If we consider animals to be our "pets" and treat them badly, what does this say about our values regarding life? If we kill other creatures with needless testing, it only shows a great lack of respect for life that can spill over into other areas of life, too. Schweitzer said the ethics of reverence for life "guards us from letting each other believe through our silence that we no longer experience what, as thinking people, we must experience. It prompts us to keep each other sensitive. . . . It makes us join in keeping on the lookout for opportunities of bringing some sort of help to animals, to make up for the great misery which people inflict on them" (319).

In conclusion, the rebellion against unnecessary suffering is the foundation of contemporary animal welfare. If suffering in the laboratory is considered to be necessary, then animal experimentation is justified. If animals were anesthetized before a procedure takes place or were provided with adequate pain relief before regaining consciousness, then the ethical problems could be minimized. But many procedures involve inflicting pain on conscious animals. This is unnecessary if alternative methods can be found to test the product, if the results are already available (some testing is often repeated needlessly), or if the research is badly designed so that "no meaningful conclusions are likely to result from it" (*Chemistry and Industry*, January 1999). A great deal of modern animal research is concerned with finding remedies for diseases that are sometimes preventable, such as heart disease. Advocating a reduction in animal experimentation does not have to be accompanied by an acceptance of the view that animals possess rights. But, at the very least, we ought to treat other species with respect, and this means thinking long and hard before we harm them for our benefit. We are not so separate from other living beings, as Schweitzer tells us with his ethic of reverence for life.

Walking on the Path of Righteousness: Steps Toward the Principle of Reverence for Life   Anna Blishak Peschong

The foundation of reverence for life is action, and it is the responsibility of each living person to take a positive, dynamic step toward the betterment of all living things. By taking even a single step toward goodness, whether a small, careful step or a large, powerful stride, we have the ability to set into motion a chain of events that affect the many in a positive manner and, more significantly, may stimulate a positive reciprocation that has the potential to reverberate throughout the world. It is the realization that we must consistently strive for goodness that is the first of several simple but difficult actions required to promote the principle of reverence for life. We cannot sit on the sidelines of life, existing idly as the world around us constantly lives, breathes, dies, and is born again in its daily rotation. We must take action by summoning the courage and the strength to acknowledge that ours is a world brimming with life, life that is interconnected; it is our duty to think completely and clearly about that life around us, and it is up to us, the most intelligent animals on earth, to act responsibly toward all other living things. We can look to the life of Albert Schweitzer for some suggestions on how we may live a life that promotes goodness; we can look to his life for the inspiration and the courage to take our own action, in a time and place where complacency and apathy are gradually creeping into the consciousness of humanity. We can learn from his example of the benefits of celebrating the oneness we share as humans with each other and with other living things.

Albert Schweitzer's awareness of and action regarding the common bond between all living things may have been established as early as his childhood. He grew up in an environment where he was exposed to the benefits of a community that was able to share its church between the two local religions. It was in his homeland and during his childhood that he developed an astute connection with nature and an appreciation of its power and beauty throughout his years of playing and traveling among the flora and fauna in his immediate surroundings. His parents provided a close-knit, loving home that may well have been an inspiration for promoting the oneness we share in the larger family of humanity and life.

It was also at a young age that Schweitzer took action for something he felt at the core of his being was significant enough to stand up for. For what may have been the first time in his life, young Albert thought clearly about the consequences of a negative action he and his young friend were about to take by shooting their slingshots at birds; he concluded that such an action was wrong, and although he greatly risked disapproval, teasing, and loneliness, he made his stand and did not shoot the birds. By taking such action, this young child ultimately affected the behavior and thoughts of many through his actions at that time and later, including his retelling of the story. If a child can make a conscious, risky decision for the sake of goodness, we should all feel a sense of obligation to do the same for those beliefs we know, deep within, are crucial to the promotion of goodness.

Schweitzer appreciated the ambition and heroism exhibited by Jesus. A particular passage from the Bible may have had an impact on the decisions made by Schweitzer throughout his life. This passage describes the instructions given by Jesus to his disciples to help those in need (Matthew 10.1–5): "He called his twelve disciples to him and gave them authority to drive out evil spirits and to heal every disease and sickness." The instructions Jesus gave them were "Heal the sick, raise the dead, cleanse those who have leprosy, drive out demons. Freely you have received, freely you give." These words are not unlike the words of Schweitzer when he spoke of reverence for life, and they show the courage of Schweitzer and Jesus, two brave and dynamic men who can be examples to us today as we look for the means by which we can travel through life's journey in a positive, productive way while considering the commonality we share in life and the universe.

Schweitzer has spoken of "the fellowship of those who bear the mark of pain." In this statement, he made a very clear and distinctive point about the debt we human beings have or ought to have to one another. There is a connection between us all that may be easier to recognize than other connections: the connection founded upon suffering. How often do we hear or read about a community coming together to help others in need after a natural disaster or some other type of catastrophe? There is a willingness within people to reach out to others during times of need that we do not otherwise see very often. We spend so many hours in our offices, on the freeways, running errands, all the while not giving a second thought to the lives of the man in the car next to us on the freeway or the woman standing in an aisle of the local grocery store. When we are faced with tragedies and hardships such as the bombing of the federal building in Oklahoma City or the war fought in Yugoslavia, there is a sense of coming together, whether on the smaller scale of an individual family or on the larger scale of the family of humanity. We are less inhibited about reaching out and offering to help. What is it that opens our hearts and minds during these times of need? Why is it that we act upon these basic but profound principles only at select times?

Why can we not have the desire, the compulsion to help our fellow human beings at all times, on a daily, consistent basis? Schweitzer enlightens us to some possible answers to these questions by suggesting that "those who bear the mark of pain" have "a secret bond." He reminds us that pain is a lonely, debilitating entity that we all share in one form or another, to one degree or another. At some point in each of our lives, we are faced with pain; not one person is spared, regardless of income, race, or social standing. But if kindness, warmth, and compassion are extended to those in need, the agony may be lessened, the suffering may be decreased, the burden may be shared, and our lives altogether may be enriched. There is also the suffering of species we consider below ours that needs to be lessened, from the abuse and neglect of animals to the destruction of lands and waters. As Schweitzer tells us, all life has a will to live: this reminder can serve as a tool to promote the preservation and the enrichment of the living things surrounding us.

Schweitzer suggested that upon relief of our own pain, we must reach out to others; we must carry our share of the misery in the world. The connection between all living things provides a plane on which good deeds may be felt universally, where momentum is established and goodness echoes throughout. If we each contribute even the smallest amount toward the betterment of the world and its inhabitants, we have the ability to alleviate pain, suffering, and misery. Ultimately, reaching out to those in need will have an effect greater than our initial steps, because one good deed has the potential to lead to many others, each in turn developing into more distributions of goodness.

Those who practice Jainism make a powerful statement. Jains' lives are a consistent, unflagging example of the benefit of promoting life and goodness for all living things. Jains allow no room for aggression in their lives: they will not subordinate animals, some wear masks so as not to inhale insects, and volunteers provide food to traveling monks so that a monk may eat every day of his life. We can look at Jains and ask if their lives are more complicated, more challenging, more difficult because of their complete devotion to the preservation of life. They have to think constantly about their choices and actions, but what is so difficult about that? Why should we not think wholeheartedly about the choices and actions we make every day? We spend so much time and energy considering choices such as the home in which we will live, the careers we will pursue, even the movie we will see on a Saturday night; if we redirect those decision-making skills toward situations that are less complicated and have a more profound impact on the world as a whole, we will be on our way to promoting reverence for life.

It is not for the weak or the lazy to take action. The daily choices we will be faced with may be challenging, and obstacles may impede our path in the promotion of life. When taking a step toward living the principle of reverence for life, one may face discomfort in the form of ridicule, misunderstanding, and loneliness. It takes courage and strength to act upon principles that result in personal sacrifice, but if we look at the ultimate goodness that comes from the choices and actions we make, there should be no doubt in our minds that the choice of action is a good choice; more significant, it is a necessity. Albert Schweitzer took an immeasurably large step toward the promotion of goodness when he decided to practice medicine in Africa. He was faced with adversity from the beginning, having to face his family's and friends' disapproval of his decision. Throughout the rest of his life, Schweitzer made numerous sacrifices as a result of his decision to practice medicine in Africa. His wife and daughter lived on a different continent, and as a result it appears his personal relationships with them did not grow and flourish as a husband and father might wish. We need to be aware that choices and action will not always be easy; as we have seen, so many of Schweitzer's choices were not simple.

Why should we act upon the principle of reverence for life? Is it a debt we owe, and if so, to whom or to what? Is it a sense of guilt, as Schweitzer mentioned when explaining his decision to practice medicine in Africa? Answers to these questions will vary from person to person, but one thing remains certain: reverence for life is goodness and awareness in action, and we all have the ability to practice this simple yet profound principle. The promotion of reverence for life from one living entity to the next can only bring about relief in a world infected with pain. Whether a small, simple act, such as Schweitzer's planting fruit trees near and around his hospital so that all people might take fruit as they needed it, or something complex and controversial, such as speaking out on political or volatile topics that we believe must be addressed—however we categorize our actions, we may be at peace when we know that our actions are significant because in them we promote the principle of reverence for life.

Notes

2. Affirming Reverence for Life

1. Frederick Franck, *Days with Albert Schweitzer: A Lambaréné Landscape* (New York: Henry Holt and Co., 1959).

2. Franck, *Days with Albert Schweitzer*, 110–12.

3. Albert Schweitzer, *Memoirs of Childhood and Youth,* trans. Kurt Bergel and Alice R. Bergel (Syracuse: Syracuse Univ. Press, 1997).

4. Ibid., 37 (see ch. 6).

5. Ibid.

6. James Bentley, *Albert Schweitzer: The Enigma* (New York: HarperCollins, 1992), 1–19.

7. Compare my review, "New Translation of *Memoirs of Childhood and Youth*" in *Albert Schweitzer Institute Bulletin* (1997): 5, 7.

8. The synoptic sayings source Q (from the German *Quelle,* "source") is the source assumed by most scholars to have been used (along with Mark) by Matthew and Luke in the compilation of their gospels.

9. Albert Schweitzer, *The Mystery of the Kingdom of God: The Secret of Jesus' Messiahship and Passion,* trans. Walter Lowrie (Buffalo: Prometheus Books, 1985); idem, *The Quest of the Historical Jesus: A Critical Study of Its Progress from Reimarus to Wrede,* trans. William Montgomery (New York: Macmillan Publishing Co., 1968; Baltimore: Johns Hopkins Univ. Press, 1998); idem, *The Quest of the Historical Jesus,* ed. John Bowden (Minneapolis: Fortress Press, 2001). The 1968 English edition of *The Quest* is prefaced by the excellent introduction of James M. Robinson.

10. James M. Robinson, introduction to *The Quest of the Historical Jesus* (1968 edition), xii. See also Robinson's essay "The Legacy of Schweitzer's *The Quest of the Historical Jesus*," ch. 15.

11. Schweitzer, *The Quest of the Historical Jesus,* 370–71 (slightly modified for style).

12. Ibid., 403.

13. Ibid., 182.

14. Compare, for example, John Dominic Crossan, *The Historical Jesus: The Life of a*

Mediterranean Jewish Peasant (San Francisco: HarperSanFrancisco, 1991); Robert W. Funk, *Honest to Jesus: Jesus for a New Millennium* (San Francisco: HarperSanFrancisco, 1996).

15. See my translation of the Sermon on the Mount ch. 16.

16. Albert Schweitzer, *Reverence for Life,* trans. Reginald H. Fuller (New York: Harper and Row, 1969), 65 (slightly modified for style).

17. See Schweitzer, *The Quest of the Historical Jesus,* 401; Ara Paul Barsam, " 'Reverence for Life': Albert Schweitzer's Mystical Theology and Ethics" (Ph.D. thesis, Oxford University, 2001), 166–67.

18. See Henry Clark, *The Ethical Mysticism of Albert Schweitzer: A Study of the Sources and Significance of Schweitzer's Philosophy of Civilization* (Boston: Beacon Press, 1962), 88–89. Note also the discussion in Marvin Meyer, "Albert Schweitzer and the Image of Jesus in the Gospel of Thomas," in *Jesus Then and Now: Images of Jesus in History and Christology,* ed. Marvin Meyer and Charles Hughes (Harrisburg, Pa.: Trinity Press International, 2001), 72–90; and Ara Paul Barsam, " 'Reverence for Life,' " 112–48. Barsam cites an important footnote Schweitzer included in *The Kingdom of God and Primitive Christianity* (ed. Ulrich Neuenschwander, trans. L. A. Garrard, New York: Seabury Press, 1968), 128, which indicates further developments in Schweitzer's reflections upon the historical Jesus: "In the section on the secret of suffering in my *Geschichte der Leben-Jesu-Forschung...*, I still believed that in the pre-Messianic tribulation a load of guilt that encumbered the world and was delaying the coming of the kingdom could be expiated by believers, and that Jesus therefore, in accordance with the Servant passages, regarded his vicarious sacrifice as an atonement. As a result of further study of late Jewish eschatology and the thought of Jesus on his passion, I find that I can no longer endorse this view."

19. Albert Schweitzer, *Out of My Life and Thought: An Autobiography,* trans. Antje Bultmann Lemke (Baltimore: Johns Hopkins Univ. Press, 1998), 235.

20. Clark, *Ethical Mysticism,* 89 (slightly modified for style).

21. David L. Dungan, "Reconsidering Albert Schweitzer," The Christian Century 92 (1975): 879.

22. Albert Schweitzer, *Christianity and the Religions of the World,* trans. Johanna Powers (New York: Henry Holt and Co., 1939); idem, *Indian Thought and Its Development,* trans. Mrs. Charles E. B. Russell (Boston: Beacon Press, 1936).

23. Schweitzer, *Indian Thought and Its Development,* 85.

24. Schweitzer, *Christianity and the Religions of the World,* 87.

25. See Ara Paul Barsam, "Albert Schweitzer, Jainism, and Reverence for Life," ch. 14.

26. Cited in L. M. Singhvi, *The Jain Declaration on Nature* (Cincinnati: Federation of Jain Associations in North America, 1990), 7.

27. *Sources of Indian Tradition,* ed. William Theodore DeBary, Introduction to Oriental Civilizations (New York: Colombia Univ. Press, 1958), 61.

28. Cited in Singhvi, *The Jain Declaration on Nature,* 13.

29. Schweitzer, *Indian Thought and Its Development,* 82–83.

30. Albert Schweitzer, *The Philosophy of Civilization,* trans. C. T. Campion (Buffalo: Prometheus Book, 1987), 282.

31. Albert Schweitzer, *A Place for Revelation: Sermons on Reverence for Life,* ed. Lothar Stiehm and Martin Strege, trans. David Larrimore Holland (New York: Macmillan Publishing Co.; London: Collier Macmillan, 1988), 10 (see ch. 4).

32. See Mike W. Martin, "Rethinking Reverence for Life," ch. 12.

33. See James Brabazon, *Albert Schweitzer: A Biography* (New York: G. P. Putnam's Sons, 1975), 258. Brabazon has now completed a second edition of his biography of Schweitzer (Albert Schweitzer Library, Syracuse Univ. Press, 2000).

34. Schweitzer, *The Philosophy of Civilization,* 311, 318.

35. Albert Schweitzer, *Goethe: Five Studies,* trans. Charles R. Joy (Boston: Beacon Press, 1961), 18.

36. "Albert Schweitzer—Hélène Bresslau: The Years Prior to Lambaréné, Correspondence, 1902–1912," trans. Antje Bultmann Lemke, forthcoming from Syracuse Univ. Press. See ch. 3.

37. Compare Brabazon, *Albert Schweitzer,* 303–4.

38. See chapter 26 of Schweitzer, *Philosophy of Civilization,* and other discussions of reverence for life in the present volume.

39. Schweitzer, *Philosophy of Civilization,* 309 (see ch. 5).

40. Martin, "Rethinking Reverence for Life," ch. 12.

41. Albert Schweitzer, *The Story of My Pelican,* trans. Martha Wardenburg (London: Souvenir, 1964).

42. Schweitzer wrote this letter from Lambaréné to Jack Eisendraht in 1951; see Schweitzer, Letters, 1905–1965, ed. Hans Walter Bähr, trans. Joachim Neugroschel (New York: Macmillan Publishing Co., 1992), 218. Ara Paul Barsam also cites this letter, ch.14.

43. Brabazon, *Albert Schweitzer,* 246, citing Schweitzer, *Philosophy of Civilization,* 80.

44. Schweitzer, *Philosophy of Civilization,* 312.

45. Matthew 7.12 (Q); Luke 6.31 (Q); Gospel of Thomas, saying 6.

46. Mark 12.31; Matthew 22.39; Luke 10.27 (citing Leviticus 19.18); Gospel of Thomas, saying 25; Matthew 5.44 (Q); Luke 6.27 (Q).

47. Schweitzer, *A Place for Revelation,* 11 (see ch. 4).

48. Compare, for example, Robert O. Ballou, ed., *The Bible of the World* (New York: Viking Press, 1939).

49. See Alice Bergel, "Philosophy with 'Calluses on Its Hands,' " *Albert Schweitzer Institute Bulletin* (1997): 4, 6, reviewing Claus Günzler, *Albert Schweitzer: Einführung in sein Denken* (Munich: C. H. Beck, 1996).

50. Compare Schweitzer, *Goethe: Five Studies,* 51.

10. The Assessment of the Life and Thought of Albert Schweitzer in Germany and Africa

1. W. E. B. DuBois, "The Black Man and Albert Schweitzer," in *The Albert Schweitzer Jubilee Book,* ed. A. A. Roback (Cambridge, Mass.: Sci-Art, 1946), 121–27, esp. 121.

2. John Gunther, *Inside Africa* (London: Hamisch Hamilton, 1955), 697–719; Gerald McKnight, *Verdict on Schweitzer: The Man Behind the Legend of Lambaréné* (New York: John Day Co., 1964).

11. The Significance of Reverence for Life Today

1. Albert Schweitzer, *Leben, Werk und Denken, 1905–1965: Mitgeteilt in seinen Briefen,* ed. Hans Walter Bähr (Heidelberg: L. Schneider, 1987), 322.

2. Albert Schweitzer, *Gesammelte Werke,* ed. R. Grabs (Zurich and Munich: C. H. Beck, 1974), 5: 159.

3. G. R. Taylor, *Das Selbstmordprogramm* (Frankfurt am Main: S. Fischer, 1971).

4. J. Dahl, "Der wahre Preis des Stroms," *Natur: Das Umweltmagazin* 7 (1990): 98.

5. Hans Jonas, "Technik, Freiheit und Pflicht," in *Friedenspreis des Deutschen Buchhandels 1987* (Frankfurt am Main: Buchhändler-Vereinigung, 1987), 37.

6. Ibid., 42.

7. Concerning the concept cf. C. Amery, *Das Ende der Vorsehung: Die gnadenlosen Folgen des Christentums* (Hamburg: Rowohlt, 1972), 233.

8. Amery, *Das Ende der Vorsehung,* 234.

9. Robert Spaemann, "Laudatio," in *Friedenspreis,* 27.

10. Amery, *Das Ende der Vorsehung,* 236.

11. Cf. Erich Gräßer, "Ehrfurcht vor allem Lebendigen," in *Studien zu Albert Schweitzer: Gesammelte Aufsätze,* ed. Andreas Mühling (Bodenheim: Philo, 1997), 25.

12. Bernhard Rambeck, *Mythos Tierversuch: Eine wissenschaftskritische Untersuchung* (Frankfurt am Main: Verlag Zweitausendeins, 1990), 203–5.

13. Albert Schweitzer, "Appell an die Menschheit," in Schweitzer, *Werke,* 5: 576.

14. Jonas, "Technik," 37.

15. Jonas, *Das Prinzip Verantwortung: Versuch einer Ethik für die technologische Zivilisation* (Frankfurt am Main: Suhrkamp, 1979), 47.

16. Jonas, "Technik," 40.

17. Jonas, *Prinzip,* 28–29.

18. Ibid., 28.

19. Ibid., "Technik," 40.

20. Ibid., 29.

21. Schweitzer, *Gesammelte Werke,* 5: 117; cf. Erich Gräßer, "Ethik bei Albert Schweitzer," *Studien,* 64–78. See also, above, Schweitzer's sermon in translation, ch. 4.

22. Schweitzer, *Leben,* 328. Therefore the sentence "Every traditional ethics is anthropocentric" (Jonas, *Prinzip,* 22; cf. 29) is to be corrected.

23. Jonas, *Prinzip,* 29.

24. Schweitzer, *Gesammelte Werke,* 5: 125.

25. Jonas, *Prinzip,* 63–64.

26. Schweitzer, *Gesammelte Werke,* 5: 164.

27. Ibid., 1: 171.

28. Ibid., 2: 714.

29. Ibid., 2: 387.

30. Albert Schweitzer, *Kultur und Ethik: Kulturphilosophie* (Munich: C. H. Beck, 1923), 2: iii.

31. Ibid., 2: xxii.

32. Schweitzer, *Gesammelte Werke,* 5: 171.

33. Ibid., 5: 373.

34. Quoted in R. Brüllmann, *Treffende Albert-Schweitzer-Zitate* (Thun, Switzerland: Ott, 1986), 179.

12. Rethinking Reverence for Life

1. Although I disagree with substantial parts of their interpretations of Schweitzer, the following philosophers provide insightful discussions: J. Baird Callicott, "On the Intrinsic Value of Nonhuman Species," in *The Preservation of Species: The Value of Biological Diversity,* ed. Bryan G. Norton (Princeton: Princeton Univ. Press, 1986), 153–55; John Kleinig, *Valuing Life* (Princeton: Princeton Univ. Press, 1991), 47–56; Lawrence E. Johnson, *A Morally Deep World* (New York: Cambridge Univ. Press, 1991), 134–41; and Joseph R. DesJardins, *Environmental Ethics: An Introduction to Environmental Philosophy* (Belmont, Calif.: Wadsworth, 1993), 147–51. An additional indication of renewed interest in Schweitzer is inclusion of his writings in several widely used texts: Tom Regen and Peter Singer, eds., *Animal Rights and Human Obligations,* 2d ed. (Englewood Cliffs, N.J.: Prentice Hall, 1989); Susan J. Armstrong and Richard G. Botzler, eds., *Environmental Ethics* (New York: McGraw-Hill, 1993); Louis P. Pojman, ed., *Environmental Ethics: Readings in Theory and Application* (Boston: Jones and Bartlett, 1994).

2. Cf. the definitions of these terms given by DesJardins, *Environmental Ethics,* 144–46.

3. Parenthetical page references to Schweitzer are as follows: C: *The Philosophy of Civilization,* trans. C. T. Campion (Buffalo: Prometheus Books, 1987); L: "The Ethics of Reverence for Life," *Christendom* 1 (winter 1936): 225–39; O: *Out of My Life and Thought,* trans. Antje Bultmann Lemke (New York: Henry Holt and Co., 1990); R: *Reverence for Life,* trans. Reginald H. Fuller (New York: Harper and Row, 1969).

4. Especially illuminating is Gabriel Langfeldt, *Albert Schweitzer: A Study of His Life and Thought,* trans. Maurice Michael (London: George Allen and Unwin, 1960).

5. Of course, Schweitzer's optimism is the polar opposite of Schopenhauer's thoroughgoing pessimism. Nevertheless, Schopenhauer's influence is unmistakable in passages where the entire world (not just life), and especially inorganic crystals and snowflakes, is said to manifest the will-to-live (C 282, R 115). Such passages are also ubiquitous in Arthur Schopenhauer, *The World as Will and Representation,* trans. E. F. J. Payne, 2 vols. (New York: Dover Publications, 1966).

6. Cf. James F. Doyle, "Schweitzer's Extensions of Ethics to All Life," *Journal of Value Inquiry* 11 (1977): 45.

7. Albert Schweitzer, *Memoirs of Childhood and Youth,* trans. C. T. Campion (New York: Macmillan Publishing Co., 1961): 27–31.

8. Hans Walter Bähr, ed., *Albert Schweitzer: Letters, 1905–1965,* trans. Joachim Neugroschel (New York: Macmillan Publishing Co., 1992), 350.

9. Bähr, *Letters,* 336.

10. See Albert Schweitzer, *Goethe: Five Studies,* trans. Charles R. Joy (Boston: Beacon Press, 1961).

11. Schweitzer was quite capable of the aesthetic distancing involved in making humorous ascriptions of human features to animals. See Albert Schweitzer, *The Story of My Pelican* (London: Souvenir, 1964).

12. After criticizing Schweitzer, Callicott, "Intrinsic Value," 156–62, makes a suggestive appeal to "bio-empathy." My interpretation of Schweitzer brings their views closer together. I also see Schweitzerlike appeals to empathy in John A. Fischer, "Taking Sympathy Seriously: A Defense of Our Moral Psychology Toward Animals," in *The Animal Rights/Environmental Ethics Debate: The Environmental Perspective,* ed. Eugene C. Hargrove (Albany: State Univ. of New York Press, 1992), 227–48; Kenneth E. Goodpaster, "On Being Morally Considerable," *The Journal of Philosophy* 75 (1978): 308–25; and Paul Taylor, *Respect for Nature* (Princeton: Princeton Univ. Press, 1986).

13. These charges are more justified with regard to Schweitzer's cousin, Jean-Paul Sartre. There are some striking parallels between Schweitzer's "elemental" ethics of sincerity with oneself and Sartre's existentialist ethics of honesty with oneself. Unlike Sartre, however, Schweitzer retains a conception of objectively defensible values.

14. Cf. Henry Clark, *The Ethical Mysticism of Albert Schweitzer: A Study of the Sources and Significance of Schweitzer's Philosophy of Civilization* (Boston: Beacon Press, 1962), 38–52.

15. Albert Schweitzer, *Indian Thought and Its Development,* trans. Mrs. Charles E. B. Russell (Boston: Beacon Press, 1936; London: A. and C. Black, 1951; Gloucester, Mass.: Peter Smith, 1977), 83.

16. Bähr, *Letters,* 287.

17. Schweitzer occasionally discusses rights, as noted by Antje Bultmann Lemke, "Moderator's Introduction," in *The Relevance of Albert Schweitzer at the Dawn of the Twenty-First Century,* ed. David C. Miller and James Pouilliard (Lanham, Md.: University Press of America, 1992), 83–84. Making human rights more prominent, however, might have helped him

avoid the great blemish on his career: his support for colonialism and his paternalism toward Africans. See Albert Schweitzer, *On the Edge of the Primeval Forest,* trans. C. T. Campion (New York: Pyramid Books, 1961), 99. Also see Manuel M. Davenport, "The Moral Paternalism of Albert Schweitzer," *Ethics* 84 (1974): 116–27.

18. Albert Schweitzer, *The Animal World of Albert Schweitzer,* trans. and ed. Charles R. Joy (Boston: Beacon Press, 1950).

19. Schweitzer became a vegetarian only in his late eighties, four decades after initially formulating his philosophy of reverence for life. James Brabazon, *Albert Schweitzer: A Biography* (New York: G. P. Putnam's Sons, 1975; new ed., Syracuse: Syracuse Univ. Press, 2000), 463.

20. Schweitzer also occasionally formulates rough rules of conduct toward persons, such as the principle that good fortune obligates (C 321). Cf. Herbert Spiegelberg, "Good Fortune Obligates: Albert Schweitzer's Second Ethical Principle," *Ethics* 85 (1975): 227–34. Ultimately, however, these rules are grounded in virtues and ideals of character. See my essay "Good Fortune Obligates: Gratitude, Philanthropy, and Colonialism," *Southern Journal of Philosophy* 37 (1999): 57–75.

21. There is also an authenticity in passages such as the following: "By helping an insect when it is in difficulties, I am only attempting to cancel part of man's ever new debt to the animal world" (C 318). Without his metaphysics, however, the compensation is at most symbolic.

22. Louise Jilek-Aall, *Working with Dr. Schweitzer: Sharing His Reverence for Life* (Blaine, Wash.: Hancock House, 1990), 189–90.

23. Kleinig, *Valuing Life,* 55.

24. I thank Kurt Bergel and Alice R. Bergel for their helpful comments on an earlier draft of this paper.

13. Jainism and Ethics

1. Alfred North Whitehead, *Process and Reality* (New York: Macmillan Publishing Co., 1924), 513.

2. Jagmanderlal Jaini, *Outlines of Jainism* (Cambridge: Cambridge Univ. Press, 1916).

3. Vilas Adinath Sangave, *Jaina Community* (Bombay: Popular Book Depot, 1959), 303–4.

14. Albert Schweitzer, Jainism, and Reverence for Life

1. Albert Schweitzer to Jackson Lee Ice, unpublished correspondence, July 7, 1952, Archives of the Albert Schweitzer Institute, Connecticut. Lee later published *Schweitzer: Prophet of Radical Theology* (Philadelphia: Westminster Press, 1977). I am thankful to the Schweitzer Institute for access to its archival materials and library.

2. Schweitzer to Ice, unpublished correspondence, July 7, 1952.

3. Ibid.

4. It is interesting to note that Jain scholar Natubhai Shah translates *ahimsa* as "non-violence and reverence for life." However, Shah uses "reverence for life" without adequate differentiation from Schweitzer's understanding of the ethic. See Natubhai Shah, *Jainism: The World of Conquerors* (Brighton: Sussex Academic Press, 1998), 1: 108.

5. Schweitzer, *Memoirs of Childhood and Youth,* trans. Kurt Bergel and Alice R. Bergel (Syracuse: Syracuse Univ. Press, 1997), 37.

6. Ibid.

7. Ibid.

8. Ibid., 37–38.

9. Ibid., 39.

10. Ibid., 73.

11. Ibid., 41.

12. George Seaver, *Albert Schweitzer: The Man and His Mind* (London: A. and C. Black, 1947), 11.

13. Schweitzer, *Memoirs of Childhood and Youth,* v.

14. See Charles R. Joy's introduction to Schweitzer's memorial address delivered at the one hundredth anniversary of Goethe's death in Albert Schweitzer, *Goethe: Five Studies,* trans. Charles R. Joy (Boston: Beacon Press, 1961), 13–26.

15. Schweitzer, *Goethe: Five Studies,* 24.

16. Quotations from Goethe's *Wilhelm Meister* in Charles R. Joy's introduction to Schweitzer, *Goethe: Five Studies,* 24.

17. Ibid., 25.

18. Ibid.

19. Schweitzer uses the terms "infinite Being," "universal Will-to-Live," and the "infinite Will-to-Live" interchangeably in his philosophical works to refer to God. In a letter to Oskar Kraus, he writes, "Hitherto it has been my principle never to express in my philosophy more than I have experienced as a result of absolutely logical reflection. That is why I never speak in philosophy of 'God' but only of the 'universal Will-to-Live.' But if I speak in the traditional language of religion, I use the word 'God' in its historical definiteness and indefiniteness, just as I speak in ethics of 'love' in place of 'reverence for life.'" See Oskar Kraus, *Albert Schweitzer: His Work and His Philosophy* (London: A. and C. Black, 1944), 42.

20. Schweitzer discusses his intentions to complete two further installments of *The Philosophy of Civilization* at the end of the preface to *Civilization and Ethics.* He produced a partial manuscript of the third volume that has recently been published in Germany.

21. Albert Schweitzer, *Indian Thought and Its Development,* trans. Mrs. Charles E. B. Russell (London: A. and C. Black, 1951), vi.

22. Schweitzer, *Indian Thought and Its Development,* 83.

23. Ibid., vi. Similarly, in *Memoirs of Childhood and Youth* and *Out of My Life and Thought,* Schweitzer recounts the significance of his early exposure to Schopenhauer and how, since childhood, Indian thought interested him. For an account of the influence of Buddhist thought on Schopenhauer, see Dorothea Dauer, *Schopenhauer as Transmitter of Buddhist Ideas* (Bern: Herbert Lang and Co., 1969).

24. Schweitzer admired Tagore's work and devotes a section of his text on Indian thought to his philosophy.

25. Albert Schweitzer to Asiatic Society, Calcutta, India, February 10, 1965, in Hans Walter Bähr, ed., *Albert Schweitzer: Letters, 1905–1965,* trans. Joachim Neugroschel (New York: Macmillan Publishing Co., 1992), 351.

26. Albert Schweitzer to Prime Minister Lal Bahadur Shastri, New Delhi, India, November 29, 1964, in Bähr, *Letters,* 348.

27. Schweitzer, *Indian Thought and Its Development,* 10.

28. Ibid., 83.

29. Ibid., vi.

30. Ibid., viii.

31. Albert Schweitzer, *The Philosophy of Civilization,* trans. C. T. Campion (Buffalo: Prometheus Books, 1987), 304.

32. Schweitzer, *Out of My Life and Thought: An Autobiography,* trans. Antje Bultmann Lemke (Baltimore: Johns Hopkins Univ. Press, 1998), 232.

33. Schweitzer, *The Mysticism of Paul the Apostle,* trans. William Montgomery (New York: Henry Holt and Co., 1931), 297.

34. Ibid.

35. Schweitzer, *The Philosophy of Civilization,* 302.

36. Ibid., 305.

37. Albert Schweitzer, *Aus meinem Leben und Denken* (Hamburg: Richard Meiner, 1931), 190.

38. Schweitzer, "The Ethics of Reverence for Life," in Henry Clark, *The Ethical Mysticism of Albert Schweitzer: A Study of the Sources and Significance of Schweitzer's Philosophy of Civilization* (Boston: Beacon Press, 1962), 229; see above, ch. 8.

39. In 1844 the second edition to Schopenhauer's text was published, which focuses on primacy of the will.

40. Arthur Schopenhauer, *The World as Will and Representation,* trans. E. F. J. Payne (New York: Dover Publications, 1966), 2: 244.

41. Immanuel Kant (on whom Schweitzer completed his doctoral dissertation in philosophy in 1898) criticized claims to knowledge, through reason, of that which is beyond sense experience. In *Critique of Pure Reason* (1781), Kant distinguished between ultimate realities *(noumena),* "things" as they are "in themselves" *(Ding-an-sich),* and *phenomena,* or things as they are known for us by the senses and the human mind. According to Kant, rationalistic

claims to knowledge, through pure reason, of that which lies beyond sense experience are foundationless, and hence the differentiation between noumenal and phenomenal worlds delineates the border of knowledge.

42. See Schopenhauer's chapter "On the Objectification of the Will in Nature Without Knowledge" for his discussion of the connection between the "will" and metaphysics.

43. Schweitzer, *The Philosophy of Civilization*, 236.

44. The will-to-live as an evaluative concept rose to importance in the late nineteenth century in reaction to scientific materialism and Kantian idealism. The "vitalist" philosophy of Henri Bergson, elucidated in his *Creative Evolution* (1907), stated that evolution was actuated by an "élan vital," or creative life force. The élan vital, unknown to the natural sciences, animated all life. To the vitalists, as well as to Schweitzer, the will-to-live is known by intuition, as opposed to being known by concepts or through abstract reasoning. In *The Philosophy of Civilization,* Schweitzer writes that he agrees with Bergson that "philosophizing means experiencing our consciousness as an emanation of the creative impulse which rules in the world." Both argued that the will-to-live received its life from "the creative impulse," or God. The "élan vital" or "will-to-live," given from God, is woven into the fabric of existence and *sine qua non* of life.

45. Schweitzer's reasoning strongly resonates with the Jain concept *attanam upamam katva.* This notion, as expressed in the *Acaranga Sutra,* can be loosely translated as "you know others because you know yourself first." I am thankful to Professor P. S. Jaini for helping to explain this concept.

46. Lee Ellerbrock, as quoted in Henry Clark, *The Ethical Mysticism of Albert Schweitzer: A Study of the Sources and Significance of Schweitzer's Philosophy of Civilization* (Boston: Beacon Press, 1962), 28.

47. Schweitzer, *The Philosophy of Civilization,* 276.

48. Ibid., 76.

49. Ibid.

50. Ibid., 271.

51. Clark, *Ethical Mysticism,* 32.

52. Albert Schweitzer, *A Place for Revelation: Sermons on Reverence for Life,* ed. Lothar Stiehm and Martin Strege, trans. David Larrimore Holland (New York: Macmillan Publishing Co.; London: Collier Macmillan, 1988), 15–16.

53. Schweitzer, *The Philosophy of Civilization,* 312, 78 (my italics).

54. Andrew Linzey, *Christianity and the Rights of Animals* (New York: Crossroad, 1991), 7.

55. Schweitzer, *Indian Thought and Its Development,* 263.

56. Ibid., 1.

57. Ibid., 1, 2.

58. Ibid., 42.

59. For Jains, the *sallekhana* (sacred death), or voluntary fasting unto death, is considered the most auspicious way to die for those who are spiritually prepared. Often misunderstood

as suicide, Jains view this "holy death" not as suicide but as a ritualized leaving of the body, the purpose of which is spiritual advancement.

60. Schweitzer, *Indian Thought and Its Development,* 7–8. Schweitzer's thought corresponds closely with the section "Karma Yoga, or The Path of Action" from the Bhagavad Gita: "No one can attain freedom from activity by refraining from action; nor can he reach perfection by merely refusing to act. One cannot even for a moment remain really inactive; for the qualities of nature will compel one to act whether he will or not. . . . Even the maintenance of the body would be impossible if one remained inactive." *Bhagavad Gita,* trans. Shri Purohit Swami (Boston: Shambhala Publications, 1994), 28.

61. Jainism propounds a different understanding of activity and karma that challenges the applicability of Schweitzer's remarks to the Jain worldview. Part 4 discusses this theme further.

62. S. Radhakrishnan, *Eastern Religions and Western Thought* (Oxford: Oxford Univ. Press, 1991), 74.

63. In a letter (November 29, 1964) to Prime Minister Lal Bahadur Shastri, Schweitzer acknowledges several Indian friends, including Prime Minister Jawaharlal Nehru, Charles F. Andrews, and Mahatma Gandhi, whom he contacted through Andrews. He writes, "So those were my Indian friends. Little by little they were joined by others because I was seriously studying Indian thought, to which I felt drawn." It is unclear as to what extent his interaction with these men involved discussions of Indian religious ideas. See Bähr, *Letters,* 349.

64. In the preface to *Indian Thought and Its Development,* Schweitzer acknowledges Moritz Winternitz's texts on Indian literature and assistance in response to questions, the works of Romain Rolland, and conversations with Andrews.

65. In Indian traditions, the "ethical life-affirmation" is subject to the "caste" duties of *svadharma.* See P. S. Jaini, "Values in Comparative Perspective: *Svadharma* Versus *Ahimsa,"* in *Sramana Vidya: Studies in Buddhism* (Sarnath and Varanasi, India: Central Institute of Higher Tibetan Studies, 1987), 111–22.

66. Schweitzer, *Indian Thought and Its Development,* 8.

67. Ibid., 3.

68. Ibid., 117.

69. Ibid., 8–9 (my italics).

70. Ibid., 10.

71. P. S. Jaini, *The Jaina Path of Purification* (Berkeley and Los Angeles: Univ. of California Press, 1979), 1.

72. See *Acaranga Sutra* 1.1.2, 1.5.5, in *Studies in Jaina Philosophy,* ed. Nathmal Tatia (Banaras: Jain Cultural Research Society, 1951), 18.

73. Jainism claims immemorial antiquity. Its last leader, Lord Mahavira, restored an ancient faith but is not held to have originated it. He is held to be the last of twenty-four *Tirthankaras* (or Fordmakers, the people who show the crossing to the other shore of existence). According to Jain tradition, Mahavira (great hero) was born in 599 B.C.E., though

some scholars put his date fifty or more years later. At the age of thirty he, like the Buddha, renounced the world to lead the life of a wandering holy man to search for happiness. After twelve years of penances and austerities, he gained release from this world to a state of omniscience. At age seventy-two Mahavira is held to have attained final *moksha* or *nirvana*.

74. W. J. Johnson, *Harmless Souls* (Delhi: Motilal Banarsidass Publishers, 1995), 1.

75. Jaini, *The Jaina Path of Purification,* 166 (Jaini's emphasis).

76. Ibid., 167.

77. *Dasaveyaliya Sutra* 4.1. Jaini, *The Jaina Path of Purification,* 20.

78. Johnson, *Harmless Souls,* 50.

79. Ibid., 63.

80. The ascetic must accede to delimitations placed on his or her way of life: he or she cannot light fires or plough the ground, must drink filtered or boiled water, must inspect his or her surroundings carefully to avoid injury to other *jivas,* and so on to prevent accidentally taking life in any form.

81. Shah, *Jainism: The World of the Conquerors,* 1:111.

82. Unlike Schweitzer, Jainism deems euthanasia of all beings wholly unethical and prohibited. Schweitzer neglects to note that the Jain commitment to nonviolence is reflected in active concern with the prevention and alleviation of suffering. For instance, an attempt by the eighteenth-century monk Bhikhanji to found a sect based on the doctrine of total nonassistance to any living being (except mendicants) was met with protest by nearly the entire Jain community. Bhikhanji's theory was that saving the life of an animal makes one responsible for all the violence the animal commits in the future and therefore should be avoided. He also believed that such assistance involves interest in the result and, thereby, karmic attachment. Bhikhanji is an example of what Schweitzer sees as the logical progression of world negation. Bhikhanji highlights the difficulties inherent in Jainism's espousal of total renunciation (leading to *moksha*) and the importance afforded to compassionate and charitable behavior (leading to rebirth in the realm of heaven). Although the canonical teachings may well be seen to justify Bhikhanji's interpretation, his thought has been rejected as a form of *ekanta* (one-sidedness) that violates the spirit of *anekantavada* (doctrine of manifold aspects and views).

83. This term is not found in the *Tattvartha Sutra* and is a later development in Jain thought.

84. The *Acaranga Sutra* (5.1) asks one to consider himself or herself to be in the position of the person or being to whom injury is being caused. See Jaini, *The Jaina Path of Purification,* 111.

85. In Schweitzer's defense, Jaini maintains that such efforts are mainly a response to the ecological movement in the West and not clearly expressed in early Jain texts.

86. Schweitzer, *Indian Thought and Its Development,* 79.

87. Ibid., 78.

88. Ibid., 79.

89. Ibid.

90. Ibid., 81.

91. Ibid., 82–83 (my italics).

92. Ibid., 83.

93. Schweitzer, "The Ethics of Reverence for Life," in Clark, *Ethical Mysticism,* 188, and above, ch. 8.

94. Schweitzer, *The Philosophy of Civilization,* 241.

95. Schweitzer to Hans Walter Bähr, January 2, 1962, in Bähr, *Letters,* 314.

96. Bahr, *Letters,* 314.

97. Schweitzer, *Indian Thought and Its Development,* 81, 83.

98. Ibid., viii.

99. Ibid., 83.

100. Ibid., 83–84.

101. Schweitzer, *The Philosophy of Civilization,* 312.

102. Note the similarity between Gandhi's claim that the "world is bound in a chain of destruction" and Schweitzer's view that the "world is a ghastly drama of the will-to-live divided against itself." Also noteworthy is Gandhi's use of the term "will-to-live" as well as his recognition that life "exists by violence," both of which resonate with Schweitzer's views. Gandhi elaborates: "The saying that life lives on life has a deep meaning in it. Man cannot live for a moment without consciously or unconsciously committing outward *himsa.* The very fact of his living—eating, drinking, and moving about—necessarily involves some *himsa,* destruction of life, be it ever so minute. A votary of *ahimsa* therefore remains true to his faith if the spring of all his actions is compassion, if he shuns to the best of his ability the destruction of the tiniest creature, tries to save it, and thus incessantly strives to be freed from the deadly coil of *himsa.* He will be constantly growing in self-restraint and compassion, but he can never become entirely free from outward *himsa.* "

Again, he states, "In life it is impossible to eschew violence completely. Now the question arises, where is one to draw the line? The line cannot be the same for every one. For, although essentially the principle is the same, yet everyone applies it in his or her own way. . . . What is good under certain conditions can become an evil or sin, under different conditions. . . . At every step he has to use his discrimination as to what is *ahimsa* and what is *himsa.* " Schweitzer was well acquainted with Gandhi's thought on this subject and specifically these lines to which he makes passing reference. He remarks that "Gandhi arrives at the admission that the commandment not to kill and not to injure cannot be carried out in entirety, because man cannot maintain life without committing acts of violence." There is a strong sense in which Gandhi's union of "the idea of *ahimsa* to the idea of activity directed on the world" reflects his own development of *ahimsa* into an ethic in accord with his understanding of the will-to-live and life-affirmation. Gandhi's own application of *ahimsa* may be traced back to Jain influences. He grew up in the area of Gujarat, long influenced by Jainism, and was influenced by the Jain teacher Srimad Rajachandra, whom he mentions with great respect in his autobiography. Rajachandra was born and raised in Vaishnava, but his mother was a *sthanakvasi* (nonimage-worshiping) Jain. His views thus appealed to Gandhi. Gandhi writes, "Three persons have influenced me deeply, Tolstoy, Ruskin, and Rajachandra: Tolstoy through his books . . . and Rajachandra through intimate personal contact." Because Rajachandra was a spiritual mentor to Gandhi, it was his example that led Gandhi to utilize *ahimsa* to gain independence for India. Mahatma Gandhi, in Charles F. Andrews, *Mahatma Gandhi's Ideas* (London: George Allen and Unwin, 1929), 138; Mahatma Gandhi, in Moritz Winternitz, *A History of Indian Literature,* trans. S. Ketkar and H. Kohn (Calcutta: University of Calcutta, 1933), 85; Mahatma Gandhi, *Collected Works of Mahatma Gandhi,* 32: 4 (Delhi: Government of India, 1958–1976); Schweitzer, *Indian Thought and Its Development,* 230, 234.

103. Schweitzer, *Indian Thought and Its Development,* 83.

104. Schweitzer, "The Ethics of Reverence for Life," in Clark, *Ethical Mysticism,* 187.

105. Ibid.

106. Ibid. (Schweitzer's emphasis).

107. Ibid.

108. Gandhi, in Andrews, *Mahatma Gandhi's Ideas,* 140.

109. Jaini claims that the latter is not possible without the first, hence the Jain emphasis on the former.

110. In his commentary on this passage, Jaini notes that the form this "devotion" may take is indefinable. Jain mendicants maintain that they do serve others by their presence, which is a witness to the spiritual process for the laity. Schweitzer, *The Philosophy of Civilization,* 314.

111. Schweitzer, "The Ethics of Reverence for Life," in Clark, *Ethical Mysticism,* 184.

112. Albert Schweitzer, *Christianity and the Religions of the World,* trans. Johanna Powers (New York: Henry Holt and Co., 1939), 51.

113. Schweitzer, *The Philosophy of Civilization,* 284.

114. Ibid., 285.

115. Linzey, *Animal Theology,* 6.

116. Kraus, *Albert Schweitzer,* 42.

117. Lois Daly, "Ecofeminism, Reverence for Life, and Feminist Theological Ethics," in *Liberating Life: Contemporary Approaches to Ecological Theology,* ed. Charles Birch, William Eakin, and Jay B. McDonald (New York: Orbis Books, 1994), 106.

118. Schweitzer to Jack Eisendraht, 1951, in Bähr, *Letters,* 218.

119. Schweitzer, *Out of My Life and Thought,* 235.

120. At the conference at Chapman University where this work was first presented, Schweitzer's daughter, Rhena Schweitzer Miller, emphasized that her father was most concerned that each person reflect and decide for himself or herself which harmful actions are a "necessity."

121. Schweitzer, *A Place for Revelation,* 27.

122. Albert Schweitzer, *On the Edge of the Primeval Forest,* trans. C. T. Campion. (London: A. and C. Black, 1922), 11.

123. Schweitzer, *Indian Thought and Its Development*, 83.

124. Schweitzer, "The Movement for the Protection of Animals," in *The Animal World of Albert Schweitzer*, trans. and ed. Charles R. Joy (Boston: Beacon Press, 1950), 186.

125. Clark, *Ethical Mysticism*, 102.

126. Schweitzer, *The Philosophy of Civilization*, 317.

127. Ibid.

128. Schweitzer, *Out of My Life and Thought*, 236 (my italics).

129. For instance, Schweitzer writes: "I rejoice over the new remedies for sleeping sickness, which enable me to preserve life, where once I could only witness the progress of a painful disease. But every time I put the germs that cause the disease under the microscope I cannot but reflect that I have to sacrifice this life in order to save another." Schweitzer, *Out of My Life and Thought*, 236.

130. Schweitzer, *The Philosophy of Civilization*, 318.

131. Albert Schweitzer, *The Teaching of Reverence for Life*, trans. Richard and Clara Winston (New York: Holt, Rinehart and Winston, 1965), 23.

132. Schweitzer, *The Philosophy of Civilization*, 57 (my italics).

133. Ibid., 310.

134. Schweitzer, *The Teaching of Reverence for Life*, 47.

135. Schweitzer to Oskar Kraus, November 7, 1931, in Bähr, *Letters*, 124 (Schweitzer's emphasis).

136. For further discussion on the properties of sense-beings, see "The Nine Categories of Fundamental Truths," in Mrs. Sinclair Stevenson, *The Heart of Jainism* (London: Oxford Univ. Press, 1915).

137. Jaini, *The Jaina Path of Purification*, 103.

138. Ibid., 241–42.

139. Ibid., 242.

140. Schweitzer, "The Ethics of Reverence for Life," in Clark, *Ethical Mysticism*, 182.

141. Ibid., 183 (Schweitzer's emphasis).

142. Schweitzer, *The Philosophy of Civilization*, 309.

143. Ibid.

144. Schweitzer, "The Ethics of Reverence for Life," in Clark, *Ethical Mysticism*.

145. Ibid., 194.

146. Hermann Jacobi, *Sacred Books of the East*, 22:3, in Stevenson, *The Heart of Jainism*, 95.

147. Jaini, *The Jaina Path of Purification*, 103.

148. Ibid.

149. Schweitzer, *Indian Thought and Its Development*, x.

150. Ibid.

151. Ibid.

152. Keith Ward, *A Vision to Pursue: Beyond the Crisis in Christianity* (London: SCM Press, 1991), 208.

153. Paul Tillich, *Christianity and the Encounter of World Religions* (New York: Columbia Univ. Press, 1963), 30.

154. Keith Ward, *Religion and Revelation: A Theology of Revelation in the World's Religions* (Oxford: Clarendon Press, 1994), 341.

155. Schweitzer, *Indian Thought and Its Development*, ix.

156. Ward, *A Vision to Pursue*, 213.

157. Schweitzer, *Out of My Life and Thought*, 240.

158. Ibid., 239.

159. Schweitzer to Rabindranath Tagore, August 15, 1936, in Bähr, *Letters*, 142.

160. Schweitzer, *Indian Thought and Its Development*, viii.

161. Schweitzer received several letters from individuals in India and Asia endorsing reverence for life. See also Natubhai Shah's recent two-volume series, *Jainism: The World of Conquerors*, for frequent reference to Schweitzer and reverence for life.

15. The Legacy of Schweitzer's *Quest of the Historical Jesus*

1. The page references are to Albert Schweitzer, *The Quest of the Historical Jesus: A Critical Study of Its Progress from Reimarus to Wrede,* introduction by James M. Robinson (New York: Macmillan Publishing Co., 1968), slightly modified here for style.

Bibliography

Ahimsa. KRMA-TV, Denver, 1987, videocassette.

Amery, C. *Das Ende der Vorsehung: Die gnadenlosen Folgen des Christentums.* Hamburg: Rowohlt, 1972.

Andrews, Charles F. *Mahatma Gandhi's Ideas.* London: George Allen and Unwin, 1929.

Armstrong, Susan J. and Richard G. Botzler, eds. *Environmental Ethics.* New York: McGraw-Hill, 1993.

Bähr, Hans Walter, ed. *Albert Schweitzer: Letters, 1905–1965.* Translated by Joachim Neugroschel. New York: Macmillan Publishing Co., 1992.

Ballou, Robert O., ed. *The Bible of the World.* New York: Viking Press, 1939.

Barsam, Ara Paul. " 'Reverence for Life': Albert Schweitzer's Mystical Theology and Ethics." Ph.D. thesis, Oxford University, 2001.

Bentley, James. *Albert Schweitzer: The Enigma.* New York: HarperCollins, 1992.

Bergel, Alice R. "Philosophy with 'Calluses in Its Hands.' " *Albert Schweitzer Institute Bulletin* (1997): 4, 6.

Bergel, Kurt. "Albert Schweitzer's Reverence for Life." *The Humanist* 6 (1946): 31–34.

Bergson, Henri. *Creative Evolution.* Translated by Arthur Mitchell. New York: Henry Holt and Co., 1907.

Betz, Hans Dieter. *The Sermon on the Mount.* Hermeneia; Minneapolis: Fortress Press, 1995.

Brabazon, James. *Albert Schweitzer: A Biography.* Second edition. Syracuse: Syracuse Univ. Press, 2000.

Brüllmann, R. *Treffende Albert-Schweitzer-Zitate.* Thun, Switzerland: Ott, 1986.

Callicott, J. Baird. "On the Intrinsic Value of Nonhuman Species." In *The Preservation of Species: The Value of Biological Diversity,* edited by Bryan G. Norton, 153–55. Princeton: Princeton Univ. Press, 1986.

Clark, Henry. *The Ethical Mysticism of Albert Schweitzer: A Study of the Sources and Significance of Schweitzer's Philosophy of Civilization.* Boston: Beacon Press, 1962.

Cousins, Norman. *Albert Schweitzer's Mission: Healing and Peace.* New York and London: W. W. Norton and Co., 1985.

Crossan, John Dominic. *The Historical Jesus: The Life of a Mediterranean Jewish Peasant.* San Francisco: HarperSanFrancisco, 1991.

Dahl, J. "Der wahre Preis des Stroms." *Natur: Das Umweltmagazin* 7 (1990): 96–98.

Daly, Lois. "Ecofeminism, Reverence for Life, and Feminist Theological Ethics." In *Liberating Life: Contemporary Approaches to Ecological Theology,* edited by Charles Birch, William Eakin, and Jay B. McDonald. New York: Orbis Books, 1994.

Dauer, Dorothea. *Schopenhauer as Transmitter of Buddhist Ideas.* Bern: Herbert Lang and Co., 1969.

Davenport, Manuel M. "The Moral Paternalism of Albert Schweitzer." *Ethics* 84 (1974): 116–27.

DeBary, William Theodore, ed. *Sources of Indian Tradition.* Introduction to Oriental Civilizations. New York: Columbia Univ. Press, 1958.

DesJardins, Joseph R. *Environmental Ethics: An Introduction to Environmental Philosophy.* Belmont, Calif.: Wadsworth, 1993.

Doyle, James F. "Schweitzer's Extensions of Ethics to All Life." *Journal of Value Inquiry* 11 (1977): 45.

DuBois, W. E. B. "The Black Man and Albert Schweitzer." In *The Albert Schweitzer Jubilee Book,* edited by A. A. Roback, 121–27. Cambridge, Mass.: Sci-Art, 1946.

Dungan, David L. "Reconsidering Albert Schweitzer." *The Christian Century* 92 (1975): 874–80.

Fischer, John A. "Taking Sympathy Seriously: A Defense of Our Moral Psychology Toward Animals." In *The Animal Rights / Environmental Ethics Debate: The Environmental Perspective,* edited by Eugene C. Hargrove, 227–48. Albany: State Univ. of New York Press, 1992.

Franck, Frederick. *Days with Albert Schweitzer: A Lambaréné Landscape.* New York: Henry Holt and Co., 1959.

Funk, Robert. *Honest to Jesus: Jesus for a New Millennium.* San Francisco: HarperSanFrancisco, 1996.

Gandhi, Mahatma. *Collected Works of Mahatma Gandhi.* Delhi: Government of India, 1958–76.

Goetz, Bernhard. *Albert Schweitzer: Ein Mann der guten Tat.* Göttingen: W. Fischer, 1955.

Goodpaster, Kenneth E. "On Being Morally Considerable." *The Journal of Philosophy* 75 (1978): 308–25.

Gräßer, Erich. "Ehrfurcht vor allem Lebendigen." In *Studien zu Albert Schweitzer: Gesammelte Aufsätze,* edited by Andreas Mühling, 25–33. Bodenheim: Philo, 1997.

———. "Ethik bei Albert Schweitzer." In *Studien zu Albert Schweitzer: Gesammelte Aufsätze,* edited by Andreas Mühling, 64–78. Bodenheim: Philo, 1997.

Gunther, John. *Inside Africa.* London: Hamisch Hamilton, 1955.

Günzler, Claus. *Albert Schweitzer; Einführung in sein Denken.* Munich: C. H. Beck, 1996.

Hollman, Reimar. "Zum 100. Geburtstag Albert Schweitzers. Willkommenes Alibi einer inhumanen Welt." In *Neue Hannoversche Zeitung,* Hanover, January 1975.

Ice, Jackson Lee. *Schweitzer: Prophet of Radical Theology.* Philadelphia: Westminster Press, 1971.

Italiaander, Rolf. *Der weiße Oganga Albert Schweitzer: Eine Erzählung aus Äquatorialafrika.* Hanover: T. Oppermann, 1954.

Jacobi, Hermann. *Sacred Books of the East.* Vol. 22, edited by F. Max Müller. Delhi: Motilal Banarsidass Publishers, 1989.

Jaini, Jagmanderlal. *Outlines of Jainism.* Cambridge: Cambridge Univ. Press, 1916.

Jaini, P. S. *The Jaina Path of Purification.* Berkeley and Los Angeles: Univ. of California Press, 1979.

———. "Values in Comparative Perspective: *Svadharma* Versus *Ahimsa.*" In *Sramana Vidya: Studies in Buddhism,* edited by N. H. Samtani, 111–22. Sarnath and Varanasi, India: Central Institute of Higher Tibetan Studies, 1987.

Jilek-Aall, Louise. *Working with Dr. Schweitzer: Sharing His Reverence for Life.* Blaine, Wash.: Hancock House, 1990.

Johnson, Lawrence E. *A Morally Deep World.* New York: Cambridge Univ. Press, 1991.

Johnson, W. J. *Harmless Souls.* Delhi: Motilal Banarsidass Publishers, 1995.

Jonas, Hans. *Das Prinzip Verantwortung: Versuch einer Ethik für die technologische Zivilisation.* Frankfurt am Main: Suhrkamp, 1979.

———. "Technik, Freiheit und Pflicht." In *Friedenspreis des Deutschen Buchhandels 1987,* 33–46. Frankfurt am Main: Buchhändler-Vereinigung, 1987.

Kleinig, John. *Valuing Life.* Princeton: Princeton Univ. Press, 1991.

Kraus, Oskar. *Albert Schweitzer: His Work and His Philosophy.* Translated by I. G. McCalman. London: A. and C. Black, 1944.

LaFleur, Willaim R. *Liquid Life: Abortion and Buddhism in Japan*. Princeton: Princeton Univ. Press, 1994.

Langfeldt, Gabriel. *Albert Schweitzer: A Study of His Life and Thought*. Translated by Maurice Michael. London: George Allen and Unwin, 1960.

Lemke, Antje Bultmann. "Moderator's Introduction." In *The Relevance of Albert Schweitzer at the Dawn of the Twenty-First Century*. Edited by David C. Miller and James Pouilliard, 83–84. Lanham, Md.: Univ. Press of America, 1992.

Linzey, Andrew. *Christianity and the Rights of Animals*. New York: Crossroad, 1991.

Martin, Mike W. "Good Fortune Obligates: Gratitude, Philanthropy, and Colonialism." *Southern Journal of Philosophy* 37 (1999): 57–75.

———. "Rethinking Reverence for Life." *Between the Species* 9 (1993): 204–13.

McKnight, Gerald. *Verdict on Schweitzer: The Man Behind the Legend of Lambaréné*. New York: John Day Co., 1964.

Mbondobari, Sylvère. "Archäologie eines modernen Mythos: Albert Schweitzers Nachruhm in europäischen und afrikanischen Text- und Bildmedien." Ph.D. thesis, University of Bayreuth, 2001.

Meyer, Marvin. "Albert Schweitzer and the Image of Jesus in the Gospel of Thomas." In *Jesus Then and Now: Images of Jesus in History and Christology*, edited by Marvin Meyer and Charles Hughes, 72–90. Harrisburg, Pa.: Trinity Press International, 2001.

———. "How to Become a Gentle Heretic: Albert Schweitzer on Jesus and Buddha." Chapman University Honors Lecture, Orange, Calif., November 2000.

———. "New Translation of *Memoirs of Childhood and Youth*," *Albert Schweitzer Institute Bulletin* (1997): 5, 7.

Miller, David C., and James Pouilliard, eds. *The Relevance of Albert Schweitzer at the Dawn of the Twenty-First Century*. Lanham, Md.: Univ. Press of America, 1992.

Ndaot, Séraphin. *Le procès d'un prix Nobel, ou Le médecin du fleuve*. Paris: La Pensée Universelle, 1983.

Pojman, Louis P., ed. *Environmental Ethics: Readings in Theory and Application*. Boston: Jones and Bartlett, 1994.

Radhakrishnan, S. *Eastern Religions and Western Thought*. Oxford: Oxford Univ. Press, 1991.

Rambeck, Bernhard. *Mythos Tierversuch: Eine wissenschaftskritische Untersuchung*. Frankfurt am Main: Verlag Zweitausendeins, 1990.

Regen, Tom, and Peter Singer, eds. *Animal Rights and Human Obligations*. 2d ed. Englewood Cliffs, N.J.: Prentice Hall, 1989.

Robinson, James M. Introduction to *The Quest of the Historical Jesus: A Critical Study of Its Progress from Reimarus to Wrede,* by Albert Schweitzer. Translated by William Montgomery. New York: Macmillan Publishing Co., 1968.

Rouch, Jane. "Le scandale de Lambaréné." *Jeune Afrique* (1962): 14.

Sangave, Vilas Adinath. *Jaina Community.* Bombay: Popular Book Depot, 1959.

Schmied, Luise Maria. *An den Ufern des Ogowe.* Berlin: A. Holz, 1956.

Schopenhauer, Arthur. *The World as Will and Representation.* Translated by E. F. J. Payne. 2 vols. New York: Dover Publications, 1966.

Schweitzer, Albert. *Albert Schweitzer's African Sermons.* Edited and translated by Steven E. G. Melamed. Syracuse Univ. Press, 2002.

———. *The Animal World of Albert Schweitzer.* Translated and edited by Charles R. Joy. Boston: Beacon Press, 1950.

———. "Appell an die Menscheit." In Albert Schweitzer, *Gesammelte Werke,* edited by R. Grabs, 5: 564–77. Zurich and Munich: C. H. Beck, 1974.

———. *Aus meinem Leben und Denken.* Hamburg: Richard Meiner, 1931.

———. *Christianity and the Religions of the World.* Translated by Johanna Powers. New York: Henry Holt and Co., 1939.

———. "The Ethics of Reverence for Life." *Christendom* 1 (winter 1936): 225–39. Reprinted in Henry Clark, *Ethical Mysticism: A Study of the Sources and Significance of Schweitzer's Philosophy of Civilization,* 180–94. Boston: Beacon Press, 1962.

———. *Gesammelte Werke.* Edited by R. Grabs. 5 vols. Zurich and Munich: C. H. Beck, 1974.

———. *Goethe: Five Studies.* Translated by Charles R. Joy. Boston: Beacon Press, 1961.

———. *Indian Thought and Its Development.* Translated by Mrs. Charles E. B. Russell. Boston: Beacon Press, 1936; London: A. and C. Black, 1951; Gloucester, Mass.: Peter Smith, 1977.

———. *The Kingdom of God and Primitive Christianity.* Edited by Ulrich Neuenschwander, translated by L. A. Garrard. New York: Seabury Press, 1968.

———. *Kultur und Ethik: Kulturphilosophie.* 2 vols. Munich: C. H. Beck, 1923.

———. *Leben, Werk und Denken, 1905–1965: Mitgeteilt in seinen Briefen.* Edited by Hans Walter Bähr. Heidelberg: L. Schneider, 1987.

———. *Letters, 1905–1965.* Edited by Hans Walter Bähr, translated by Joachim Neugroschel. New York: Macmillan Publishing Co., 1992.

———. *Memoirs of Childhood and Youth.* Translated by Kurt Bergel and Alice R. Bergel. Syracuse: Syracuse Univ. Press, 1997.

————. *Memoirs of Childhood and Youth.* Translated by C. T. Campion. New York: Macmillan Publishing Co., 1961.

————. *The Mystery of the Kingdom of God: The Secret of Jesus' Messiahship and Passion.* Translated by Walter Lowrie. Buffalo: Prometheus Books, 1985.

————. *The Mysticism of Paul the Apostle.* Translated by William Montgomery. New York: Henry Holt and Co., 1931.

————. *On the Edge of the Primeval Forest.* Translated by C. T. Campion. London: A. and C. Black, 1922; New York: Pyramid Books, 1961.

————. *Out of My Life and Thought: An Autobiography.* Translated by Antje Bultmann Lemke. New York: Henry Holt and Co., 1990. Reprint, Baltimore: Johns Hopkins Univ. Press, 1998.

————. *The Philosophy of Civilization.* Translated by C. T. Campion. Buffalo: Prometheus Books, 1987.

————. *A Place for Revelation: Sermons on Reverence for Life.* Edited by Lothar Stiehm and Martin Strege. Translated by David Larrimore Holland. New York: Macmillan Publishing Co.; London: Collier Macmillan, 1988.

————. *The Quest of the Historical Jesus: A Critical Study of Its Progress from Reimarus to Wrede.* Translated by William Montgomery. New York: Macmillan Publishing Co., 1968; Baltimore: Johns Hopkins Univ. Press, 1998. Complete English edition, edited by John Bowden. Minneapolis: Fortress Press, 2001.

————. *Reverence for Life.* Translated by Reginald H. Fuller. New York: Harper and Row, 1969.

————. *The Story of My Pelican.* Translated by Martha Wardenburg. London: Souvenir, 1964.

————. *The Teaching of Reverence for Life.* Translated by Richard and Clara Winston. New York: Holt, Rinehart and Winston, 1965.

———— and Hélène Bresslau. "Albert Schweitzer–Hélène Bresslau: The Years Prior to Lambaréné, Correspondence, 1902–1912." Translated by Antje Bultmann Lemke. Forthcoming from Syracuse Univ. Press.

———— and Alice Ehlers. *A Friendship in Letters.* Translated and edited by Kurt Bergel and Alice R. Bergel. Lanham, Md.: Univ. Press of America, 1991.

————. Letter to Jackson Lee Ice. Unpublished correspondence, July 7, 1952. Archives of the Albert Schweitzer Institute, Conn.

Seaver, George. *Albert Schweitzer: The Man and His Mind.* London: A. and C. Black, 1947.

Shah, Natubhai. *Jainism: The World of Conquerors.* 2 vols. Brighton: Sussex Academic Press, 1998.

Singhvi, L. M. *Jain Declaration on Nature.* Cincinnati: Federation of Jain Associations in North America, 1990.

Spaemann, Robert. "Laudatio." In *Friedenspreis des Deutschen Buchhandels 1987,* 17–37. Frankfurt am Main: Buchhändler-Vereingung, 1987.

Spiegelberg, Herbert. "Good Fortune Obligates: Albert Schweitzer's Second Ethical Principle." *Ethics* 85 (1975): 227–34.

Stevenson, Mrs. Sinclair. *The Heart of Jainism.* London: Oxford Univ. Press, 1915.

Tatia, Nathmal, ed. *Studies in Jaina Philosophy.* Banaras: Jain Cultural Research Society, 1951.

Taylor, G. R. *Das Selbstmordprogramm.* Frankfurt am Main: S. Fischer, 1971.

Taylor, Paul. *Respect for Nature.* Princeton: Princeton Univ. Press, 1986.

Thomas, M. Z. *Unser großer Freund Albert Schweitzer.* Munich: Franz Schneider, 1960.

Tillich, Paul. *Christianity and the Encounter of World Religions.* New York: Columbia Univ. Press, 1963.

Vethake, Kurt. *Das weiße Haus im Dschungel.* Kiel: Neumann and Wolff, 1955.

Ward, Keith. *Religion and Revelation: A Theology of Revelation in the World's Religions.* Oxford: Clarendon Press, 1994.

———. *A Vision to Pursue: Beyond the Crisis in Christianity.* London: SCM Press, 1991.

Whitehead, Alfred North. *Process and Reality.* New York: Macmillan Publishing Co., 1924.

Winternitz, Moritz. *A History of Indian Literature.* Translated by S. Ketkar and H. Kohn. Calcutta: Univ. of Calcutta, 1933.

Index